CONFESSIONS OF AN ACTOR

CONFESSIONS
OF AN ACTOR

Laurence Olivier

ORION

An Orion paperback
First published in Great Britain by
Weidenfeld & Nicolson Ltd in 1982
This paperback edition published in 1994 by
Orion Books Ltd,
Orion House, 5 Upper St Martin's Lane,
London WC2H 9EA

A CIP catalogue record for this book is available
from the British Library.

ISBN: 1 85797 493 X

Printed and bound in Great Britain by
Clays Ltd, St Ives plc

For my family

CONTENTS

ILLUSTRATIONS

Henry V on stage in 1937 (Mander & Mitchenson Collection)
Coriolanus at the Old Vic, 1937–8 (Angus McBean/Harvard Theatre Collection)
Macbeth at the Old Vic 1937–8 (author's collection)
Macbeth at Stratford, 1955 (author's collection)
Hotspur in *Henry IV, Part 1*, 1945–6 (John Vickers)
Richard III with Joyce Redman and Nicholas Hannen (John Vickers)
Portrait of me as Richard III by Mervyn Peake (author's collection)
My first Lear, with Alec Guinness as Fool, 1946 (John Vickers)
In *Caesar and Cleopatra*, 1951 (Angus McBean/Harvard Theatre Collection)
With Vivien in *Antony and Cleopatra*, 1951 (Rex Features)
Malvolio in *Twelfth Night*, 1955 (Angus McBean/Harvard Theatre Collection)
The death of Coriolanus, 1959 (Angus McBean/Harvard Theatre Collection)
Titus Andronicus with Vivien, 1955 (Angus McBean/Harvard Theatre Collection)
With Lilian Harvey in my first film, 1930 (author's collection)
With Vivien in *Fire Over England* in 1936 (National Film Archive)
With Lionel Barrymore in *The Yellow Passport* (Len Sirman/Camera Press)
With Merle Oberon in *Wuthering Heights* (National Film Archive)
With Joan Fontaine in *Rebecca*, 1939 (Len Sirman/Camera Press)
With Greer Garson in *Pride and Prejudice*, 1940 (BBC)
In *Lady Hamilton* with Vivien, 1941 (Rex Features)
A scene from *Henry V* (Len Sirman/Camera Press)
My moment of courage in *Hamlet* (National Film Archive)
Richard III with Ralph Richardson, 1954 (National Film Archive)
With Jennifer Jones in *Sister Carrie* (Len Sirman/Camera Press)
Othello striking Maggie Smith as Desdemona (Camera Press)
Desdemona and Othello between shots (Terry O'Neill/Camera Press)
Working with Marilyn Monroe in 1956 (Popperfoto)
Directing Joan and Alan Bates in *Three Sisters* (Norman Gryspeerdt/author's collection)

First visit to Chichester Festival Theatre (Pierre V-Manery/author's collection)

With Joan and George Devine at the Royal Court Theatre (Zoë Dominic)

With Lord Chandos (Central Press Photos)

With architect Sir Denys Lasdun (Keystone Press)

My introduction to the House of Lords (Zoë Dominic)

CONFITEOR

Bless me, Reader, for I have sinned.

Since my last confession, which was more than fifty years ago, I have committed the following sins . . .

PART ONE

CHAPTER ONE

How It Began

For my father, saving was a craving. This is no idle jingle but the plainest statement of fact.

He had, of course, many run-of-the-mill opportunities to indulge this obsession. At the end of every month a feast awaited him as bills came flooding in. We did enjoy the luxury of toilet rolls, though we were encouraged and constantly reminded to be as sparing as possible in their use; and there were always the daily commodities to be examined with a keen master's eye: gas, coal, light, heat, butcher, baker, grocer, fishmonger, greengrocer, wine merchant – he was insistent on his glass of port at the end of lunch or dinner. For a while after Christmas there would be the occasional thimbleful of cherry brandy and an occasional whisky (Black and White always) for the occasional visitor; there was always a small barrel of ale in the cellar/silver-cleaning/lamp-cleaning room, of which a limited amount was allowed to my brother and me.

One of the more obvious manifestations of what I am afraid we may as well call parsimony was apparent in the size of his helpings at mealtimes. He was a brilliant carver – he used to say that parsons' sons always made the best carvers. His own father was a parson's son too, though he had enjoyed considerably ampler means, living under the protection of the wealth that seems to have come by nature to most families of gentlefolk born in the last century. My father, being the youngest son of a youngest son (eight in his family, ten in my grandfather's), naturally came off worse than anyone to date.

His gift for carving was extraordinary and I am lucky

enough to inherit a share of it, though not with a like driving sense of economy – at least I sincerely trust not. It was fascinating to watch the rare delicacy with which he performed his task; he could cut three razor-thin slices of meat, laid beautifully with one slice half-covering another, then make you feel richly provided for in the extreme by saying with purring assurance, 'There, get outside that and you won't do badly'; in truth you could have got outside it in a very few seconds indeed. I have always sworn that he was able to make a chicken do for six, leaving enough for cold at tomorrow's lunch and drumsticks for breakfast the following morning. All of which is a helpful skill for a parson living on the lowest imaginable income.

His driving sense of economy extended to every area. There was one particular commodity that used to strike us, familiar as we all were with the rigidity of the general idea, as unacceptably eccentric: that was his preoccupation with the conservation of water; not only hot water, which involved an expenditure of fuel, but cold water too – any water.

I have no reason to believe that Letchworth Garden City was especially subject to drought; whereas ten days without rain in Berkhamsted and the headlines would announce 'water by the bucket in Berkhamsted'. The climate of Letchworth, according to my memory, was as damp as most other places in England, but water came under the axe as surely as coal, gas or electricity. I have been informed by the proper official department of that borough that in 1923 the water rate was somewhere in the region of a penny-halfpenny per thousand gallons. This would work out as something less than a pound per annum. I am pretty sure my father would be careful enough not to use more than ten gallons of water in his bath, so the amount that any one bath could have cost him is incalculably low.

My sister, being not merely the only young woman in the family after our mother died but also the eldest of us children, was allowed the privilege of a bath by herself and to herself. We three males, father, elder and finally younger son, had no such luxury, but seemingly were required to pay for our sister's privilege by jumping into the same water one after the other: Father first of course, then my elder brother Dickie, and finally me. By this time the water had got into such a state that it could hardly be described as a cleansing agent.

However, on the particular evening I have all this time been preparing to describe, the mood in the bathroom was unaccustomedly sad, in fact suffused with the sure heaviness of grief. There were only two in the bathroom, not the cutomary three. My father and I had that morning accompanied my beloved brother to Waterloo to see him off to be a rubber planter in India for possibly nine years. I felt tearful enough, goodness knows, on my own account; life without Dickie seemed too dreadful to contemplate. However, even at the supremely selfish age of sixteen I felt more concerned for my father, whom I knew to be preoccupied with the unbearable question: what were the chances of his ever seeing his elder son again?

Lowering myself into the water which was, I noticed unhappily, a little cleaner than usual, I snatched the hot tap on for the allotted number of seconds, and after a minute or so I asked my father how soon I might reckon on being allowed to follow Dickie to India. My father's answer was so astonishing that it gave me quite a deep shock: 'Don't be such a fool, you're not going to India, you're going on the stage.' 'Am I?' I stammered lamely. 'Well, of course you are,' he said: and as he went on I realised not only that he had been thinking of me quite deeply, which was something I had long ago decided he never did, but that he had been following these thoughts through in pleasingly creative and caring ways.

'You will leave school at the end of this summer and sometime, at whatever date for such things is ordained, you will go to Elsie Fogerty's school.' This was one of many establishments at which my sister who was six years older had already studied. 'You will of course achieve a scholarship – she will see at once that you are a born actor. You will no doubt have to recite one or more pieces and she will no doubt talk to you afterwards, at which time you will find an opportunity to explain what you may perhaps find a tricky little subject to broach, but the fact is that you have to *insist* that you are given the scholarship. Otherwise there is really no hope of your being able to enter the school, and what is more, you are afraid – and this you may find a little trickier than anything yet – you have been instructed to say that it is equally essential that you also be given the £50 bursary as well as the benefit of the scholarship or there will still be no hope of your being able to attend, as your father has no means which will enable him to pay for you to live in London. You ought to be able to live in London quite decently on what I'm able to give you. I remember when I was a young man you could, in the City, get a perfectly decent meat pudding for fourpence.' (My father was talking about 1890.) This new life of mine was to start in 1924, six years after the end of the Great War.

I gulped hard at all this hopelessly unreal optimism and clung to the main point, which was that I was going to be free, free and independent – quite hungry, I expected, but Free.

And that is how it was that, sitting in two or three inches of lukewarm water which was none too clean, on the orders of an eccentrically surprising father, my fate was sealed.

CHAPTER TWO

Cradle to Choirboy

There were almost as many beautiful moments in the film of *Gone With The Wind* as there were in the original novel by Margaret Mitchell. Olivia de Havilland gave a perfect performance as Melanie. In one highly dramatic scene the Unionists were breaking into the house when the only people at home were the ladies and their ageing black nanny-retainer. The invaders were scouring the rooms for secret documents and anything they could cram into their pockets. The ladies, led by Melanie, were playing as cool as they were able to in the terrifying circumstances. Melanie snatched up a book and began reading it aloud, giving a splendidly brave impression of enjoying a perfectly normal, quiet evening.

The book she had grabbed was *David Copperfield*, and she started at the opening paragraph, so that we heard her beautiful voice reading what must be one of the most familiar passages in literature in her lovely lilting Southern cadences: 'Whether I shall turn out to be the hero of my own life, or whether that station will be held by anybody else, these pages must show. To begin my life with the beginning of my life, I record that I was born (as I have been informed and believe) on a Friday, at twelve o'clock at night. It was remarked that the clock began to strike, and I began to cry, simultaneously.'

In almost every detail I could use the same description with regard to my own birth. But if the clocks did chime as I was born at 26 Wathen Road, Dorking, Surrey, on the morning of 22 May 1907, it would have been five o'clock that they were striking.

My father used to describe how he was frying sausages for Dr Rawlings and himself when the doctor appeared in the kitchen doorway bearing a tiny but healthy-looking infant in his arms, as yet unwashed and smeared with blood. My father's telling of this always indicated a sense of slight disgust as Dr Rawlings placed me in his arms. After a decent enough pause, he handed me back and returned his attention to the sausages. I think the doctor must have murmured some suggestion that perhaps he might like to pay a brief visit upstaris, so with a wee bit of hesitation he put the sausages to one side and with a hint of slightly guilty reluctance followed the doctor. He found my mother turned away towards the wall; she had now given way to her utter exhaustion and made no sign. He gave a little tender stroke to the damp forehead and led the doctor back to their sausages.

The slight disgust that he felt at his first viewing of me seemed to me and, I feel sure, to my mother, to last all my boyhood until my heaven, my hope, my entire world, my own worshipped Mummy died when I was twelve. From this I learnt that great suffering could sometimes implant in some mysterious way an unexpected strength. I have managed to cling to that belief throughout my life, and in any really appalling circumstances it has given me a small, narrow shelf that could afford me a moment's rest, a borrowed moment of strength like the loan of oxygen that we feel on taking a deep breath. At this particular time my only sister Sybille (French spelling for all our names, *please*) told me that she had been present as my mother was nearing her end and heard her make my father promise to be as kind as he could to me, her baby. She heard him promise to do his utmost to obey this deathbed wish; and I became aware of some signs of this effort as time crawled by.

Most people, I believe, have some very early memory and it is reckoned that the majority of these haunt the area of a first spanking. That is not my earliest memory, it is my second, when I was three. My earliest is of when I was two and is corroborated by my memory of a view through a window, which establishes the place as Dorking. I was being dried after my bath in front of this window – it must have been summer time as it was open and it was sunny outside. I was gazing down at my four-year-old brother in his smock making a determined attempt to climb the trellis-work. My strong impression is that he did not make any very remarkable success in this gallant venture. We did not move from Dorking to London until 1910, when I was three.

From the age of five until I was nine my Mummy had, more often than it pleases me to remember, to quell the natural anguish which she suffered at what was to her the dreaded prospect of spanking me for one inveterate and seemingly irresistible sin, that of lying. It was apparently impossible for me to resist this temptation. It was a compulsion in me to invent a story and tell it so convincingly that it was believed at first without doubt or suspicion.

After three or four years of the monotonous exchange of sin and punishment, it eventually pierced my sluggish little brain that this operation really did hurt her more than it hurt me. I noticed at last while I was removing the necessary garments that she was in a state of high distress. She caught me staring at her and said, 'How I wish you wouldn't persist in making this hateful business necessary. I do detest it so.' I resolved that on this occasion I would grit my teeth and not cry out until I could stifle my cries no longer. She stopped after the fourth stroke; I was surprised as I was expecting six. She said, 'Yes, it should have been six really but you were so brave I couldn't go on.' This amazed me; I had always assumed that if a person did not cry out the punisher would continue, unsatisfied until the expected reaction was brought forth.

I thereupon resolved that she should never again be made to suffer in this way and that I would forever remove the cause of it all. And so my habit of lying ceased . . . for a time, anyway.

I used to wonder why it was that my father did not take on the responsibility, as happened with most sons, but left it to my mother to whom it caused such suffering. I felt sure in my heart, and still do, that she would not risk giving his displeasure full rein in case he did not know when to stop. He had been a schoolmaster with a lasting reputation for severity before taking Holy Orders. How much the nobler, then, my mother's voluntary self-punishment.

If my wonderful Mums had lived to watch me at work, at times more glowingly fortunate than I would have dared to imagine, I have sometimes wondered whether she might not have come to the conclusion that those years of habitual lying were due to an instinct for some initial practice in what was to become my trade. Let it not be thought that I am attempting to find any excuse whatever for my early wicked tendencies, but it might, as is said west of the Atlantic, it might well figure.

I was five and entering my mendacious phase when I dragged into the nursery on the top floor of 22 Lupus Street, Pimlico, a huge (to me) wooden chest. I doubt if its length measured, in fact, more than four feet and a few inches. I placed it conveniently against one of the windows, whose curtains could be nicely arranged round and across the front of it. Goodness knows what my performances consisted of. I can't remember writing, certainly not memorising anything; my shows were probably imitations of plays I had seen at my brother's choir school; *Box and Cox*, in which my brother would join me, and, highly important, the Hubert and Arthur scene from *King John*. The audience was composed of my mother, with occasionally my sister or a visiting auntie or friend. For lighting, my footlights were candles set into round cigarette tins, beautifully cut out by my father, who was always ready to do any service requiring his wonderfully skilful hands. I remember him looking in once very briefly but I never played to an empty house so long as my mother was at home.

Nowadays people often ask my wife Joan, 'How do you know when Larry is acting and when he's not?', and my wife will always reply, 'Larry? Oh, he's acting all the time.' In my heart of hearts I only know that I am far from sure when I am acting and when I am not or, should I more frankly put it, when I am lying and when I am not. For what is acting but lying, and what is good acting but convincing lying? But what elevates this condition of life to the assumption of a vocation? I think we may not get recognisably closer than one of our youngest amusements – the game of 'pretends'.

The more intelligent of my young colleagues, in ceaseless talks pathetically seeking some rationalisation of our lives, agree that their choice of métier was to satisfy an urgent need to 'express themselves'. When my turn comes I cannot boast that degree of intellectuality; in honesty I have to confess, rather shamefacedly, that I was not conscious of any other need than to show off.

Why I was sent to quite so many prep schools I had not yet discovered; I only knew that the number was grist to the predictable mill of fault-finding schoolmasters who could add my history to my other faults: 'How many schools do you say you have already been to before you came here?' I dreaded answering because of the extra weight it lent to the admonition that was inevitably to follow: 'All those schools and you don't even know . . .?'

The fact is that my mother nursed a private ambition that I should follow my brother's successful entry into the choir of All Saints, Margaret Street, near Oxford Circus in London. This extremely High Anglican church possessed a rarely fine group of choristers reputed, and I believe with justice, to be the finest of all choirs in London. It was a small choir, consisting of only fourteen boy sopranos, two altos, two tenors and two basses, but the balance was perfectly achieved. It was my repeated failure to win a place in this wonderful singing machine that pushed me, time and time again, to some new prep school, which my patient mother would only regard as a temporary measure until the glorious moment came when her patience would be rewarded and I would pass muster. Meanwhile she would keep training me with the utmost diligence, playing for me on her piano.

Another reason for these changes may have been financial. Her own income varied much between a reliance on her modest inheritance and the times when her more well-to-do brothers would perceive her plight and provide for her awhile. My poor father's situation as an assistant priest at St Saviour's, Pimlico, must have made him wretchedly unable to provide for his children in the way that he would have hoped in his earlier life.

I have always thought that the initial trouble between me and my father was that he couldn't see the slightest purpose in my existence. There, in splendid relief, was his beautiful daughter, his eldest child, and three years younger was his son and heir and the only one he needed thank you very much. Everything about me irritated him. I was an entirely unnecessary extra burden on the exchequer; he would describe how the enormous amount of porridge that I consumed at breakfast put him in a bad temper for the whole day; he found himself staring in disagreeable fascination at the seeming distension of my stomach, gaining such an increase in dimension that it would force my chair further away from the table. These considerations, one is bound to remark, were all matters of hard materialism. One must add that the undisguisedly frank favouritism of my mother for her Baby could not have been a helpful influence in soothing and smoothing my father's shredded patience.

My mother was lovely – there is no photograph that I have ever seen that has revealed this in anything like its true measure. She was also undeniably a favourite among her own generation, gifted with a delightful wit and serenely high spirits. These qualities enabled her to make a joke of our somewhat strange family situation. My sister and brother understood that I alone needed her special protection; in spite of the gaps between our births – 1901, 1904 and 1907 – I cannot imagine a more truly fond and close trio than were we three: Sybille (Baba), Gerard Dacres (Dickie or Bobo) and Laurence Kerr (Larry or Baby). Baba was wonderfully kind to her brothers and pitched into household responsibilities for our beloved but greatly overstressed Mummy. Dickie was my own special hero throughout my entire boyhood until the sad, heavy day of his departure for what seemed a lifetime in India.

At long last I was offered a place in the choir. In my last two years there, enjoying my glory as solo-boy, I also learned, a little bit, to act. In this we were all blessed with the gift of angels in our master, the Reverend Geoffrey Heald. This young and gifted priest, one of five assistants, had already achieved immediate fame as a preacher, adding brilliantly witty touches to the high dramatic tirades with which he admonished his congregation for their sins of omission and dilatoriness. I remember well a particularly daring spur of dramatics in a voice of terrifying thunder, 'Sloth . . . is a sin of the flesh . . . LIKE LUST!' rendering his congregation tremulously helpless and weeping. He took great risks in his scoldings, at one time daring to lambast them with: 'It's no use you sitting there, looking like dried *haddocks*.' Geoffrey Heald (Father Heald to all, of course) could without question have been an actor of the highest distinction had his great talent not been exceeded by the firm strength of his steadfast, constant, *live* spirituality.

As a chorister of All Saints I received a musical education of great worth, which has given me for ever a passion and an appreciation for this most God-given of the arts. All Saints' music repertoire was especially rich. Our training was nursed in the great hierarchy of classical composers, way skywards above the usual Church of England aspirations: Mozart, Handel, Bach, Beethoven (Masses in C *and* D), Schubert, Mendelssohn, Gounod, Dvorak, Palestrina, supported also by the more usual Attwood, Tallis, Tinel, Silas, Wesley, Stainer and Stanford, masses, evensongs, choral services of every kind, anthems and requiems. All these and more were presented for the rapture of the congregation which attended this highly fashionable, unimaginably beautiful though small place of worship, which catered to the religious fulfilment of the Very High Anglican.

With the presence of Geoffrey Heald on the staff the standard of dramatic endeavour was far more ambitious than in the days of my brother; under his influence our choirboy acting took on a new dimension. My first opportunity was accidental – whose isn't? I had been cast for the Second Citizen in *Julius Caesar*, our Christmas play. At the early rehearsals I found myself delightedly and undoubtedly scoring, eliciting enthusiastic laughter from boys and clergy alike. Our Cassius was not happily cast and Brutus, an older boy named Ralph Taylor, whose mother was the actress Mary Forbes and who was showing himself to be a born actor, was switched to Cassius. I, in whom my masters apparently saw like potentialities, was raised from Second Citizen to Brutus, and the original Cassius was made to feel happier as the Second Citizen. The show consisted of the first half of the play, finishing at Act III scene ii, line 264, generally conceded to be the best of *Julius Caesar* before the cogency of the story disintegrates. The last scene was Antony's incitement of the citizenry to vengeful mutiny.

Our performances were graced by highly august persons, one staggering example of which was none other than the magical Ellen Terry. Also there was Sir Johnston Forbes-Robertson, to whom my father wangled an introduction. Sir Johnston was, of course, courtesy itself, seeing my father's dog-collar and priestly silk tunic under his frockcoat. My father reported that Sir Johnston said to him, 'My dear man, your boy does not play Brutus, he *is* Brutus.' I cannot vouch for the truth of this anecdote – indeed, I have never myself believed it.

The production was successful enough to be revived. I was nine the first year we presented a show; I felt quite an old hand the following year when I was ten.

The third show was a *conversazione* – all the boys doing turns or songs; mine was '. . . he sipped no sup and he craved no crumb as he sighed for the love of a lady.' The fourth year (I was twelve) I played Maria in 'Scenes from *Twelfth Night*'. We lost our Sir Toby due to sudden illness and the part was played by a churchwarden's daughter called Ethel McGlinchy, a name which, wisely following the trend, she changed to Fabia Drake – a name much revered in later years by all audiences at Stratford-upon-Avon. This casting was an odd variation of the Elizabethan tradition: boy was playing girl, but girl was also playing boy. Ellen Terry came to that too, and I was told she 'chuckled at every line' I spoke – a palpable exaggeration from an overfond reporter; my memory is of an extremely forced Maria, who steadfastly refused to bubble deliciously.

The following year came the main quarrel scenes of Petruchio and Katharina from *The Taming of the Shrew*; Geoffrey Heald was a stunning Petruchio and I was allowed to be his Kate. In the subsequent year the whole play was undertaken. Father Heald's direction was brilliant, and he injected into my consciousness a conviction that I was, in fact, being a woman. This production made such an impression that we were invited to the Shakespeare Memorial Theatre at Stratford-upon-Avon to give a special matinée – I remember it was for Shakespeare's birthday in 1922. That, of course, was an amateur appearance, but my first sniff of a real theatre from 'that' side of the footlights.

At the end of my last term Geoffrey Heald, who was now the precentor (second only to the vicar), said to me, 'Well, Larry, next Sunday will be your swan song. What shall it be: "Oh for the Wings" or "Trinity and Unity"?' I chose the latter in which I particularly fancied myself. It was the solo of the famous Wesley anthem referred to by all choirboys of all time as 'I Saw the One Two Three Four, Sitting upon a One Two Three Four'. My swan song was a disaster of a kind that was to be a recurring one. These crises were unpredictably sporadic and have been a nightmare to me all my life in public appearances, as will be seen. The cause seems always to be the same – a measure of fright, which is apt to follow any feeling of over-confidence.

The initial onset of this treacherous phenomenon happened thus. The first half of the anthem's chorus themes were coming to an end and the solo was looming near. I yielded to the wicked inclination to make a boastful gesture for the benefit of the rest of the choir. I folded my music and placed it upon the choir-desk in front of me, took off my glasses and placed them alongside. Nonchalantly folding my arms, I raised my head at an aloof angle towards some imagined distant clouds, and started the opening strains of 'Oh Trinity, Oh Unity'. After the first two or three bars a sense of guilt about my conduct began to assail me. It went further; it consumed me. My voice faltered, the breath left my being and could not be retrieved, my throat closed up and I was forced to stop. The organ ploughed on and, after a couple more bars, the shock of what had happened resulted unexpectedly in a merciful relaxation and I was able to find some breath again and proceed. Confidence mounted and the end was reached as normal.

The Evensong over, we gathered in the vestry and Geoffrey, who had conducted the service, volunteered with unbelievable tactfulness: 'Poor Larry, you were overdoing it from an excess of zeal in the procession and you strained your voice. That was it, wasn't it?' I can still feel the flood of gratitude with which I gazed at him. It was all over and everything would be all right now.

There was a pocket of slight doubtfulness, though, in my mind that was to lurk there, never to be totally dismissed.

The time had now come for me to take the step up – regarded as a steep one by generations of English school-boys for some hundreds of years – to public school.*

St Edward's was not in 1921 regarded very brilliantly among the regnant high-class English public schools. It was one of a small group called the Woodard Schools. Canon Woodard was a wealthy and worthily-intentioned force among the Holy Orders. He felt about those in his profession as the actor Gadd does in Pinero's *Trelawny of the Wells*: 'What I say is this: why can't an actor in private life be simply a gentleman?' Now, parsons in the last century were generally the youngest sons of gentlemen whose other numerous sons had gobbled up the more rewarding professions, including the armed services. The youngest son

---

* For non-English readers the term 'public school' creates an extraordinary paradox. It is by no means public; it is on the contrary the most private and inaccessible class of school in the world, entry to which in many cases requires years of being 'put down' for it, or generations of family connections as previous pupils.

was condemned to a life of poverty from two directions: he received the smallest portion of the family inheritance, and was the poorest paid by his enforced choice of profession.

Added to this, the highest standard of classical education was necessary to pass the examination imposed upon the would-be clerk in Holy Orders. When my own father (Winchester and Oxford) was school-mastering he had to use every spare minute for four years in preparation for making the attempt. Throughout these years my mother and he remained patiently engaged, which meant strictly what it said in those days.

Canon Woodard thought earnestly about such unkind fates and was concerned that lack of means might lead to second-rate education and so indicate a lack of gentility. He therefore devoted his life to the creation of institutions to be known and referred to as 'public schools', with the attendant rider 'for the sons of gentlemen'. In these Schools special terms were offered to parsons' sons, who could afterwards boast 'a public school education'. Consequently, these great establishments embellished the already rich English skyline: Lancing College in West Sussex, St Edward's (the Martyr) School in Oxford, and Ardingly in East Sussex.

I am told from every quarter in scholastic circles that St Edward's is now handsomely regarded and highly placed by any public school standards, attended I believe by more than 500 boys. It enjoyed no such glories in 1921. With a roster of precisely two hundred and sixteen and very little reputation academically, its one and only claim to fame lay in the name of one Old Boy: Kenneth Grahame, the author of *The Wind in the Willows*. It was just not the sort of school in those days that one was inclined to boast about.

My brother, who was at Radley, was as kind as could be about it, to be sure; but he felt, I knew, some pity for his underprivileged younger brother. Though Radley seemed to bear a rich crown to me, it was itself a long way from 'the first five': Eton, Harrow, Winchester, Westminster and Rugby. It was to the last of these famous schools that my mother had planned to send me; it was one of the things I was told she had spoken about to my father in her final days.

After she died in 1920, my father was allowed to sell the glorious Queen Anne rectory in Old Letchworth, where the twelfth-century St Mary's Old Church stood in lovely serenity, and we moved to a decent but jerry-built house in the new and growing Letchworth Garden City. Here he was within reach of what was considered by its position in the new part of town to be the much more important and commodious St Michael and All Angels, which was indeed rewarded with an infinitely larger congregation than the old gem standing alone in the fields two or three miles outside the new town.

The move was good for him in that he was less haunted than he might have been by the anguish of his great loss. In some to me ever-mysterious way, this move also enabled him to take a house on Guernsey for our summer holiday – a whole night's sea voyage from Southampton – which gave us all an exciting change and blessed relief from our grievous situation.

Never once in my life did I dare venture to ask my father about his own life, let alone question his motives or conduct. Consequently his sudden turn of generosity, particularly with our liquid refreshment – before any meal possibly half a glass of 'this new Italian vermouth', and half a glass of port afterwards – was puzzling to me. My father's wine glasses were naturally and properly full ones. From time to time he was wont to explain away such luxuries by saying, 'Of course I couldn't do any of this if I hadn't got rid of the Old Rectory.' I don't think the Old Rectory enjoyed more than a staff of one, aided formerly, of course, by my mother and sister. There was no longer any such help, as my sister was starting a somewhat brief career as an actress. In the new rectory we now had a favoured parishioner, Amy Porter – 'Ames'. She was a decent enough cook who had an uncommon skill in needlework, a trade she had followed for many years and of which my sister, about to go on the stage and therefore in urgent need of a wardrobe, was able to take advantage.

In those days all 'artistes' were expected to provide their own wardrobe, and the more extensive this was the more likely one was to get work. My step-mama, Ronnie, gave me a second-hand half evening dress suit (dinner jacket, black tie), thus enabling me to get my first job. Full hunting attire, it was conceded, the management should provide, this being regarded as 'costume', though most people elected to bring their own tights (for obvious reasons). From my own resources, I had to have full evening dress, full morning dress and a short black coat, plus-fours, sports jacket and blazer with grey and white flannels, dressing-gowns and night attire, as well as all suitable socks, shirts, shoes, collars and ties.

My sister read us her first application for a job with Dobell's Irish company, in which she asked £3 10s per week while agreeing to provide one ball dress, one simple evening dress and all day clothes 'except for shoes and stockings'. The answer came that she would receive £3 and must provide her own shoes and stockings.

Apart from his meagre stipend, my father as parish priest received quite a handsome honorarium, as was the custom, in the 'Easter offering'. This came from the collections on Easter Day, when every parishioner felt obliged to dip his hand extra deeply into his pocket or her purse. Roman Catholics feel quite reasonably scathing that the clergy of the Church of England should be paid by the state: all too possibly it recalls the *Vicar of Bray* and political control of religious dogma.

When my father died early in 1939 and my very dear step-mother telephoned me the saddest news of her life-time, she found me in Indianapolis where I was playing a pre-New York try-out of Behrman's *No Time for Comedy*. It was a situation from which no theatre person could extricate himself; there was no way that I could return home to give her a helping hand.

One is apt to forget there were no intercontinental flights in those days; only in 1940, in response to Churchill's plea 'Lend us the tools and we will finish the job', did a trans-Atlantic air service start from North America, taking off from Newfoundland and landing at Shannon. My father's funeral would have been long over by the time I arrived if I had crossed by sea. My step-mother assured me there was nothing whatever I could do and that she was able to manage everything perfectly; knowing and loving her as I did I was able to believe her.

The event, however, did cause deep consternation in my spirit. I am sure that to anyone fortunate enough to be brought up in a close and loving family the death of one's old man feels something like a blunt biff to the nose. Having suddenly no protective influence between oneself and death, and finding oneself alarmingly in the vanguard of life, feels more strange than the first day at school; one feels the new 'atmosphere' to be unfriendly, nasty, draughty.

It is impossible, too, to avoid intense fits of recalling the past. Such bouts are mercilessly penetrating in their self-questioning; when did I ever have the guts to confront my father about anything, to tell him his attitudes were stupid, childish, wrong, sometimes close to being wicked in their dangerous prejudices and ignorance? I remember his once declaring with the firmness of blind faith that Bernard Shaw was the reincarnation of the Devil! (I had been in a couple of Shaw plays by this time and pretended not to hear.) I thought back in envious admiration of my sister's complete fearlessness of him; she would oppose him directly; her brilliant eyes staring into his, she would blaze. Her feebler brothers offered her no support – just a weak deprecating, 'Oh, I say, Baba . . . that's a bit . . .', to avoid a row at any cost.

It was during the Guernsey holidays that some rethinking took place on the matter of my public school. We met two or three pleasant enough youths who were already at St Edward's; also three boys from the choir were destined to go there.

I could see that my father was very struck by this solution to what was obviously an economic problem. Every visiting acquaintance was challenged: 'Don't you think Teddie's

School would be ideal for this boy?' They all nodded obediently and vigorously, indicating that from what they had heard it was a good place. In the face of such an overwhelming weight of 'voluntary' opinion the small morsel of courage that was mine was not enough to rise up and protest, 'But father, what about Rugby?' I could guess that he was shying away from the formidable fees, and though my mother was supposed to have made provision, quite likely she had not been able to make enough.

Such was the lot of my generation (this is 1921, remember) that in such matters we did what we were told, though perhaps not in every case with such a glaring lack of fight as was shown by me. I was glad and relieved that the thing was settled; I was anxious most of all to feel I was getting on with my life. And so to St Edward's I went.

On arrival I was struck by three light blows. I was forced into the choir and, although I had loved All Saints, I felt I had had enough of being a choirboy. There was no appeal, this was an order. I was also informed a day or two later that their solo-boy's voice was well and truly on the way out as he was close on sixteen; I could look to be taking over from him any time. I knew enough of ordinary school life to know that these two factors would be a strong guarantee against any chance of popularity. I should confess now that the wish for this treacherous glory had and has been obsessive all my life; not perhaps consistently, since my desire to be my own boss has been strong in me from the start of my professional life and has done a great deal to diminish my earlier weakness, but it was strong in me at fourteen. The third slight blow was that the boys I knew, or thought I knew, either from my old school or as pleasant holiday companions, were chill and remote in these changed circumstances. It was a little like the volunteer recruit who, on discovering that his former favourite barman in civilian life is now his sergeant-major, greets him in the friendliest of fashions on his first parade.

I felt unpopular, and knew that I was consciously being made to feel so from my first moments at S.E.S. I felt quite stunned in my miserable abasement. My first two or three terms were much preoccupied by the puzzlement of why this should be. My housemaster, who was always kind to me though not always in the most helpful ways, did not make my life any easier by appointing me the vice-president of my large form-room in the second term, replacing another boy who remained, discarded on my account, in the same form-room – not very easy to handle. I should, of course, if I had had a grain of sense, have refused it; but apparently I had not yet learned about grains of sense; besides, the promotion carried the weight of authority and was supported by the Warden, who wished me luck and said, 'Show 'em what you're made of.' I'm afraid in the circumstances this turned out to be very flimsy material indeed.

With hindsight, I suppose that the allowable feeling of superiority conferred by solo-singing, plus my giddily successful acting opportunities, had lent my exterior a hint of show-off; and the female roles had varnished it with an extra coat of girlishness. All of which is a polite way of explaining away the fact that I was universally known as 'that sidey little shit Olivier'. I very soon caught the attention, rapidly followed by the attentions, of a few of the older boys. The prefects themselves, in the dignity of their exalted positions, were above such things.

I did not in any way welcome such attentions; I knew well enough what they spelt. My first experience of that had been a somewhat frightening one. Calling at the All Saints church house one day before I joined the choir, I was stopped by a large boy, an old choirboy, who offered to show me the stage upstairs where the choir school plays were performed. I was dressed in a kilt, Kerr tartan (my second name, as was my father's, is Kerr; no one has ever found the Scottish connection), with the velvet jacket and silver buttons, a customary Sunday outfit inherited from my brother. This boy flung me down on an upper landing, threw himself on top of me and made me repeat again and again, 'No, no, let me go, I don't want it.' This I did willingly enough, but it only increased his ardour. His 'exercises' were getting more powerful when to my relief he thought he heard someone coming up the stone stairs. He pushed me down these and himself disappeared further up towards the top of the building. I rushed down, tearful and trembling, in desperate search of my mother, into whose arms I gratefully flung myself. On the way home she asked me the lad's name, which she recognised; a year or two back he had come to a birthday party for me to which Mummy had invited all fourteen boys. She made me promise to tell her if anything of the kind should ever happen again.

The reactions I provoked two years later, at St Edward's, were seemingly shared by the entire school, quite instantaneously.

I was a flirt.

I was ostracised.

I had had more than the normal amount of chastisement at All Saints. I had been there about a year when a new master arrived. He was a shell-shocked, wounded hero home from the war – a type most dreaded by all schoolboys at the time. Their heroic gallantry was soon discovered to be wretchedly underemployed and found expression in the indulgence of sadistic tendencies. He had soon fastened his prime interest on me (I reportedly sang like an angel and was as pretty as was needed to attract the worst in certain males).

He arrived at the school armed with a specially fashioned strap. We boys thought: 'Oh, he's been thinking a lot about punishments then.' The object of his strapping exploits was of course me. With my trousers down I was made to bend over – 'Bend more tight, more tight,' he always said; angled to his satisfaction, he laid it on to my bare flesh until my screams reached the vicarage across the courtyard.

To the vicarage across the courtyard, my adored brother as head boy made his way. He saw the vicar and protested that his brother was being picked out for quite unjust and infinitely more frequent punishment than anybody else. 'It's not fair,' he shouted at the vicar's raised eyebrows.

The highest authority was now apprised that the kind of man spoken of as a 'sadist' was on his staff. The wretched culprit disappeared with surprising suddenness; he had only quite recently joined the priesthood and just a few days before this occurrence had celebrated his first Mass. With my experience of this type of punishment in my old school I saw no reason to feel alarmed by the probability of more of the same at my new one. I was surprised by the size of this miscalculation.

The senior prefects of public schools had had enough time and painful personal experience to look forward to exercising this most significant expression of their authority. The strength behind their cane-strokes was so powerful that I suffered pain such as I had not known possible. I never had much of a gift for the stiff upper lip, and in these circumstances I was quite unable to bear it like a man; my reactions were therefore unusually, stridently, vociferous. Other boys, when they knew that I was for it, would gather in the quad outside the sixth-form room for the entertainment provided by my plaintive performances. It took me almost two years to learn to bear such intense pain in the way that was expected of me.

My three years there, however, were not without an occasional pleasant patch. I always knew that, much as I longed for it, popularity was not to be within my compass. In the first place I was absolutely no good whatsoever at games, in spite of wildly heroic dreams; even those who only shone in their work were objects of some respect. For me, my three or four years were to be just an endurance test. My sky would brighten here and there no doubt; soon my voice would break and one formidable cause of wretchedness would disappear. I could still enjoy the two subjects I loved, English and History. In the spring I was allowed to row for my house (Set D) in the School Torpids (Toggers), which I loved. I would get older bit by bit; eventually I would be one of the older boys.

During my last Christmas term, 1923, what I had dreaded more than anything loomed up like a horrible spectre. I was told that I was to be in the school play – no argument about it – which was destined to be *A Midsummer Night's Dream* and, horror upon horror, I was cast as Puck; *Puck*, to *that* audience! It was now that I discovered a priceless gift in myself. At times when prospects have seemed altogether without hope (for example the part of Sergius in *Arms and the Man*), some deep-seated truculence in my nature has asserted itself. A small, sharp poniard of steel passes through my brain and a voice seems to come from my lips, saying, 'So that's *it*, is it? *This* dismally wretched part, this *utterly hopeless, so-called* opportunity. Okay. *Right.* In that case – I don't know yet how, but I'll knock their bloody eyes out with it *somehow*.'

Puck was obviously a success throughout the show. I can't think of anything in particular that I did with it beyond the most obviously high-spirited things. Our unloved but not really bad old toadstool of a senior master, bearded and elfin, immemorially enthroned as the producer* of whatever the school play happened to be, had arranged a much-admired innovation. I was to dance about among the audience, up and down the aisles and to and fro among the cross-sections, making surprise appearances, my face lit from underneath by two torch-lamps which were fixed to a harness round my chest. But there and then I learnt that Shakespeare could look after himself and look after, too, the actor who trusts him. At the end there was no particularly marked applause for me, but I knew well the school tradition – fair dos for all.

* The title of 'producer' enjoyed its original distinction at this time, meaning the person who ordered the actors' moves, prescribed their inflections, set the tempo and generally interpreted the author's intentions. In the old actor-manager days this was part of the stage-manager's job, carried out, of course, in accordance with his chief's desires. This new influence in the theatre was made significant at the turn of the century by Granville Barker in England, Fay in Ireland, Copeau in France, Reinhardt in Germany, Stanislavsky in Russia, Frohman in New York, etc. Gradually, under the influence of the silent film as well as that of Broadway, the meaning of 'producer' changed emphatically. It was seized by the no doubt deserving individual whose money, influence or ownership of the play entitled him to it. It took most of the 1950s for the British theatre to be generally converted to this usage.

The title of the person with the more technical métier became the 'director', who on film by tradition claimed the position of honour in the credits, namely the last before the beginning of the photographed story.

But next day, because of the heretofore unknown, undreamt of number of boys that were not only willing but anxious to walk round the quad with me, their arms through mine, I realised what had happened. Popularity was measured by the quantity of schoolmates who queued up to be seen walking round the quad with a favoured one.

Unbelievably, indeed, I was at long last popular. But it was too late: already too late. Only a few days later came my brother's departure to India, and I found myself sitting in shallow, dirty bath water, listening agog to my father giving me full and thrilling instructions regarding my future.

CHAPTER THREE

Rough, Not Ready

During that spring term of 1924 at St Edward's I had got permission to leave school for a day in London to try for a scholarship at the Central School of Speech Training and Dramatic Art, in the Albert Hall. This Victorian coliseum boasts four projecting architectural features forming four separate covered entrance porches. Looked at from the front, the right-hand one of these housed at this time the stage of the Central School, its auditorium sweeping away from the stage on each side in the way dictated by the circular form of the huge building, making a design eccentrically unlike that of any other theatre I have even known. It was uncommonly narrow from front to back, accommodating at the most six rows.

I was directed by an obliging commissionaire to my destination. On the way up I peeped through a door and found myself gazing down at the vastest expanse I had ever seen or imagined inside a building. I had a moment of terror that I would be obliged to stand on that tiny platform in front of that magnificent organ and that the place would be filled with – how many would it hold – four, five thousand? The thought was mercifully dismissed. I shook off my apprehensions and continued in search of the great lady of whom I had such hopes.

Elsie Fogerty was not a tall woman, and she possessed the slight thickness of set to be expected in late middle age. She was smartly dressed with a carefully chosen hat; dark-haired with some assistance, her head was arresting, even distinguished, but not handsome or very attractive. Her eyes were strong, very dark, almost almond-shaped, but by no means always kindly. Her looks were those of a serious person; her nose was right for her face, sizeable with an even downward curve. Her voice was predictably remarkable; its pitch was that of a richly skilled bass baritone. Though respect was instantly and always commanded, I never felt drawn to her with any kind of affection, although she very often, and markedly on this occasion, made a special effort to be kind to me.

Having memorised the speech that had been set for me in the intervals between school and games hours, I had also thought hard about the dramatic expression; I tried in every way I could to make it a performance, and 'All the world's a stage' must have been given more powerful utterance than I realised at the time. When it was over I was beckoned down to sit with Miss Fogerty at her table. She obviously found my efforts commendable enough, because without any beating about the bush she informed me that the scholarship was mine. I suspected that the fact that my sister was a former and reportedly favourite student of hers might have lent a little weight; if that was so, then God bless my darling old Sybille. About the bursary? She might discuss that in a while. She had listened attentively to my set piece and was disposed to discuss it fully, without being taxingly critical, except about my being over-gesticulative. This may perhaps provoke a smile, and the wish that Miss Fogerty had lived a few years longer. The fact was, I suppose, that I was anxious to show that I was not shy of physical expression and had prepared myself to display examples of this on every line. 'For instance', I remember her saying, 'when you say "sudden and quick in quarrel" it is not necessary to make fencing passes.'

Before I left she gave me one unforgettable, very special word of advice, which has been imprinted for ever in my memory. I can't think when, if ever, I have heard or known such a penetrating foray into the hazardous area of an actor's psychological weakness. I had noticed her during my recitation shading her eyes top and bottom in order to peer at me with greater intensity. She now leant towards me and said, 'You have weakness . . . *here*,' and placed the tip of her little finger on my forehead against the base of my remarkably low hair-line, and slid it down to rest in the deep hollow of my brow-line and the top of my nose. I felt immediately the wisdom of this pronouncement. There was obviously some shyness behind my gaze. This was a thing I comprehended so completely that it shadowed my first few years as an actor. I am not imputing to Elsie Fogerty the responsibility for a psychological block – it was simply not like that; I knew it was true, there *was* a weakness there. It lasted until I discovered the protective shelter of nose-putty and enjoyed a pleasurable sense of relief and relaxation when some character part called for a sculptural addition to my face, affording me the relief of an alien character and enabling me to avoid anything so embarrassing as self-representation.

In respect of the prophetic insight of Elsie's gesture, I would ask my critics to look back in benign remembrance on the staggering array of false noses that have been remarked upon me; one for Romeo, believe it or not, in 1935. I remember John Gielgud being upset about this and begging me to take the thing off. I was obdurate. He then sent for Bronson Albery as managing director of Wyndham Theatres to try to insist upon my obedience. I made some highly dramatic utterance like, 'Perhaps you would like to have it taken from me by force? But then, how would you force me on the the stage? Better let me keep on the nose, Bronnie.' (I had been on familiar terms with him since *The Circle of Chalk* in 1929, and I felt he was fond of me.)

After Miss Fogerty finished her comments, I gulped and forced myself to obey my father's instructions and say he could not afford for me to come to her without the bursary as well as the scholarship. She looked at me narrowly and said, 'That seems to mean that without our bursary you cannot become an actor?' I nodded miserably. At last, with a suitable show of hesitation, she granted the gift to my grateful relief, and I was able to tell my father that both his conditions had been met. He did not, as I remember – consistently, I suppose, with the confidence of his predictions – express any surprise or joy.

* * *

I did reasonably well at the Central, but as usual did not take full advantage of all that I could have learnt. There were classes in movement, voice, diction and every aspect of the job. I was particularly idiotic in my inattention to most of the lectures, foolishly and indolently not making proper notes on subjects which should have been, and later were, of the most intense fascination to me, such as theatre history, or the plays of Molière and Rostand in French. Elsie even managed to get the great Jacques Copeau to give us a lecture. Unfortunately he started in French which was way beyond my school standard and I let my imagination wander until something he said raised an appreciative murmur from my brighter fellow students. This seemed to please him, and to make sure his meaning should be understood by all, he repeated this one sentence in English. I have been grateful all my life for this happy chance. He was obviously describing the foundation of his company and said, 'There is only one way to begin to do a thing and that is to do it.' Somehow more appealingly precise and apt even than, 'That we would do we should do when we would,' from Claudius.

I just wanted to get on with the *acting* – natural enough, but how senseless; these studies would not come my way again, except as spare-time pleasures.

People often ask me what are my hobbies, what do I do for pleasure? I can never think of anything. I get strong feelings of guilt about taking a holiday; I am filled with unease if I am doing anything other than working. Work is life for me, it is the only point in life; and with it the almost religious belief that service is everything. I am sometimes in contact with sad people who ask me, 'What am I living for, what is the point of my life?' The answer 'Work' is not always applicable. I answer promptly, if a little sententiously, 'Service; if you can only achieve an ideal in that, if everybody could, then no one from the Queen to the humblest scrub-lady could ever feel they were living for nothing.'

After a year at the Central I scraped through to a 'halved' gold medal. I have suspected that this was perhaps wafted my way by Elsie, who may well have felt the need to justify that old scholarship/bursary embarrassment. My winning 'number' was Shylock (to be played in a very different vein some fifty years later), with Peggy Ashcroft as Portia, and we were supposed to split the medal, each taking away a notional half of it (nothing of metal ever emerged).

I had been fortunate in finding work for myself during both the Christmas and the Easter holidays, which enabled me, when I had seriously to look for employment, to say that I had had professional experience. In fact both jobs might have been read as semi-amateur, since both productions were presented in St Christopher's School theatre, an excellent and useful playhouse in, of all places, Letchworth Garden City. In each case the cast was professional and I was paid a proper salary – it was possible to live very reasonably on £4 per week. The first job was humble enough for me to claim that I started at the veritable bottom: I was second assistant stage manager and general understudy in a play for children, the name of which has never failed to bring a smile to the lips of the average profane grown-up – *Through the Crack*.

During this first job I went to visit 'our old Ames' – Amy Porter – to take her a couple of tickets I had scrounged. I felt it incumbent upon me to explain the importance of my job as she would not be seeing me at all 'up there'; but, I told her, 'When you hear the bell during the interval in the tea-room, you will know . . . *my finger will be on it!*'

Letchworth was enjoying a certain notoriety as a try-out place for modest managements, and a second job, during my Easter holiday, was also found there. Norman V. Norman was a formidable actor, enjoying what must have been for him a felicitous last come-back, making late splashes as Sir Anthony Absolute for Playfair in Hammersmith and the King in *Henry VIII* for Sybil Thorndike in 1925–6. His wife, Beatrice Wilson, an underrated actress and an angelic woman, was the second best Lady Macbeth I ever remember*. I was Lennox (quite a step

* The best in my seriously considered opinion was Vivien Leigh.

up) and a much more experienced assistant stage manager now.

On leaving 'The Hall', as the Central School was generally called, I turned immediately and with grim determination to the necessity of finding work. This involved daily visits to every agent in the Charing Cross Road, Shaftesbury Avenue and the Leicester Square district. I studied *The Stage, The Era* and Thursday's *Daily Telegraph*, which obligingly ran a theatre page one day a week – being forever regarded as the theatre-conscious newspaper in London, into whose useful columns my 'card' was inserted in every issue: 'Laurence Olivier' (very careful checking every time for correct spelling) 'at liberty.' A little later (1926), '*The Farmer's Wife* No 1 Tour – Next week, Plymouth.' Then in rosy times, 'Birmingham Rep. Next week, *Uncle Vanya* (name part).' It was reasonably cheap, three shillings a line I think, but it made quite a hole in £3, and a yawning void in nothing – only one half-sandwich at the Warwick Avenue coffee-stall for supper for a week.

Being still steeped in orthodox religion, I went back to All Saints as an acolyte every Sunday, and the vicar once noticed me in the vestry looking poorly from undernourishment, and wrote to my father advising that perhaps he should spare me £1 per week for a few weeks. This made the difference between life and death for a while, during which time I could address myself with renewed vigour to the deadly serious business of getting work.

One day I was called to read a part stylishly named 'Armand St Cyr' to Julian Frank, who was occasionally referred to as a 'lucky' manager – which meant that occasionally *he* was lucky, not necessarily you. It was a playlet called *The Unfailing Instinct*, written by Julian Frank himself (by no means an attractive creature, but kindly enough through his queer Jewish shrewdness) to provide a vehicle for Miss Ruby Miller, his star for the first try-out of *The Ghost Train*, which was thought to be a little on the short side for the provinces, where audiences liked to get their money's worth. This curtain-raiser had to be specially tailored for Miss Miller, giving her an opportunity, by contrasting material, to show what she reckoned to be her staggering versatility. She was, in this, 'Zee Grande Fraunsh Actrice', who had been prevailed upon by an old lover to give a gracious interview to a young boy – me – still in his teens, who had developed an adoring craze for her. Within a giddily short space of time she had divined that I was none other than her own son. I don't think I'll go on, I might spoil it.

I have never forgotten what I endured on my first entrance ever upon an unquestionably professional stage. It would have permanently shattered most, and would have been taken by many another as a warning that further attempts to be an actor were clearly out of the question; but not this little turkey-cock. The occasion was a special Sunday night charity show at the Hippodrome in Brighton, a very ample house.

On this particular night it was filled to capacity to do honour to the all-star bill, which was one of unusual glamour comprising no less than Alice Delysia, Ada Reeve, Lily Morris, Gertie Gitana, Harry Lauder, Billy Bennett, George Robey, Billy Merson, the Houston Sisters, Lorna and Toots Pounds, Scott and Whalley, Ruby Miller and all. Ours was the straight act on the bill – and the comics and the trick-cyclists, all the most brilliant talents imaginable, would gather in the wings to watch the 'legits', greatly and reverently impressed. Ruby's call to stardom had been *A Little Bit of Fluff* in the middle of the Great War. This great period was the last the music-hall was to enjoy.

John Osborne has always maintained that the end of the music-hall really did spell the end of our country's greatness. This was, of course, the sub-text of his play *The Entertainer*. He claims, it seems to me with justification, that one great property of the music-hall was that through it could be clearly traced the tides of changing public taste.

*   *   *

Every stand-up comedian relied to a great extent upon current topicalities; besides a liberal sprinkling of gossip of all kinds, politics provided the ripest field for comment. By noting the way in which these jokes were received – whether they brought the house down or misfired, or if indeed they were greeted with boos or hisses – the spectator, particularly if he happened to be a wise politician, could avail himself of this ready-to-hand testing ground, as could any student of social history.

Incidentally, I have my own convictions about the cause of the extinction of this treasured form of entertainment. When I was preparing to start my work on *The Entertainer*, John Osborne took me to the half-dozen or so remaining music-halls in the country, and I noticed this: that the scattered audiences generally remained relaxed, leaning back in their seats, and only if some *diseuse* moved or danced away from the microphone did they lean forward in a posture of interest and watch the figure on the stage with marked attention. I was struck by two related things. The stand-up act with a microphone clasped in his hand had a weapon of unbeatable calibre, thereby taking from the audience the right to send him cowering off the stage in response to their mercilessly vociferous refusal to have further patience with him. Thus the solo artist had robbed himself of his own gallantry. The admiration that the audience would have happily given to deserving cases would no doubt have been forthcoming, but not with that unsportingly unbeatable weapon clasped in their hands.

We were in the Brighton Hippodrome on a Sunday evening in the autumn of 1925.

I passed through the stage door and the stage doorkeeper said sharply, 'Name, please? Oh yes, you're new, aren't you? Well now, I've been told to warn you: be careful the way you make your entrance. This is the old type set. The doors in the set are framed right out – the same width all the way round, top, both sides *and bottom*. That means across the bottom of the doorway there is a sill – ooh – four and a half to five inches high. It's quite difficult not to trip over this, see?' The stage doorkeeper turned away to

his books again. Taking my small suitcase containing my
ready-made dinner jacket, shirt, shoes, studs, etc., and a
tin with a few sticks of Leichner greasepaint in it, a tin of
Cremine, a towel and a piece of soap, I went up to the
topmost floor to dressing-room No 12; here were quite a
few old actors, already at their make-up. After a while one
said, 'Listen, laddie' (no, *honestly*) 'it's possible you may
not have come across this,' and told me about the sill. I said
it was kind of him but I did know about it. Dressed,
made-up and ready (rather too much black under the eyes),
I sat and waited for the first time for my call, praying that
my name would be pronounced correctly. Eventually, the
sharp knock and the boy's voice, 'Mister Oliver, please.' I
sighed in disappointment and realised I was probably in for
quite a battle with this problem.

Six years later I was under contract to RKO in Hollywood; Schnitzer, the big boss (his brother was head of
Western Wardrobes), sent for me to deliver a nasty threat:
'If y' don' change that name o' yours, we just can't do
noth'n wid yer – may's well letcha go. Just change that "u"
to a doubleya in the normal way 'n take that goddam extra
"i" outa'v'ya second name, huh? Lawrence Oliver – wut's
wrong withat? Y' c'n say it, y' c'n read it, it's easy, it's
catchee, we c'n *use* ya, we c'n build y'*up*! Wadya say?
C'mon, kid, now get goin', willya?'

I confided in my agents, who understood. If I was really
prepared to take risks for what was a reasonable bit of
pride, they supposed, okay, it was up to me. I hated
'Lawrence Oliver' and loved my own name, I told them; I
felt it had a little distinction; besides a slight difficulty with a
name was supposed to make it more memorable. Frank
Joyce and Myron Selznick were just emerging from the
crammed snake-pit – they had recently made a dazzling
new deal for Constance Bennett, sister of Joan and Barbara, and supremacy was within their grasp. I was lucky to
belong to them (you belonged to your agent, your agent
didn't belong to you). They travelled quickly on and up to
become, I think, the biggest of the empires among actors'
agencies.

I changed over to the William Morris Agency after a few years. The big pull there, apart from the high respectability of their reputation, was a very small-sized man with a very large-sized talent, a genius at his trade who was their representative, named Johnny Hyde. After all too short a time of association he became ill, and in hospital Vivien and I went to visit him. There was an unusually attractive, pretty blonde girl standing by his pillow who retired immediately we appeared; she was later to become a dazzlingly famous star whose name was Marilyn Monroe. Johnny died soon after and then we weren't thinking about agents for quite a bit; just the war, Europe, home.

Back for another glimpse of 1925.

The call-boy was on the lowest rung of the theatrical ladder, though advancement was quite possible; I imagine that Claude Rains must be the most spectacular example of one who started life as a call-boy. I followed the one who had called me 'Mr Oliver' down the back-stage stairs of the Brighton Hippodrome. On the way he said, 'Oh, you have to be careful, the entrance is a bit awkward.' 'I know, thanks,' I said. This was getting tedious.

Some of my generation may remember an ancient ghost of a habit that still haunted *les grandes dames* of our theatre in our early days. It was a device, we assumed, deliberately cultivated to lend dignity, grandeur, hauteur, not to say majesty to their image as leading ladies, which was accomplished by raising their beautiful skirts and seemingly sailing across the threshold on their entrance. It was born of forgotten years early training in how to cope with *that sill* somehow, without looking undignified.

I stepped on to the stage, which as I had guessed was pretty sizeable. Several yards away the stage manager was beckoning me from the traditional left-hand prompt corner. (Stage-right prompt corners were unusual, except for odd places like the Birmingham Rep.) I came up to him and said, 'I know, you're going to tell me about that old sill, aren't you?' He waved me impatiently round the back of the set to the upstage right entrance at the end of the back wall of the set, which of course flapped about like a becalmed sail; I waited two or three yards up right of it for my cue from the stage. There was a friendly stagehand standing near me. My cue came and I started forward, the stagehand just touched me on the sleeve and pointed to the bottom of the door; it was my turn to wave someone impatiently away. I gave the canvas door a push and strode manfully through it.

Of course I did a shattering trip over the sill, sailed through the air, and before I knew what was happening to me I found my front teeth wedged firmly between a pink bulb and a blue one in the middle of the footlights. I was appearing before a very ample house, which means that an audience reaction of any kind makes a thunderously loud noise to one on the stage facing it. The particular reaction stunned me for a second or two by its volume. I scrambled to my feet dusting myself off, and stood a while blinking at the audience; then turned and blinked at Ruby Miller, who was pro enough not to have turned a hair. I looked back once pleadingly to the audience, but they were not to be robbed as easily as that of their biggest laugh for ages.

In the many years between then and now I have delightedly played in numerous comedies and have often had cause to cast my mind wistfully and longingly back to that moment. I have flattered myself that I could generally fetch the size of laugh that I thought I, or the comic situation, merited, but I have sighed in vain; never, never in my life have I heard a sound so explosively loud as the joyous clamour made by that audience. Whenever I may have thought that I had reason to feel pleased with myself, the recollection of my first entrance on to a professional stage has restored my sense of balance at once.

I made my wretched way upstage right to Ruby and took my place beside her on the sofa, leaving her with her wonderfully skilled sense of timing to bring that laugh to a halt – which she did with the confident assurance of a conductor bringing his orchestra to an abrupt silence with a sharp sweep of his baton.

Finally, my part of the scene concluded, I rose, bent to kiss Ruby's hand, and got myself off, avoiding the sill this time, to the pleasing accompaniment of a merry little round of applause from that most generous of audiences. At this my head swelled in an alarming resurgence of over-confidence.

The next day being Monday, Ruby, Julian and I had an early start to get to Manchester to join *The Ghost Train* on one of its early try-out tours, with our sketch at the beginning as a curtain raiser. I had to understudy in *The Ghost Train* too, and stand in a doorway backstage centre, dressed as a policeman with a painted moustache (I was a long way from the audience; Leichner No 7).

In those days a manager was permitted to take quite a few weeks out of a tour, in this case as much as every other week, and keep you under contract meanwhile. This tour, which totalled twelve weeks, in fact amounted to only six. Half of the engagement was therefore subject to the 'No Play, No Pay' clause (Stage Guild contract) so that if, as was my case, your salary was agreed at £4 per week, you only averaged £2 per week and you did not get rich, fat, or save a penny-piece out of that.

At the end of this 'tour', Julian decided to call a halt for a while and the company was laid off. Eventually *The Ghost Train* found the right 'road' into London, entirely recast, where it hit the jackpot and enjoyed a very long run – 'lucky Julian Frank'.

Again I joined the elbowing throng of the unemployed. After more weeks of alternate hope and despair I scraped a job with the Lena Ashwell Players; whereupon I wrote, at the suggestion of Mr Ponting, my Castellain Road land-lord, A Very Formal Notice Indeed to all my agents and interviewers: 'Mr Laurence Olivier begs to thank you for your extreme kindness in the matter of his employment but is anxious that you should not trouble yourself more than is necessary and therefore wishes to advise you that he has been engaged by the Lena Ashwell Players.' This, if you please, in far from the most exquisitely neat handwriting and on the most ordinary sheets of the plainest paper.

Miss Ashwell, having enjoyed a name of considerable renown, had fallen prey to the inducements of actress management. Her company was the scrappiest mixture: would-be West End actors desirous of a change from constant disappointments, a few really scruffy old derelicts, and a handful of desperate hopefuls like myself. There was no sort of influence to pull the company together, Miss Ashwell was no Lilian Baylis, and she liked to remain unseen and mystifying, just a vaguely feared figure in an upstairs office. I was engaged to play Antonio in *The Tempest* – not exactly a golden opportunity – and three parts (it hardly matters which) in *Julius Caesar*.

Miss Ashwell obeyed the dictates of a social conscience and sent her company not to the provinces, not even to the suburbs, but to unthought-of parts of London. One-night stands in such places as Deptford, Ilford, Islington, Shadwell, Shoreditch, Limehouse and a few others that the memory boggles at. You had to pay your own fares to all these places, which was quite a consideration for one starting from Maida Vale, out of £2 10s per week, and I was back to near-starving conditions. We were always playing in boarded-over swimming-baths, plus the occasional town hall, dressing sometimes in the bath cubicles or, quite often, in the lavatories. I'm afraid it was I who rechristened the company 'The Lavatory Players'. Very commonly, the company, divided into sex-segregated halves, had to do what they could in the wings. As a concession, there was one exception: you were given your fare to Watford, where you did a full week, staying (and paying) at a pub. After two or three weeks of such dates, you were given a *bonne-bouche* – three weeks at Miss Ashwell's headquarters, the Century Theatre in Archer Street, Notting Hill (no relation to other, more recent theatres or companies taking that name).

These conditions had an appalling effect on company discipline. Giggles prevailed, in some cases so uncontrollably that the play had to stop and someone – often from the prompt corner – had in desperation to make a quick cut past the danger-point. One night something damned unfortunate occurred. I was opening *Julius Caesar* as Flavius at the Century, giving utterance to his famous opening lines.

*   *   *

Pinned to the black velvet backdrop were two or three dismally dreary-looking wreaths. When safely playing away from headquarters in the outer sticks of London, I discovered that if, while pulling down and discarding these tributes to Caesar, I gave the wreaths a cunning twist and quickly tore downwards, I achieved a much more satisfying tear in the black velvet; thus for the benefit of Marullus and conceivably a member or two of the audience, the naked bottoms of the female members of the cast in the act of changing were 'unintentionally' revealed.

When Marullus's opportunity came he was given the privilege of stepping on to a grey-painted beer-crate. One night, on his climactic line, '. . . *knew you not* Pompey?' an extra burst of energy brought his long pants down from under his toga and they fell straight down, imprisoning his feet; more malevolent still, they continued downward to the floor draping themselves snugly round the beer-crate, immobilising his feet. The poor man was powerless to move in any direction. I lost all control and, gallantly leaving my partner to his fate, got myself, quaking hysterically, from the stage. The crowd quickly melted away. Eventually, in response to Marullus's desperate gesticulations, all alone and palely loitering, the stage manager at last brought the curtains together.

A message came to me that night that Miss Lena Ashwell would be expecting me in her office at eleven next morning; I was warned that, as the worst of luck would have it, she had looked into the front of house and caught that most shaming of scenes. I feared the worst, and no sooner had I entered her office than that was just what I got. It is, perhaps, a little sad that the only time she ever spoke to me was to dismiss me from her company. I don't believe I said one word back to her.

In a way my misfortune brought something like a sense of relief; the conditions, the feeling of constant strain, and for what reward? Again, near-starvation terms. Still, it had been a tiny something; now it was a tiny nothing.

At the same time I must admit that my history of indulging this weakness for giggling is lamentable, and one that will be examined in due course; but at the moment we are too much concerned with the tortured problem of ways and means. I resolved that I would now have to do what I had so long resisted: ask my old friends for a job.

Canon Thorndike, Sybil's father, had been a crony of my father's, and Sybil had found some sweet reason to befriend my sister, her near namesake. I think they must have found common ground in their connection with Elsie Fogerty, who had taught both of them at various times. Sybil and her husband Lewis Casson were so liberal in the flower of their acquaintanceships that a true and lasting friendship soon ripened between their family – their children were slightly younger than us – and ourselves.

Lady Wyndham helped Sybil to set up in management with Lewis and Bronson Albery in 1922, Lewis being her permanent producer/director (she refused to work for anyone else, I believe, until 1944). In 1924 she had a huge triumph as Bernard Shaw's Saint Joan. I now had in the following year to go and see Lewis and blatantly ask him for a job. 'All right,' he said, 'spear-, halberd- and standard-bearer, all the understudies you can undertake without looking ridiculous, and second assistant stage manager in *Henry VIII* at the Old Empire in Leicester Square, at a salary of £3.' I knew well, exactly how well, one could live on that figure. I pleaded for another pound, as I was to be part of the stage management, resolving, of course, to accept whatever figure he would declare to be his final offer.

My first week's money turned out to be £3, and I resigned myself to the usual penny-pinching existence – it was next to impossible to save in London and I was in great need of a new suit. My father had said when I first moved to town, 'Well, I mean, you can either walk everywhere and save bus fares, or bus everywhere and save shoe-leather; you'll have to try it and see which is cheapest.' And now, working all day and late into the evening, I was going to need a bit more to eat probably, and as for my shoes 'the welt had gone', as they used to say. But after the first week of the actual run at the old Empire my envelope on the Friday contained £4; I checked quickly to see if there had been a mistake – but no. It was like a great weight being lifted from my shoulders.

Special performances of Shelley's *The Cenci* were added to the bill of *Henry VIII* and I was given the part of an old servant to Orsino (Arthur Wontner). Somehow I managed to make an impression with this tiny bit; Sybil used to refer to it from time to time over the next forty years. My father had by this time married my stepmother, and though we were as close as we could be in these changed circumstances, Sybil and Lewis seemed like my second parents.

We worked together a great many times. The last was in the film *The Prince and the Showgirl*, for which I was careful to have a rehearsal period. After one week of this Sybil said to me, 'She's awfully sweet, this girl, but when's Marilyn coming?' 'It *is* Marilyn,' I said. I explained to her something it had taken me quite a few years to grasp: that for certain rare people, whose gifts were almost invisible to the naked eye, a miracle took place in the tiny space between the lens and the negative. After working a very short time with Marilyn Monroe, I learned to trust this miracle and stopped gnawing my fingers by the side of the camera.

Sybil died in her nineties, showing unbelievable courage in permanently agonising pain; the whole of her right shoulder was in splinters. I would beg her to take painkillers, but 'No', she said, 'I don't want to get woozy.' It was as if she were doing some sort of penance; my God – Sybil – a penance! What in God's name for? When she died, I felt I had lost my mother all over again.

So, at the end of 1925, I seemed to be breathing a newly exciting kind of air; among the host of serious actors of all ages in the top male dressing-room I already felt the *cachet* of being a member of Miss Thorndike's company, many of whom had willingly stayed on after the triumph a year or so before of the glorious *Saint Joan*. In 'my' prompt corner (downstage left, of course) which was up three steps to a snug round box with a near-perfect view of the stage, its brightly lit prompt-book shelf and my own glorious array of light switches all round the top of me, there were cue switches to the switchboard, the orchestra, the prop room, and seemingly every part of the house. There were two small lamps above each pair of switches – a red for warning, a blue for go. I felt it really was my property, since my place there was only taken by one of the others when I had to be on stage carrying my spear or serving drinks in the banquet scene.

In this latter scene I was able to pay very special attention to the delicious Angela Baddeley, the elder of two ravishing sisters, the younger being the delicious Hermione. All the young men in the company were madly in love with Angela, including the young Carol Reed, who was playing the non-speaking part of her courtier. We met a good deal at understudy rehearsals; ours was a most delightful, but far too seldom enjoyed friendship over many years. I was much impressed and overawed when he once took me to visit his mother, Mrs Reed. It had begun to be whispered even in those early days that his natural father was none other than Sir Herbert Beerbohm Tree; indeed the extraordinarily brilliant look in Carol's eyes was unmistakably Tree's. Years later, when Carol, David Lean and I, forgivably perhaps, fancied ourselves the three bright boys of Denham Studios, I went to see him in that beautiful block of old houses in the King's Road; there one quailed a little under the full glare of those eyes that blazed from the magnificent full-length portrait of his resplendent father. In these later years we could never escape the mutual reminders of how, back in 1925–6, he as the outraged courtier kept waving away this impudent fellow, and how the impudent fellow would persist as long as he dared before there was danger – not from a furious King Henry so much as from a more greatly feared authority – the scrutiny of an ever-watchful eye from the front of house.

I was deeply interested in my job on the stage management; it has always been my boast that as a stage manager I surpassed any that I have known. I was even slightly sad when it seemed that I was being thrust into the realms of acting; it staggers me a little that I could ever have nursed such thoughts.

I recall in particular one sorry incident that could have blotted my otherwise scrupulously clean copy-book with a less kindly and imaginative management. It was a misfortune that can reasonably be attributed to an unexpected moment when there was too much to do. It occurred during *The Cenci*. I should normally have been one of those discovered in the trial scene when the curtain went up. At this performance the Murderer was indisposed, and the part had to be taken by my immediate superior, who would normally have been in charge of the prompt corner at this moment so that I could go on stage with my spear. There was nothing for it but to ring the curtain up, grab my spear and shin on to the stage in a brave attempt to look as if I had been there all the time. So far so good. I signalled to the flymen on the curtain, switching on first the red and then the blue cue lights, and rushed into position downstage left in time, I felt sure, to have hoodwinked the audience. The scene proceeded. But at the climax of the Murderer's impassioned appeal the curtain suddenly came down, just as Sybil was taking breath to launch into her diatribe.

I was stunned and utterly mystified; nobody moved, and in three or four seconds the curtain went up again, apparently all by itself. I racked my brains during the rest of the scene and all at once it came to me: I had switched on the lights for the curtain up and reached my position in the fleetest time . . . but I had not given myself time to switch those lights off again! The flymen, coming back from the pub as always in good time for the end of a scene, saw both lights on and dashed to pull down the curtain. The head flyman, who was an exceptionally experienced and intelligent backstage worker, was also an extremely game one; having keenly observed the play, he saw at once the mistake that had been made and, without regard for his safety, he vaulted over the fly-rail, seized the 'up' rope with both hands and brought the curtain up again, while he landed in reasonable safety upon the stage below.

I still have my diary for 1926 and read there that the last performance of *Henry VIII* was given on Saturday 20 March. Its first performance was on 23 December 1925, which gives it a run of twelve and a half weeks. On present reckoning this would spell disaster, but the feeling in the company was that we were all part of a splendid success. The venture would have amply paid for itself in that time, and what if it hadn't made a fortune? Well, it was a rarely performed piece; Irving had done it, certainly with Ellen Terry, but I know of no other noteworthy presentation. For Sybil it could only have meant a gain for her reputation.

I certainly felt no cause for despondency. According to what I can decipher from my diary, in which the majority of entries are in fading pencil, that extra pound had made an astonishing difference to my life; I went for my haircuts to Topper's, occasional meals at Alexis, a charming and excellent little restaurant in Lisle Street, opposite the stage door of the old Empire; on 4 February I bought a pair of brown shoes, a blue suit and also an umbrella. To treat myself to a real splash of life I went boldly to the Chelsea Arts Ball, borrowing a costume that Geoffrey Heald had worn in the old days as Petruchio, and with a pair of 'Boccaccio shoes' borrowed from the wardrobe.

On Monday 8 March I seem to have achieved a much desired objective, for my entry that day reads: 'Barry Jackson? Phone.' Barry Jackson was a stage-struck millionaire who ran the best provincial theatre in the country, the Birmingham Rep. This would seem to suggest that some discussion had been going on with one or another of his representatives; the most likely for me would have been Walter Peacock, B.J.'s casting director, who was very friendly and two or three years later became my agent.

I wasn't exactly within the magic circle of my heart's desire yet – that means I was not yet a member of Sir Barry Jackson's Birmingham Rep, but I was under the same banner; I was engaged to play the small but fairly telling role of the Minstrel in *The Marvellous History of Saint Bernard*, a beautiful parable play by the French dramatist much in vogue just then, Henri Ghéon. I was also to understudy the name part. Our two leading players were Robert Harris and Gwen Ffrancon-Davies.

I had a shock when I joined the throng looking at the

board one morning early on in rehearsals and read, much to
my consternation, that the first understudy had been taken
from me and given to Denys Blakelock, an infinitely better-
known actor than me. I was much upset by this unkind
change. I decided I would beard the lion, in this case our
'producer'. This gentleman seemed to be the smallest lion
imaginable: a short man, his black hair neatly sleaked, his
face rather chubby, very white and a little greasy, and his
clothes tastefully dandyish – he always wore gloves. I
asked him to tell me why this hurtful change had been
made; to my amazement he said that I gave the impression
of feeling self-conscious in the passages requiring pure
religious feeling. I knew that this was simply not possible; I
was deeply and devotedly religious, and capable of con-
veying the aura of saintliness far less self-consciously than
most people. I was pretty sure in my simple but already
suspicious mind that there must be more to it. I did not have
long to wait.

Valerie Taylor was a beautiful actress with a most unusual quality of delicate simplicity; you could indeed
describe it as a saintly sort of warmth of personality, and
her looks supported this. Already a young actress of
some distinction, she was 'Valerie' to everyone within the
shortest of times from the first meeting. A week or so after
the start of rehearsals our diminutive producer beckoned
me into the stalls and asked if I had been in a couple of plays
in which Valerie had attracted some attention. 'No,' I said,
'I wasn't.' 'Well,' he said, 'I find it extremely unsuitable for
you to call Miss Taylor "Valerie"!' My God, I thought, I
never expected that anyone would make their jealousy so
palpably obvious as that. I felt certain it was a case of
'despised love', and promptly went to tell Valerie about it.
She laughed and said, 'Oh, you mustn't take any notice of
that, he's just a silly little man.' Not until 1950, in the first
play of my tenancy of the St James's, did Valerie and I work
together again, in Fry's *Venus Observed*; her part was the
most significant of the three leading ladies', and quite
perfect she was too.

The run of *Saint Bernard* was irrecoverably interrupted.

It was 1926 and there in my diary, in large pencilled letters, is 'STRIKE??!' on 3 May. On the fifth, '*St Bernard* closes after matinée – *pro tem*?'

The General Strike was the worst in the history of Great Britain and paralysed the country for almost two weeks. Many members of the middle classes helped to keep essential services going. I got a job on the underground, after taking care to fit myself up with a fine pair of plus-fours, not wishing to be out of the picture and guessing, quite correctly, that this would be almost a uniform among the volunteers. (I have constantly been told in the last few years that I was on the wrong side and should be ashamed of myself.)

I was taken on as a gateman, there being no automatic gates on the tube trains then. The gates were opened by pulling towards you, one in each hand, two round-handled levers; they were closed by pushing the handles away from you. The drivers were student engineers, or sometimes specialists from the Services. The steam trains were operated mostly by boilermen ratings or Petty Officers E from the Navy; bus drivers and conductors, usually in pairs (depending on the district), were the toughest rugger-playing types from the universities, armed with police truncheons and, in a few extra-nervous cases, with their own shotguns. Some of these jobs were really dangerous, particularly in the rougher parts of London. We gatemen encountered no more than mockery, which could be quite humorous. I found to my surprise that I was being paid £5 a week for a job I had imagined would not be paid at all. At the Kingsway I had managed to 'up myself' to £6 10s.

Quite soon after the General Strike was over, the run of *Saint Bernard* was finally brought to a close with a curtain speech by Barry in a rare fit of petty bitterness. It went something like this: 'Ladies and gentlemen. I have to thank you for the support that you have given to this play, which, out of sixty-three performances, has actually paid at only ten of them. Thank you *so* much. Goodnight.'

This shocked us all, I think; it really did seem a bit rough on that particular audience, who had paid and sat attentively, to blame them for the many audiences who had ignored the offering altogether. It taught me to be very careful about venting my feelings on the paying public. There has been, I think, but one occasion on which I have addressed an audience in terms of reproof. I was playing the smallish part of the Chorus in *Antigone* (1949), and it was extraordinary that the uncontrolled coughing from that particular house should have upset me so much; but on account of my colleagues, who were suffering dreadfully from the barrage, I just could not restrain myself from remonstrating with those whose bad-mannered thoughtlessness was inflicting such torment on my fellows. Afterwards I felt by no means sure that I had done the right thing, though the other actors were pleased enough; after more thought I felt that I had been wrong. There are quite a number of instances of actors addressing their audiences in the middle of the play. None that I have heard tell of make very amusing reportage and generally the instance is regrettable.

At curtain-fall, on the other hand, a brief curtain speech that is witty and apt can be most agreeable. Shaw made a famous Shavian riposte when, during a small lull in the well-deserved plaudits after the triumphant first night of *Arms and the Man*, there came the sound of a single 'Boo'; the audience was reduced to a horrified silence in which, looking towards the man who made the comment, Shaw said, 'I agree with *you*; but who are we among so many?' George Robey once made a joke which a man in the audience felt was too near the knuckle; he stood up and made his way across the auditorium to the exit. Robey stood staring at him and then proceeded to walk parallel with the man all the way to the proscenium arch, and just as the offended man reached the exit door Robey spluttered in his best shocked manner, 'Ai say . . . you didn't think I meant *that*, did you?' (Collapse of offended party.)

At the best of times, no one would in wisdom cross swords with Noël Coward unless well prepared with a last word. At the end of one of Noël's less happy first nights, the applause was warm and strong from his friends, but his friends had not shown up in the numbers that might have been expected and such plaudits as there were petered out for lack of encouragement. In the quiet that followed, a voice from the gallery shouted, 'We expected better!' Noël replied instantly, 'So did I,' turned his back to the audience and remained thus, bowing his thanks to the company until the curtain came down for the last time.

While at the Kingsway, whose fortunes were clearly insecure, I had applied to Birmingham Repertory Company for consideration as one of the two juveniles in a No 1 tour of *The Farmer's Wife*. It was a play I loved dearly, but I had also taken note of the fact that the No 1 tour spent two weeks at the Royal Court Theatre in London to give the resident company there a summer holiday. *The Farmer's Wife* ran for three years at the Court, and ran three concurrent tours for five years; No 1 covering the main provincial towns of Manchester, Glasgow, Edinburgh, etc.; No 2, Wolverhampton perhaps, Bolton, Huddersfield, etc.; No 3, Hartlepool, Ashby de la Zouche, Wigan and, according to the season, seaside towns like Rhyl, Colwyn Bay and Clacton-on-Sea, and, if pushed for dates, even such places as Aylesbury, Worcester, Chichester, Marlborough, Hythe, and so on. By comparison with present conditions, one might think that work would have been limitless, with not enough actors to fill the empty places; and we have not yet taken account of the Reps in almost every town in the country, and the touring actor-manager Reps – even the smallest places had their seasons. One does not have to ponder for long on the reason for this *richesse*. There was nowhere for the people, ever drawn by the herding instinct, to go to but a church service, a travelling circus or the country fairs.

Despite all this, unemployment in the profession even then was prodigious; I found starting my career in 1925 a sore anxiety, as my sister had before me. Then came the movies, regarded only as a curiosity until the early 1930s. The present state of the profession is that there are 26,000 people represented by British Equity, out of which roughly 800 are fairly continuously in work, a decent majority of that number almost constantly, the rest sporadically. These figures include the West End, any touring going on, such films as are left, and television. I am given to understand that the situation is almost identical in America. It may be easier to appreciate the situation if I say that 2½ per cent work, 97½ per cent do not. The profession has always been overcrowded; you might well expect this to have been realised by now, but it possesses a fatal fascination for too many people, and there seems to be no effective way of scaring them off.

Back to 1926, to the tour of *The Farmer's Wife*. I was too late to get the advantage of the two summer weeks at the Court, but each of these tours – the late summer into winter ones – had the same sort of exchange-weeks season at their end; this time the three weeks occurred over Christmas, not at the Court but in Birmingham. My hopes rose; if I played it right, if I made a tremendous show of how intensely enthusiastic I was, I might be taken on.

The tour lasted twenty weeks without incident but with a good share of fun and laughter. A tour can be instructive; apart from the healthy practice of the work, there was the fascination of seeing such a variety of places in my own country. There was, too, one fresh intellectual experience: someone had got hold of a copy of Stanislavsky's masterpiece *My Life in Art*. In the charmingly warm way of lengthy tours, this book was passed round the company; my turn was fortunately an early one, and it was a source of great enlightenment to me.

It became a matter of much amusement for those who had read it to watch the changes in behaviour and attitude growing on the one presently reading it. It was quite easy to tell whereabouts in the book the new reader had got to. For instance, when some young scallywag, who habitually rushed through the stage door ten minutes before he was due to go on, was suddenly found to be coming into the theatre an hour or even two before curtain-up; taking an extremely careful further hour or more to assume his make-up, and wandering thoughtfully about the set, touching the furnishings affectionately and familiarly; then sitting silently in the dressing-room, refusing to take part in any conversation but sitting quietly and concentratedly to wait for his call – well, the rest of us knew he had got to the 'Salvini' chapter.

My only regret during *The Farmer's Wife* tour was that I did not fall in love and get married. I was dying to get married so that I might, with the blessing of God, enjoy sex, the thought of which was beginning to obsess me unremittingly. You might well think that it would interfere with my work; it did not, to any damaging extent. There were no romantic adventures, oh no, most certainly not – without marriage that would have been a mortal sin and I was well and truly steeped in religious thinking. This should, of course, have dealt with the sexual thinking and sent it packing. But I was not, it seemed, made of the stuff of the martyrs, and more often than not the sexual thoughts won. With this uneasy compromise I continued in my religious convictions and practices until the age of twenty-three – the day I was married, in fact; make of that what you will.

The professional dream that had fortified me for so long came true, and I was engaged for the next season by the Birmingham Rep. Such an event as this allowed me to enjoy the confident feeling that my time of slowly taking off was past. As Cressida says to Pandarus, 'So let it now; for it has been a great while going by,' (*Troilus and Cressida*, Act 1, scene ii).

CHAPTER FOUR

Gags and Giggles

Overwhelmed with joy as I was, I was also young and idiotic enough to make a hideous and unforgivable blot on the last performance of the very first offering of my first season with the Birmingham Repertory Company. The evening was composed of a double bill, a curtain-raiser as silly as it sounds, *Something to Talk About*, not up to Eden Phillpott's usual standard, followed by Synge's *The Well of the Saints*.

The last incident of this kind had resulted in my being fired by Lena Ashwell only two years before. You would think that for an eighteen-year-old such a lesson would be one that he would never forget, but I fear that turkey-cocks have a short memory.

On this last night I nursed an insane determination to make none other than Melville Cooper, known always as George, giggle. He was a brilliant comedian, well able to handle any situation, the lead in *The Farmer's Wife* for three years, a thoroughly established member of the company and the pride of Birmingham Rep. (In later years we were together in the films *Rebecca* and *Pride and Prejudice*.) I thought it a delicious idea to make him giggle. He was playing the Burglar who has invaded the rich home of an asinine family who, after much idiotic blather, come to the conclusion that they should let the Burglar go because, after all, he has given them 'Something to Talk About'.

The Burglar turns once more at his exit for a final reassurance of the family's sincerity; I should have said something like, 'My dear chap, you have our word – the word of a Throstle' (or whatever). However, at this final

performance out came a phrase well-rehearsed to myself
over the last two or three days: 'My dear chap, we Throstles
are Freemasons, Frothblowers and Gugnuncs!' It was not
entirely unfunny at the time, all the epithets were in
popular currency; but so pathetically green was I that it had
not occurred to me that the high-ups might well be out front
on the last night. It did get a pretty good laugh from the
audience for whom the piece had not exactly been a riot up
to then; George conceded me the merest half-guffaw, but
the one who laughed most and so nakedly the longest – I
thought it would never stop – was me.

My producer that season, W. G. Fay, shouted up for me
as I was reaching my room; I hurried, scared and guilty,
down to his office. I found a furiously incensed and enviably
voluble Irishman (the brother of the great Frank Fay of the
Dublin Abbey Players), and he did not lack for expression
or vehemence. He was infinitely more wounding and
memorably effective than had been Miss Ashwell two years
previously; I did not forget this reprimand.

Next morning I was hauled up before Barry Jackson's
representative at Birmingham, Bache Mathews. He indulged in no abuse. He even allowed himself a hint of
kindly understanding, thereby adding further to my already
sincere admiration for this superb management. 'You see,'
he said, 'we can quite possibly forgive the giggles, they are,
after all, a form of hysteria, and hysteria is a weakness to be
pitied rather than punished. It was the . . . er . . . that . . .
er . . . gag. A gag is an element of the music-hall. Those
places can be thought to house quite a useful form of lighter
entertainment, finding outlets for many and varied talents
. . but . . . er . . . Sir Barry has the greatest reverence for
all that is highest in Drama. He has, in fact, built a temple to
it here, to nurture and explore its riches, its styles and
versatilities, and possibly find new creations for it. He did
not aim to build a music-hall, and is bound to feel affronted
by any attempt to turn it into one.'

The size of my enormity flashed upon me. Sir Barry
Jackson was born into money from, one was told, the
Maypole Dairies; it is interesting to reflect that a com-

panion in trade, Miss Horniman of the great tea family, had already made a landmark with her little Gaiety Theatre in Manchester, 'Miss Horniman's Rep', from which many a fine theatre figure emerged – Sybil Thorndike for one started there in 1912: among other parts she was the original Beatrice in *Hindle Wakes*.

Our theatre's debt to the northern part of England should not be forgotten, with due acknowledgement to that other great nursery, the Liverpool Rep. Think of the host of comics, the glories of the music-hall, whose northern talents stand in such formidable apposition to the cockney geniuses, the cheeky chappies and the sparrers. Further-more, how would our more seriously-intentioned theatre boast such a flowering without the Finlays, the Finneys, the Courtenays, the Bateses, the Bennetts? And only a churl could refrain from rapturously blowing a kiss to a Plow-right.

Here was I, with guttersnipe rashness, chalking some rudeness upon Sir Barry Jackson's fine escutcheon. Were all my lofty dreams, my dizzy ambitions to betray themselves by this kind of folly?

This time I did not 'do it again'.

Well, I tried terribly hard not to.

In 1930 I was cast by Noël Coward to play Victor, of that wretched pair of 'other parts' in *Private Lives*. He smoked out the fact that I was a giggler early in the play's run. Gertrude Lawrence and he was excruciatingly funny, sometimes quite spontaneously; to Noël this gagging all belonged to the area of experimental writing. For me the play itself was quite sufficient, thank you. I could barely control myself at some of the audience laughs, even the same ones night after night.

One day Noël beckoned me to one side: 'Listen, Larry boy, you're a giggler, aren't you?' 'Yes.' 'Now you listen to me; I am going, quite deliberately, to torment this weak-ness out of you. We have three months ahead of us in London and then four months in New York; and this is what I shall do: I'm going to do everything in my power to make you giggle and corpse at every performance and when

I stop, Gertie, as you know, is quite capable of carrying on, and every time you give way I shall bawl you out in front of the company and the staff; and if nine months of that treatment do not knock this amateurish smear on your otherwise bright young talent out of you, then you'd really better start brushing up on some other trade.'

In case you can't appreciate the agonies of torment that I was put through, let me offer some samples of Noël's wicked trepans; almost invariably these were reserved for the breakfast scene, which, so entirely enjoyable to every spectator, began to be the dread of my life.

Once, having been passed the brioches by Gertrude, he examined something closely on the top of one of them, then took up his fork and flicked the 'something' off it, muttering quietly, 'He-oh – little bit o' mouse-shit.' Then came the agonising period of his conjuring up Roger, his (invisible) dog. Roger would be sitting at his right knee and Noël would carry on a great spate of idiotic converation with him, feeding him with bits of bread: 'Now Roger . . . Tru-u-u-st . . . Pay for!' Noël's fingers would be invariably snapped by Roger, who would be bitterly reproached. 'O-o-o-h, ROGER . . . how *could* you? O-o-o-o-h . . . ungrateful wicked dog! Run along now, Roger, go and bite Mr Prynne.' He would watch Roger apparently crossing under the table to me: '*Good*, Roger, now sink your teeth into those lusty ankles.' Once or twice I would react to this, but the joke was over by then.

There is a scripted situation in the play when, during the breakfast scene, Elyot decides to start up some sort of conciliation with Amanda and in the process says something funny which causes Amanda to laugh and then choke trying to smother it. I, as the wretched Victor, had to rise hastily and pat Amanda on the back – according to the unkind script direction 'much too hard'. One night she protested crossly to me, 'Oh that's enough – you great Clob!'

'Clob?' asked Noël.

Gertrude roared back at him:'Yes! *Clob*.'

'Man with a clob foot,' said Noël.

I was pretty helpless.

By the end of the London run I was all but cured; my most dangerous times were when I dared to enter the lists myself. A gag from me which was successful in corpsing one of the others would still prove almost impossible for me to control. It was much the same dreaded weakness as premature ejaculation. But soon after opening in New York I was pretty well impervious and was able, if need be, to gag with the best of them.

Towards the end of our spell in New York the atmosphere of approaching parting was heavy in the air, all of us going different ways: Gertie to London, I think, or it could have been the South of France; Noël, no doubt, to some inestimably far reach of the Empire; my wife Jill (our 'Sybil' in *Private Lives* in New York) and I were bound for Hollywood – we were but recently signed to RKO. Just once in a final pass I was permitted to know the joyous triumph of complete emancipation from a lifetime's weakness. I made Noël laugh on the stage, quite undisguisedly . . . and *did not laugh myself*. He had started a gag of variations in the pronunciation of words. It was near the end of the run and he did these things more to amuse himself than anyone else, though of course if he carried the audience with him it was all the better for them. In the last half of the last act, Victor feels it is his duty to protest forcefully to Elyot about his treatment of Amanda:

ELYOT   (*snaps*) Amanda? Amanda is a fishwife.
VICTOR   Oh, I say, look here . . .
ELYOT   A fishwife, I tell you! (*and before Victor can start again*) – A fishiff! . . . (*then interestedly to Victor*) Tell me, does one say fishwife or fishiff?
VICTOR   (*interested in spite of himself*) Oh . . . well . . . I sup*pose* . . . it might be the same as, er – mid – oh – er (*cough, cough*).

Noël corpsed, but not I; I remained straight and blithe – not a smile near my lips.

The above scrap of dialogue was a typical build-up of gags that were symptomatic of the last leg of a run in that period.

*   *   *

The management at Birmingham were not slow to give me chances. After a deliberate setback or two, obviously done to test my head for possible swelling, there came a splendid juvenile lead in *The Mannoch Family*, a new play by Murray Maclymont. They also took a big risk by giving me the name part of *Uncle Vanya* at nineteen. Vanya has to appear to be well into his forties: anyone younger could hardly resign himself to sharing with his heartbroken niece an existence of patiently waiting for death. Old dodderer parts are easier, somehow, with more recognisable eccentricities to play on.

Indeed, this character work was the accepted lot of the younger actors before 1914. The privilege of playing the *jeune premier* was in the practised hands of the middle-aged man who, by now, had the skill and knowledge to present the foibles of youth in the most stylish and attractive manner. These were the unapproachable preserves of the actor-manager. How could a youth of the actual age of the role have the reputation or the prowess required by your Hamlet, or even by your Romeo? This arrangement was accepted by audiences the world over, from the time playhouses first offered candlelit entertainment until after the Great War.

The 1920s brought forth a generation of actors, to which I belonged, who fell under the magical influence of the 'natural' actors, led by Charles Hawtrey and followed by Gerald du Maurier. They deceived us into believing that realistic acting was, in fact, realistic behaviour; those marvellous artists hoodwinked us. Their influence upon us was pretty disastrous. We all assumed that acting wasn't acting at all, it was just 'being'. We had insufficient experience to appreciate that they were such brilliant artists that they were able to conceal their special techniques. After a period of inaudible performances and mystified audiences, we were forced to reject this highly specialised school and leave it to the experts.

Vanya was immediately followed by the high comical role of Parolles in a modern-dress *All's Well That Ends Well*, and then by Tony Lumpkin in *She Stoops to Conquer*.

* * *

For the first time scraps of praise began to reach me, but in the first part of the next season, starting in September, my casting did not afford me nearly the same delight: the really moth-eaten juvenile in John Drinkwater's *Bird in Hand*. Enter, to the disapproving Innkeeper and his more human wife: 'Good evening, Mrs Greenleaf, Mr Greenleaf. I was wondering whether Joan would care for a drive; it's a *lovely* evening!' A real wet, we would have called him (there was no political slant to the word in those days). Then, the hopelessly unsuccessful second lead in Holcroft's *Road to Ruin*, and a minute part in *The Adding Machine* by the brilliant 'new' American dramatist, Elmer Rice.

It was decided to use this piece to open a Barry Jackson London season at the Royal Court. My only hope was to find some surprising element in my tiny bit. Denys Blakelock, now my close friend, was playing in *The Silver Cord* by the masterly Sydney Howard, whose American wife, Clare Eames, was an actress of some consequence in the play. Denys introduced me to her and I begged her to teach me the right East Side New York accent that was required. 'I' was being dragged by 'the Tart' I had picked up into a cemetery. Clare Eames ordered me to quote my first line to her, which I did, in the best American I could muster (no talkies yet to give us a clue): 'This? Wa-ee this heewrrh is cemetewrrhee.'

'Oh no, no, no,' she said, 'this is how it would sound in the Bowery: "Diss? Woyee diss hee-awis a cemetairwee." '

I worked ceaselessly at it to get it quite perfect. After about my third visit she seemed quite well satisfied. W. G. Fay did not like it at all and tried to talk me out of it. I pretended I could not understand what he meant. To my joyous surprise I was picked out by no less eminent a critic than St John Ervine in the *Observer*, saying something to the effect that it was only a tiny part 'but he acted'. Somewhat to his shame, I thought, Fay said, 'Y' don't wanta take any notice of that Ervine, he knows noth'n.' But it was too late; I was well away. I have thankfully applied myself with the most rigorous discipline to any required accent all my life.

My next part was Malcolm in a rash modern-dress production of *Macbeth*. The only element in it that received any approval, I blush as I write it, was me.

Next the management decided to put all their eggs into my basket and gave me the name part in Tennyson's *Harold*. It was too flat as a piece of dramatic writing for anyone to bring effective life to it: 'Oh Tostig, Tostig, what art thou doing here?' Finally, as one last test of my probable swollen-headedness, I was allotted the wretched part of the Lord in the Prologue to *The Taming of the Shrew*. Frank Pettingell, who played Christopher Sly, the young boy/wife, and I were forced to endure every performance sitting in the stage box in full view of the audience. All asides from the characters had to be addressed to us. We soon learnt ways to torment our mistakenly trusting colleagues. Ralph Richardson, a few years my senior, as Tranio was visited with very special treatment. At one time, arriving at 'our' box, he would find us all asleep; at another, we would be gazing with intense and excited interest at the stage, and when he started to speak to us we would each pick up a book and start reading.

I had finally made a breakthrough with my life-long friend Ralph. Between the end of the run of *Saint Bernard* and the start of the tour of *The Farmer's Wife* I had been hastily rushed into the poorish juvenile part in *The Barber and the Cow* for a one-week try-out at Clacton-on-Sea. It had been successfully enough received at the Birmingham Rep. for Barry Jackson to try it out further abroad. I was sent to see it at Birmingham and witness Ralph's performance in the part I was to take over from him, so that he could take over a better and older part from another actor who was unable to continue in the play.

Ralph's wife, Muriel Hewitt, known by all as Kit, had taken over from Gwen Ffrancon-Davies for a few performances in *Saint Bernard* and, following an established pattern, had bewitched every young actor in the company including me. Ralph must have been aware of the hearts that melted like snow wherever his young wife walked and I imagine it was mildly irritating to him, without in any way disturbing his self-confidence.

I resolved to try to get to know the man for whom I shared the general admiration felt by all his contemporaries. My efforts to ingratiate myself with Ralph left him chill, aloof and superior. I appreciated very well why this was: I had no gift for making friends, possibly because I could not help making my clumsy advances so obvious. My referring to his wife as 'Kitty' did nothing to advance my cause. A year of rubbing shoulders with life, trying to make friends and learning a little more about the job, took place between this first and our next meeting. Now I was established in Barry Jackson's Royal Court season, which Ralph joined to make a brilliant success as Pygmalion in Shaw's *Back to Methuselah*. Early in rehearsals I suggested to him a drink in the station bar between the stage-door passage and the stairs down to Sloane Square underground. He ordered, I think, half a pint and I asked for a gin and peppermint – 'Gin and Pep'. He asked: 'What on earth's that?' Though my every instinct warned me that effeminate jokes would not go down with this character, something emboldened me to take the risk. 'Yes,' I said, 'good for the ovaries.' To my great relief, Ralph laughed and laughed, and kept chuckling for a rewarding amount of time. Thus it was that fifty years of incomparably prized friendship took root.

As a contract player for Sir Barry Jackson, my wages were £10 a week basic, even when not working; £15 when working as normally cast; £20 for a leading part. When this short season closed, I was shifted over into my old part in *Bird in Hand*, now very successfully running at the old Royalty Theatre in Dean Street. I had a run-through with the cast, half of whom had been in it in Birmingham. One particular member of it had not. (Peggy Ashcroft, by this time, was destined for better things, namely Desdemona to Paul Robeson's Othello.) Her replacement was Jill Esmond Moore, the daughter of H. V. Esmond and Eva Moore. With incredible presumption, my immediate action upon meeting her was a decision that with those antecedents, though not *dazzlingly* attractive, she would most certainly do excellent well for a wife. I wasn't going to wait for anyone better to come along, I was desperate to get married, and I wasn't likely to do any better at my age (twenty-one) and with my undistinguished track-record, so I promptly fell in love with her. Being nobody's fool, she did not respond automatically. In fact, she took two years to agree to it and never did really respond at all.

The 1920s blossomed with well-meaning and right-thinking Sunday Play Societies in London. I can think of the names of two of them – 'The Stage Society' and 'The Repertory Players' – no repertory about it, of course, but they did take the place of Rep. for the West End actor stuck in a long run or 'an obstinate success' as they were ungratefully called. These Sunday theatre clubs were well supported by their members and they took enough money to pay for their productions – not the actors, of course – and it was a chance for the young and ambitious to show themselves off and for the established to demonstrate their versatility.

I took on all the opportunities I could grab, one of which was *Journey's End* by R. C. Sherriff, a masterpiece about the 1914–18 war. Although I could recognise the possibilities of the part of Stanhope, I told James Whale, the director, I didn't think all that highly of the play.

'There's nothing but meals in it,' I complained.

He replied: 'That's about all there was to think about in Flanders during the War.'

In furtherance of my belief that luck is as necessary to artistic success as are its companions, talent and skill, here is an example of my special brand of fortune. I have been lucky in my ill-luck. I had quite calculatedly undertaken Captain Stanhope in *Journey's End* as a sort of audition, since it was all round town that Basil Dean was in desperate search of someone to play the title role in *Beau Geste*, and would undoubtedly be scouring every Sunday show; Captain Stanhope was an ideal audition piece for this most coveted of opportunities. Maurice Evans, playing Raleigh, and I, Stanhope, were dressing together at the Apollo, and we both knew exactly what was at stake. The part of Beau was going to be given to one or other of us, as it was known that Dean had got down to his last two choices for Beau. The other two brothers had been cast for some time – Robin Irvine ('England's rising star' on hoardings all over town) for Digby, and Jack Hawkins, barely seventeen, for John.

It was not the easiest evening two leading juveniles have ever spent in the same room. The curtain came down to clamorous cheering, for the play, of course – it was obviously a dramatic achievement of historical significance – but for anyone else? If so, who? We were both wondering. A knock at the door came at last, and Dean and Angus Macleod, chief of the Daniel Mayer Company, came in. Thereupon followed the most vulgarly unkind thing I had as yet witnessed. Dean coolly requested Maurice to leave the room. I was painfully embarrassed for my partner of the evening, as he grabbed up a towel and, in his army officer's breeches and winter undervest, his face covered in grease, made the only wretched exit of his life. Dean turned to me and said, 'Well, would you like to play it?'

Colin Clive as Stanhope rode triumphantly home for two years in *Journey's End*, which was brilliantly successful wherever it played, in New York, Chicago, and in as many tours as Maurice Brown chose to send it on; The Blue Company, the Red, the Green, the Pink, the Purple – until he ran out of colours. That was the kind of dazzling whirligig a theatre success could sometimes achieve in the 1930s until about Munich time. That was what I had renounced.

In the same period of time I went through seven flops, gaining not only experience but a happy collection of critical remarks and first-night approbation which constantly remarked, to my delight, upon my versatility. Hence my boastful claim to be lucky even in my bad luck.

Beau Geste, so hard won, was a bitter disappointment to all and ran little more than a month. *The Circle of Chalk* – Dean again – with Anna May Wong, the same. *The Stran-*

ger Within, with the actor-manageress Olga Lindo, hardly much more. It was now time for some sudden excitement from out of that azure blue sky; the only cloud upon it was of the hazy pink, romantic kind from the west, for in the west 'my pleasure lay', spelt by the name of Jill Esmond, who was playing out the long run of *Bird in Hand* in New York.

Frank Vosper, an actor of much distinction and credit, was acting in his own highly successful play *Murder on the Second Floor*. For some reason he decided he didn't want to go to New York in it. One day in the Green Room Club, when he was starting to write it, he had told me the idea behind the play and I had waxed enthusiastic. Perhaps that was why he thought of me for the job now. I managed to twist Al Woods's tough old arm by trying the 'hard to get' technique, which he fell for to the extent of five hundred smackers per week plus ten weeks' guarantee. I had been strong in my act in spite of the inducement of that pink western cloud; it was considered shrewd to be demanding with New York managements, then – not any more, I think. An English leading man was thought to be fashionable and was frequently insisted upon by the reigning queens of Broadway – not any more either, I think.

I sailed on 10 August (patron saint's day, I observed reverently) on the *Aquitania*. On board were two well-known figures in the theatre – Richard Bird ('Dicky', of course) and his partner Joyce Barbour. They were very nice and good to me, though I think I was a little young for them. They took much trouble trying to teach me bridge. After a while it was clear I was making it heavy weather for them. They stopped and said, 'Now Larry, dear, just look hard at these four cards, will you?' and laid that number down on the table, all face up, so that I could see them very clearly. 'Take your time,' they said. I dutifully regarded the cards, thinking they were going to show me some trick. 'All right now?' Yes, I thought so. 'Right,' they said, and cleared them off the table and put them on top of the pack. 'Now, what were those four cards?' 'O-o-o-h, well, now . . . there was a Jack of . . . Clubs, wasn't it? And a ten of something, a red one . . . wasn't it diamonds? I'm not sure about the other two.' I paused hopefully and they regarded me gravely. 'Larry, dear, we are sorry, but you will never learn to play bridge as long as you live. No. We really can't recommend you ever to try again; just think of it as a blank spot. If people ask you to join them say no, you are sorry, you can't – and tell them this story and they won't press you, and if you let them they will either get very cross with you, they may not be as sweet as we are, or else they may be anything *but* sweet and decide to take you for a ride and take the arse off you. So, you have been "warned".'

We all dutifully stayed at the Algonquin – a first-time must for anyone from the British theatre in New York. I always stayed there until the 1960s. Since then, either I've been lent an apartment or, I don't know, perhaps the dear place has too many ghosts for me now, but I still make all possible lunch dates there; one clings to places where one has grown up over a lifetime with so many of the staff.

New York was every bit as exciting as I had hoped. I nearly wrecked my chances with Jill because of a fatally coquettish side to my character (in psychological terms, I suppose, it is a feminine trait of the worst kind – well, too late now); coyly I did not announce my presence to her until the end of her show that night, although I knew that she knew I had already arrived; it was that pitifully irresistible inclination in me to dramatise everything. I still indulge in such idiotic fantasies; my mother should really be around with slipper or hairbrush.

I had a great time in New York that first trip, living in careless extravagance on my ten-week guarantee from Al Woods, only the first five of which I had earned. Al kept me there to collect it every week, hoping, I believe, that I would get bored with the situation and agree to a settlement or get myself killed in the deadly Sixth Avenue traffic. He did not realise how ideally the situation suited me. As soon as the guarantee was all paid up I had to return home. American Equity only allowed us aliens a job after a six-month period between each engagement, and no Hollywood scouts had been attracted by our little show. Al quite understandably sent me home as cheaply as was possible within the definition of 'first-class transportation', on the *Lancastria*, a medium-small Cunarder – none of the big girls for me this time.

I had given up the flat that Ralph had rented to me for the six months before I had left. As I had no job in London there was no immediate necessity to scratch around for digs, and I took advantage of the situation to pay a duty visit to my parents.

My father, that High Anglican priest – well-known to be against priests marrying at all, unless the would-be cleric was already married at ordination, in which case we will purse our lips and leave intimate questions unasked – had had a rather slender time finding a living for some months after he himself elected to marry again in the summer of 1924. Towards the end of the year, he took the first offer that came his way. This was the rectorship of a parish of some ninety souls named Addington (not the one of golfing fame), which was engulfed in a huge landowner's park in mid-Bucks.

I had become immediately fond of my stepmama, whom most people called 'Ronnie' (from her surname Ronaldson) because she so hated the diminutive of her name, 'Izzie'; when the full new name of Isobel Buchanan Olivier became hers, her new family all started scratching around for individual names for her. I bagged her initials, so 'Ibo' it was for me; my sister invented 'Monna' because 'it sounded like her', and so it did. My brother, who did not meet her until he was on leave from India five years after the wedding, just fell in with the 'Ronnie' lot. My father, with predictable correctitude, referred to her as 'Eye-obel' to relatives or friends, but when alone would resort to all the baby 'Bees-bees' that are such a deplorable family trait.

But they were happy, ideally so, until about ten years later when I was well into my second marriage; then I felt a shadowy little *tristesse* in my father and was emboldened to question him gently. Sure enough, what I had suspected was true. When they were married he was fifty-five and she forty-five, the perfect age-difference between husband and wife, you might say. However, after ten years of marriage, she at fifty-five 'didn't want it any more', but he at sixty-five was full of beans and this withdrawal of tender intimacies was distressingly saddening to him. He never upbraided or reproached her, he just dumbly accepted what was undoubtedly a scar across his life. One felt piteously sorry for the old boy, but one does know how it is with girls between fifty and sixty.

He died before the war started in 1939, just before his seventieth birthday. She lived twenty more years, the last few of them in pain, in various hospitals. I would visit her as frequently as I could; it became more and more difficult to make out what she was trying to say through her stricken one-sided mouth. One time she made it plain that she was burning to make me understand something. I just made out 'Larry . . . you must tell them to let me go . . . .' The anguish of it was heart-rending and I took the young doctor aside and talked earnestly to him. Whether or not they might have complied in a little while I don't know, because just then a bed became available for her in a beautiful Anglo-Catholic home for the aged in Chiswick. I knew that she would achieve complete peace of mind there because she and my father had always loved the place and my father had performed the offices there many times. Though I knew that there would be little or no hope of the recent searing request being acted upon, she would be content in the spiritual comfort of religiously loving hands.

By a great stroke of luck a brilliantly effective part now came my way. This was a shell-shocked Royal Flying Corps officer in *The Last Enemy* by Frank Harvey, a respected actor. It was rather surprisingly put on and directed by Tom Walls, partner and producer with Ralph Lynn of Aldwych farce successes for ten years. He had a reputation for showing a marked preference for the race course rather than the theatre, and it was said you were lucky to catch him more than two or three times a week at the Aldwych during any racing season. Lynn didn't seem to care; he was the more popular of the two as a comedian anyway. Walls

meantime did pretty well on the turf – among his successes
in the field was the great 'April the Fifth', a famous Derby
winner at the turn of the decade. *The Last Enemy* brought
me friendly and timely establishment as a leading charac-
ter-juvenile.

When the sad last night of this fine play came after ten
weeks – a management could well retrieve the original
investment in that time with a cast of eight or so, in an
inexpensive theatre like the Fortune – I was riding up to
dress rehearsal time in John van Druten's beautiful *After
All* for just a week at the Arts. Happily and surprisingly, at
the end of a resplendent career as a dramatist, John van
Druten made a dazzling flourish as director of *The King and
I* in New York.

On the Monday following *After All*, my diary records my
first flight, 'Croydon 10.45', from the only airport in London in 1930. It took eight hours, stopping at Rotterdam and
Hanover, to get to Berlin, Neubabelsberg, where I was
engaged by UFA to do the English version to Willi Fritsch's
German juvenile in *Hocus Pocus*, renamed *The Temporary
Widow*, thereby rather giving the game away, in England.
This was the first film I appeared in – except for one day's
work as an extra for a much-needed guinea in 1925 at
Cricklewood. The excitement comes back, reading '2.30. 6,
7 Kochstrasse', and, for the evening, *Die Drei Musetiere*. I
made a determined foray into the *grosse Operhaus:
Orpheus und Eurydike, Carmen, Madame Butterfly, Caval-
leria* and *Bajazzo*. I seem to have been staying at the Hotel
am Zoo on the Kurfurstendamm, and I had 'Bank Mks
1200 (£58 14s 0d)'; and on we go into *Tosca, Tannhäuser,
La Traviata, Otello, La Bohème, Carmen* (again), *Die
Meistersinger von Nürnberg, Tannhäuser* (German version). I had a couple of weeks off from the film and went
with Felix Aylmer and one or two others to stay at the Hotel
am Stölpchensee, which was on a very beautiful lake; and
on 17 May, 10.13 Friedrichstrasse, 12.30 Flushing, 9.15
Liverpool Street.

Fiercely on the money-grab 'against the wedding', which
was now set for 25 July, I was in the middle of a film called

Too Many Crooks being shot in four nights' work. This meant that you pretended that day was night and vice versa. I shall never forget the horror of sitting down at one o'clock in the morning to a meal of boiled mutton, boiled potatoes and watery cabbage, tinned fruit and custard. It was on this job that I first met my great friend and personal manager, Laurence Evans. I was paid £60 for the four nights; well, it was better than a slap in the belly, and I was getting married on a bank balance just in credit.

There had been a significant entry in Dear Diary on Wednesday 18 June: 'Noël Coward 10.00.' Noël was sitting up in bed in exquisite Japanese silk pyjamas, finishing his breakfast. He greeted me warmly as 'Larry', so I slung in 'Noël' all over the place. Noël told me later I struck him as a little bit 'actor-y'.

He told me he was offering me the part of Victor in *Private Lives*. He said he had watched my work over the past year and had been very struck by it, but that what I obviously needed now was a shop-window, and that *Private Lives*, with himself and Gertie, would surely be it, and that I was simply to think of it like that and not to worry about the poorness of the role. After a while Jack Wilson, Noël's marvellously smartly dressed business manager, came in and hung about; later on I realised he had probably been told to come in after ten or fifteen minutes to break things up.

Now things were much improved; I could get married and have a honeymoon, knowing that I had a job to return to.

PART TWO

CHAPTER FIVE

New Wife, New World

The ceremony took place at the church of All Saints, Margaret Street, conducted by the vicar still there from my old choir school days. There was a soreness over this subject on what we may now call the other side of my family, caused by my father's stubbornness. Eva Moore, a greatly respected actress who enjoyed an enviable place in society, was Jill's mother, and she and I were now cast in that inevitably uncomfortable relationship popular only in the music-hall. She worshipped her daughter in a way that amounted to idolatry, resulting in a possessiveness which, naturally enough, soon became the cause of some considerable vexation to a young husband.

H. V. Esmond, Jill's father, who sadly died before I could meet him, was a playwright of repute as well as a skilful and fine-looking actor. Eva, I believe, was never able to forgive him for the first night of their honeymoon, which he chose to grace by getting into a drunken stupor before fumbling uncertainly into the expected proximity. As their marriage dragged itself sore-footedly along, it became clear that drink was his besetting weakness, and eventually the cause of his death. He was apt, from time to time, to disappear from his family, no one having any knowledge of his whereabouts, and when he as suddenly returned to his home he maintained an obdurate silence on his activities while absent. The news of his death came by way of a police report from Paris. He had been found dead on a bedroom floor in a small Parisian hotel. His son Jack, Jill's elder brother by some eight or nine years, nursed a lasting ill-feeling towards his mother, who, when asked if she wished the body to be brought home, replied, 'It's entirely a matter of expense.' 'For God's sake,' he growled to me long afterwards, 'the Old Man was worth a bit more than that.'

Eva had voiced a strong wish to see Jill and myself married – if there was no escaping such an occurrence – in the Chapel Royal, Savoy, because she and H.V. had been married there. This did not strike me as being the most felicitous of omens, but after the lengthy endurance test I had suffered in my efforts to marry her daughter at all, I never thought another second about it. I plunged ahead, and telephoned my father to ask him, as seemed both natural and proper, please to marry Jill and me at the Chapel Royal on 25 July.

If I expected gurgles of congratulation and delight, I was disappointed. I have never known any suggestion fall so flat. 'Across th'electric wires the dismal message came', reinforced by a special steely-steady, measured tone in the voice: 'I could not at any time enter the Chapel Royal, Savoy, as it is known that divorced people are able to be married there.' His feelings had been equally strong on priests remarrying, but he managed to conquer those all right. Eva was justifiably hurt and outraged. In my desperation I went back to my old vicar ('Prebendary' now) Mackay, who promptly said: 'There is no question, I shall marry you here in All Saints. In view of the undoubted fact that relations between your father and your bride's mother are bound to be strained now, possibly for some time to come, it would be better if he came as a guest to the wedding.' This was conveyed to my father; I can't remember if I equalled his steely-steady, measured tone; I don't think so – I could never say 'boo' to my father.

I found the ceremony very moving, standing in what I had never considered would be my rightful place in that church. I had longed to be married, but I had never imagined where. Jill in her elegant wedding dress looked more attractive than I had ever seen her, and I was conscious that in my new tailormade morning dress I looked as close to the cat's whiskers as I was ever likely to get. All Saints had given us the full choir as a present, a distinction not usually enjoyed except by the high, mighty or rich. Eva gave a splendid reception in the lovely garden of 21 White-heads Grove, which was in a part of Chelsea composed of early Georgian houses. This particular house was once, we were assured in tones of awe, the home of Madame Vestris, a great *diseuse* of the 1880s.

I made a carefully prepared but wisely short speech, and the whole day, ceremony and party went down like a dog's dinner. The time came for the newly-weds to change into their 'going away' clothes and get away as quickly as decorum would allow; the journey to Lulworth Cove was a long one. We jumped into my proud Chrysler and, waving, moved off. I managed to change up from first to second without the ghost of a sound from the gearbox, which brought a faint cheer from my younger guests. Changing silently in 1930 was either good luck or brilliant judgement. I was lucky. I was not to feel so again for some little time.

We had been most kindly lent a lovely house by Lady Fripp, a friend of Eva's, whose generous inclinations did not stop there; no doubt with the kindest intentions in the world, she left us also her two sweet, but agonisingly embarrassed, grown-up, single, young daughters as host-esses for the occasion. This made a signal addition to the bride and groom's already mounting embarrassment. Nothing for it but to lash our tired nerves with champagne and hope for the best.

The best was not for the likes of us; the journey had taken ages longer than we had imagined, we were tired out, and both of us were aware that we shared the same unspoken dread of what was expected of us before going to sleep. The two sweet Fripp girls served us supper and toyed with something on their own plates as well. None of us was capable of dealing with the degree of agonised shyness that was reached at the end of that meal. Finally, Jill and I both dived at something of the order of, 'Well, now . . . er . . . p'rps it's time we went up to our room and . . . er . . . unpacked . . .?'

I have never been able to think of that slightly pagan festivity referred to as the honeymoon as anything but disastrous, and I am sure that Jill has always felt the same. After some hesitant efforts to accomplish something we hoped would pass for foreplay – my own efforts, I knew, would not pass muster in a third-floor back room in Lisle Street, and all that would rest in my bride's memory would be an endurance test – at last we turned away from each other. I remember going to sleep with the dazzlingly selfish sulk, 'My wife doesn't suit me,' as if to some club-friend. Ah, well, all men are pigs. I was only human. I didn't ask to be born. All the 1920s patter.

It really did look like a pretty crass mistake. I had insisted on getting married from a pathetic mixture of religious and animal promptings. I have managed from time to time to convince myself that it was more wrong of Jill to give way to my desires than for me to press them. She could not and did not try to deceive herself into believing that she was in the slightest degree in love with me, and she knew that I was fully aware of it. She had admitted to me that she was in love elsewhere and could never love me as completely as I would wish. This came out only a few weeks before our wedding; of course, it was all very dramatic, and that appealed to both of us. I was able to assure myself that I was a noble enough character and was without question going to reach such divine perfection as a husband that any such petty difficulties could be outfaced. But yet you see how soon the day o'ercast. The indications were that my dreams of high sexuality were not to be realised, which was depressing and soon became oppressive. I was just not imaginative enough to find what might be the key to Jill's responsiveness.

We got back, both in having-to-make-the-best-of-it states of mind, to find my mother-in-law on the doorstep, having been in to furnish it a little. Instead of being grateful, I was scowling and furious. She should have known that I wanted none of those in-law fingers meddling in My Domain and that I was planning to buy things bit by bit as the money came in. But did I really think that a possessively adoring mother would allow the darling of her life to enter a new home that boasted no stick of furniture except a double bed? Yes, I suppose I have to admit that I really did think that; that is, if I thought about it at all. Pots and pans? Well, I mean, we could just rustle those up from round the corner as they became necessary. We did have a 'lady', a wonderful mixture of char and housekeeper – Mrs Johns, a character. We badly needed characters in our lives; we had precious little to make conversation about otherwise.

From this wedding day I kept no diary for ten years, and did not pursue my religious practices ever again. These two facts are mere coincidence and in the very depths of my soul I can find nothing in the scrappiest bit revelatory about them. In the first case I either didn't find any necessity to keep a diary – never more than a date-book anyway – or else I threw them away at the end of each year; and in the second, since the idea of bearing children did not find any welcome in my bride's eyes, it was, frankly, a choice between contraception or religious practice. In my book, it was one or t'other, not both, and so, knowing as we do that the entire purpose of my rush into marriage was nothing more commendable than a convenient passport for a rush into bed, the choice seemed to have been made for me; but I am not trying to duck responsibility by putting it like that. I knew what I was doing and chose to do it.

Rehearsals for *Private Lives* started very soon; the first reading was in Plannie Massey's house, a grand affair in the highly fashionable Wilton Crescent. Miss Adrianne Allen was to play Sybil; she had married Raymond Massey, a near-star and a much-liked Canadian who, everybody knew, was as rich as Croesus. I was not, for a little while, really to like or respect Adrianne, or 'Plannie' as Noël had christened her. I had become disenchanted with her from overhearing a conversation at the next table at the Ivy a few months before. She was talking to a friend about Ray Massey's then wife. 'My dear, I can't understand it, we were such friends and now she behaves very oddly with me.' I, who already fancied myself as a psychologist, thought I saw through that one. Here she was, having made a splendidly successful marriage for herself, and she clearly did not think very highly of me either; indeed I gave her little cause to. It was all very excitingly Top Class though, and I tried to find my way in this new world, which I did not by any means succeed in doing right away.

We only rehearsed for two weeks, as Noël and Gertie had done all their stuff on holiday in the South of France. We opened *Private Lives* at the King's Theatre, Edinburgh; then in London we opened a brand new theatre, the Phoenix, which was a special distinction, and I experienced for the first time the incredible sense of being in a West End smash success – the thronged stage door and the parties almost every night. One of the advantages of being in a tiny cast was that 'those other two' seldom got left out of an invitation. Well, it was exciting then, before blasé sophistication had set in.

No, it's not really that; it is that fifty years later parties have literally made me feel ill, even to the extent of swooning away and having to be half-carried from the room (from which, of course, everyone concludes the worst), and my poor Joan has had to take over and get me home. I have discovered that the trouble starts in the ears from the hubbub, dizziness follows hard upon this, and the shaky effort to get one's glass down on to some table provokes the body to follow in the same direction all the way to the floor. Tentative as I am of aligning myself with such dazzling company, I am told that Ingmar Bergman suffers in the same way and will never go out at all to large gatherings.

Noël pursued his ultra-chic course and took the play out of the Phoenix after only three months of playing to bursting capacity. About half-way through the run, C. B. Cochran, the pre-eminent entrepreneur of his time, started fixing up people for New York. Adrianne did not want to come, which made it easy for me to make my own engagement conditional on Jill coming along to play Sybil. In spite of Noël's strict prejudice against domestic convenience being allowed to intrude on artistic considerations, except in the case of his adored and famous Lunts, the prospect of finding and engaging two others to play those awkward parts was unattractive, and the fact that I could obviously take a load off by helping Jill break the ice in her initial rehearsals went some way to overcome prejudice. Adrianne and Ray Massey accompanied us to New York and saw all the shows that were 'musts', attended our first night and, of course, the party afterwards.

I think there was hardly an evening when Jill and I did not have to dress up for a party. At one such I had the thrill of meeting my god and goddess of the acting world. I had seen and worshipped them earlier in the summer of 1929 at the St James's in London in *Caprice* by Sil-Vara, an Austrian. It was a scintillating piece and the brilliance of Alfred Lunt and Lynn Fontanne was unforgettable and unforgotten. Many an acting couple have been held up for comparison with this pair and failed the test. Lynnie, as I may as well call her, having been happy to do so for forty years, was the most ravishing actress that can be imagined: glamorous, charming and divinely witty. Alfred, who at all times directed whatever plays they graced, was a technician of astonishing cunning, as well as possessing an extraordinarily versatile acting ability. He was thought to be the genius and she the fascinator. 'Lynn is the lantern and Alfred the light within it', as Constance Collier said. They both had greatness and limitless courage; Lynnie, at a wonderful age, is still with us and has both these virtues still. Alfred died in August 1977. I was luckily filming in Newport, Mass., and was able to fly immediately to her in Wisconsin, knowing that she might wish to feel an old friend's arms around her for a gentle while.

Lynn, by the way, was an English girl, brought up in London where she appeared in *My Lady's Dress*, among others, shortly before the war in 1914. She was young and very pretty when she joined a stock company in America where she met Alfred, and that, to coin a phrase, was that.

Just as things were drawing to a close at the Times Square Theatre, and we were starting on our last week, Jill started to suffer severe pains and appendicitis was diagnosed; she was rushed into hospital. It was immediately clear to us that it was a waste of time for me to hang around New York while she recovered – patients were not treated so briskly then as they are now after abdominal operations; they were allowed a respectful time to recover before being chivvied from their beds. Noëlie was distinctly growly when I said goodbye to him. 'You've not no artistic integrity, that's your trouble; this is how you cheapen yourself.' Then, withering with disdain, 'Hahlleewood'.

So I went ahead to get a house and a car, and make things trouble-free for Jill when she arrived, tired after the four-day journey.

I had got over like a spendthrift sigh my nearly passionate involvement with the one male with whom some sexual dalliance had not been loathsome for me to contemplate. I had felt it desperately necessary to warn him that, dustily old-fashioned as it must seem, I had ideals which must not be trodden underfoot and destroyed, or I would not be able to answer for the consequences and neither would he.

It must be exceedingly difficult to believe that, in spite of my history as a pampered choirboy, and the attentions paid to me at the next school (which, no matter how unwelcome, unfairly labelled me as the school tart), I felt that the homosexual act would be a step darkly destructive to my soul; I was firm in my conviction that heterosexuality was romantically beautiful, immensely pleasurable, and re-warding in contentment.

It is surprising that this faith should have withstood an onslaught of such passionate interest, and that this, together with the disillusionment that followed the initial experience of my early marriage, did not throw me off course or even make me waver – well, perhaps I must allow it did do that.

It would be dreadfully wrong if any of this should be taken to imply that I ever found anything in the remotest way unrespectable about homosexuality; and it is certain that he or she, in pursuit of natural inclinations, should not be pitied for a lack of romance in their lives. I am prepared to believe that the sense of romance in those of our brothers and sisters who incline towards love of their own sex is heightened to a more blazing pitch than in those who think of themselves as 'normal'. Supporting this is my firm conviction that anyone who nurses artistic pretensions must discard any sort of prejudice which might limit the broadest understanding of human nature.

Hollywood had for so long been the Ultima Thule of my dreams that I felt a little like one of the first pioneers who, having fetched up on the westernmost shores of America, had come to the conclusion that This Was It. At this time the life of Hollywood was at its most absurd; things that were considered important were in fact childish in the extreme. Intellectuality was hardly acknowledged and carefully avoided; the only thing of which you could be fairly sure was that it would always do something if you flashed your teeth and looked 'sinceerh, deerh'.

Finding a charming three-bedroomed house on the very top of Look-Out Mountain, with a view straight over and beyond Hollywood to the distant Pacific, was as fortunate a beginning as anyone could wish. We settled down happily and optimistically to the new life, disregarding the inevitable hint of mockery inseparable from any mention of the place.

Making three pictures that came to nothing took up nearly two years, which seemed and was an appalling waste of time. The little nest egg we were able to put by against future lean times was useful, but we could not feel that our careers were enhanced in the slightest.

The first film in which I was cast also included no less than Adolphe Menjou, Lili Damita and Erich von Stroheim, with me taking fourth place in equal billing (RKO were building up their small drop of new blood). Though we had interviewed representatives of all the major studios during our time in New York, we had chosen a new studio, RKO Radio, which was far less heavily encrusted with established stars than the others, and we reckoned we had more chance of promotion there. This first engagement embodied for me all the most horrific aspects of Hollywood. An extravagantly dramatic romance by Maurice Dekobra had, inevitably, been completely rewritten, but it was considered that the deal had been worth the money for the sake of the title – *The Sphinx Has Spoken*. Needless to say, by the end of the picture it was decided to change the title to *Friends and Lovers*. It may have been realised that Lili Damita was not exactly sphinx-like. The cast, apart from its eminence, was wretchedly ill-assorted. So my first Hollywood picture died the death of a dog.

Next, after a healthy pause, I was supposed to be leading man to Pola Negri in a talkie about Queen Draga, whom François I of Serbia elected to marry. Draga was shot and the King was thrown from a window; he managed to cling to the sill, pointed out to me in 1957, until his fingers, crushed by rifle butts, lost hold and he fell to the street below. This horrid occurrence brought monarchy to an end in Serbia.

Sad to say, I contracted yellow jaundice and had to give up this opportunity and go to hospital. In place of this, with yellow jaundice there came *The Yellow Ticket,* a decent old English melodrama renamed, for some odd reason of censorship, *The Yellow Passport*. This, to my great delight, cast me as leading man to my sweet friend Elissa Landi, a lovely girl and a good sort of actress; she played the fine part of my sister in *After All*, and died some years ago of dread cancer. Lionel Barrymore was the heavy lead, and it was really quite all right. After this came a truly promising picture, *Westward Passage*, with the pretty and highly respected Ann Harding, a woman of great charm, integrity and beauty. My own part had splendid opportunities and I found myself feeling the stir of optimism, but it did not last; conditions were against any seed becoming fertile.

The Depression was at its worst; it was said that on Wall Street it 'rained millionaires'. It was quite a usual occurrence for a picture in which you had been cast to start splendidly on its first morning with everyone spruce and punctual; and after an hour or so, with maybe a couple of shots in the bag and in the middle of rehearsing the next bit, two shortish men in black suits, black hats and black glasses would suddenly appear on the set, say a few words to the director, make a 'That's all' sign, or draw a forefinger across their throats in our direction, and leave as quickly as they had appeared. The murmur would go round, 'the

Banks'. We'd all go home and pray to be called again.

The big Hollywood parties were unbelievably true to their reputation – a sheer joy if you were in a mocking vein. Those glorious creatures, with their entrances and their descents down the staircase, were quite magnificent in their grace and stateliness and their confident composure – so soon to disappear without trace. After a couple of bootleg shots, and in as few minutes, all that majesty was sprawling and rolling about unable to utter a sentence that could be understood.

The more eminent and stylish the stars, on the whole, the more dignified their deportment and general behaviour; perhaps their hooch was better and they were more aware of the enemies that might be present. Even we, two innocents, had quickly learnt to be highly nervous of the press, the most frightening members of which were those heavenly twins and deadly rivals Louella Parsons and Hedda Hopper. From this second lady you might expect more kindness and understanding, as she had herself been something of a star in the silent days; but perhaps she nursed the bitterness shared by so many who had not made the bridge from silents to talkies, or perhaps she just had an intelligent appreciation that, if you were going to be a gossip columnist, you had either to be a bitch or sink into obscurity. At Christmas everybody but *everybody* gave their most expensive presents to these two females.

A few months after the RKO boss had given me a charming disquisition on my American/English accent (incidentally an American accent of sorts developed by itself from sheer aural influence), the management of our studio was taken over entirely by a very bright, spectacularly promising, youngish man called David O. Selznick, soon after to produce *David Copperfield*. Obviously he had been sent for in a desperate attempt to make some sense out of the business in spite of the crash, during even the worst of which it was possible to make money from movies, amongst other things.

Selznick quickly set about transforming the studio. He started in the good old-fashioned way (old-fashioned ways are the best) by cutting everybody's salary by half. I found this a pointedly dismal sign of the times and one which clearly spelt out the hopeless nature of our prospects. It was obvious that the thing to do was to quit as soon as conveniently possible and get back home to make a new start in work of more serious intent, for which my soul had been increasingly sharply thirsting. We had saved a bit of money, not a fortune but enough to give us a little time to size up our situation after two years away and to make sensible decisions.

It was all much more straightforward for me than it was for poor Jill. She had been promised the great star-creating part of Sydney in *A Bill of Divorcement* by Clemence Dane, originally produced by Basil Dean and played sensationally successfully by Meggie Albanesi, who died tragically young. Of course the catch in it for Jill was that, in return for this much-prized opportunity, she must sign the new deal and accept the half-salary. This worried me, because it was difficult to believe that their intentions were sincere when her emolument was to be of a size that would hardly be noticeable on their books. There was something a little suspect about it that made me anxious for her.

In these days so much taken up with overcoming our enforced indolence, we were allowed to while away the time by popping into the projection rooms whenever we felt like it. Often we would find old pictures being run for some reference point, which were always interesting, or new rushes that no one minded our seeing, or some newly-cut sequences run for an editor who welcomed odd opinions; but usually it would be a test of some new person who was a candidate for an acting contract. One of these turned out to be the first test of a very remarkable young woman indeed. Her name was Katharine Hepburn, destined to be an object of keen interest; her personality was striking, and her acting ability was of great promise and of a strange quality not easy to describe. It was a time when each of the studios was intent on obtaining its own Garbo. Greta herself belonged to MGM, Paramount had Dietrich, Fox pinned its faith on Elissa Landi; at RKO Radio (not to be

Early Years

My baby book. It does not record my first sentence: 'Why you say damn for, Mummy?'

My father, the Reverend Gerard Olivier (1869–1939), cricketer, schoolmaster, Anglican priest and a strangely opportune encourager.

My mother, Agnes (1871–1920). No photograph that I have ever seen has revealed her loveliness.

My sister, Sybille (b. 1901).

My older brother, Dickie (1904–58).

Me aged three (*right*) and seven.

To Larry
From Mother.
Jan 14.
1915.

Katharina in *The Taming of the Shrew*. On 23 April 1922, I played my first part in a real theatre, the original Memorial Theatre at Stratford.

Tony Lumpkin in *She Stoops to Conquer*, 1927.

This hung outside the Birmingham Repertory Theatre to entice passers-by, 1927.

...arriage to Jill Esmond with Dennis Blakelock as best man, 1930.
...th my eldest son, Tarquin, 1936. With my lemur Tony, 1935.

To Harry

Larry, 1929

Publicity photographs (*left*) Beau Geste, my first leading role in the West End, January 1929; I made a strenuous effort to resemble Ronald Colman in the film and RKO styled me the new Ronald Colman when I arrived. (*Below left*) The day I signed my RKO contract in early spring 1931. (*Below*) An RKO still.

Laurence Olivier

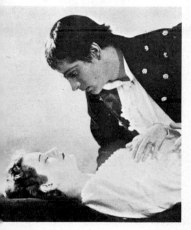

(*Left*) Peggy Ashcroft as Juliet and me as Romeo in John Gielgud's 1935 production – my first attempt at the nose, banned by Gielgud and Albery; (*Above*) as Mercutio, when I swapped roles with John; (*Below*) as Romeo with Edith Evans as the Nurse and John as Mercutio.

Cigarette cards of Sir Toby and myself.

Hamlet with Yorick at the Old Vic, 1936.

Hamlet with Vivien at Elsinore, 1937.

Sir Toby Belch with Jill in
Twelfth Night, 1937.

Henry v, 1937.

Coriolanus at the Old Vic, 1937–8 season.

confused with RKO Pathé, in Culver City, with their own quite separate list of stars), it was obvious enough who was to be their own special Garbo, and a most remarkable one too.

One day David Selznick (he was the brother of my American agent, by the way) asked me to go and see him. I went into his outer office; and then came the pearliest example ever likely to come my way of the incalculable advantages of being on familiar terms with members of other people's staff. My friend, his secretary, said (yes, she did), 'Oh, why don't you go on in, Larry dear? He wouldn't want you to be waiting out here, I'm sure.' I blew her a kiss and went on in.

Well, there I was, alone in the boss's office, and it occurred to me that there might be some reading matter of possible interest, if I searched diligently enough for it. Well (again), I sort of found myself wandering casually round his desk, and from behind his chair my attention was caught and held, by God, by a document on his blotter. This turned out to be the heads of agreement for a contract. My heart began to beat at what I read. It stated that Miss Katharine Hepburn was to be engaged on a three-year contract at a starting figure of $1,500 weekly for the first year, rising to $2,000 for the second year and $2,500 for the third year, after which, no doubt, another deal might not be too difficult to work out. Jill had been cut to $750.

It was an extraordinary discovery for me to have made at this precise moment. Thoughtfully, I continued to wait for David. He turned up eventually and found me sitting in an armchair, reading some magazines as far away from his side of the desk as anyone could be. What it was he had to say to me I don't remember, and I don't think I could have told anyone thirty seconds after I had left him and blown another kiss to my most dear friend, his secretary.

I went home and told Jill what I had sneakingly seen, pointing out that it was obvious that David would not be paying this sort of money to this interesting new girl if she was not destined for stardom; and if there were any other comparable script we would surely know about it – this sort of news did not remain a secret very long in a studio, particularly one that had as few things planned as ours had. Moreover, *Bill of Divorcement* was definitely scheduled.

Jill saw all this clearly enough but couldn't bear to believe it, which was perfectly understandable. I didn't want to stay in Hollywood anyway, couldn't afford to hang around with nothing coming in, and had received a very timely offer to do a picture with Gloria Swanson at Ealing Studios. We had always agreed that if our work took us apart, so be it. It had happened already, when she was in New York for six or more months and I was stuck in London; but for poor Jill, now, it must have seemed like two-way blackmail. We couldn't face things out with David by asking his intentions about Hepburn as we weren't supposed to have seen the test, and someone could get into serious trouble – these things were supposed to be secret, high-up stuff.

I have always believed that if you aspire to be an artist you must be prepared to make such personal sacrifices as separation readily, if not exactly cheerfully. It's tough but it's right. In 1939, when my life's pattern had changed entirely, it was Vivien's turn to force a separation. It was again David who was the villain of the piece, offering Vivien the part, so savagely desired by every star in Hollywood, of Scarlett in *Gone With The Wind* on the usual, fiendish condition that she sign a seven-year contract. Her whole professional future was at stake, and she could not refuse.

But back in 1932 there was absolutely no knowing how long it might take David to make up his mind. He was in no hurry; the contract with Hepburn might go through a history of arguments over details before being signed. After an agonising wait, Jill decided to plump for wifely rather than artistic duties.

I was happy to accept the situation, and can now only remember the grateful feelings of relief as the 'Santa Fe' aped eastwards to Chicago where we made a lightning visit to the World's Fair, then overnight on the 'Twentieth Century' to New York and thence home, 'where ne'er from France arrived more happier men.' Jill got herself a good job with UFA in Neubabelsberg, and I was quickly into my film with Gloria Swanson, the title of which was *Perfect*

Understanding, a misnomer if ever there was one; it was, I'm afraid, no great sadness to me to learn later that it had been seen only by very few people indeed.

With my next job I was lucky as could be: a lovely part with, and under the management of, our most beautiful Gladys Cooper (Lady Pearson then) in her own theatre, the Playhouse, in *The Rats of Norway* by Keith Winter. So, like a man brought round from some kind of asphyxiation, I was an actor again.

At that time, stage-acting and film-acting were thought of as two entirely different crafts, even professions. We know now that this is not by any means a true assessment; the truth is infinitely subtler. They call for the same ingredients but in different proportions. The precise differences may take some years of puzzling work to appreciate; in each case there are many subtle variations according to the character of the actor. It took me many years to learn to film-act; at least ten of these were appallingly rough and ready, from sheer prejudice and ignorance. After that, it was necessary to relearn how to act on stage, incorporating, though, the truth demanded by the cinema and thereby reducing the measure of theatricality.

I was not to make another Hollywood film until *Wuthering Heights* in 1939, but I almost did. After *Rats of Norway* I suddenly found myself back in Hollywood with heart high – only to be fired from *Queen Christina* by Greta Garbo.

I realised in the first two weeks with ever-increasing apprehension that I was not by any means making the best of myself; something was stopping me. I was too nervous and scared of my leading lady. I knew I was lightweight for her and nowhere near her stature, and began to feel more and more certain that I was for the cop. I made up my mind that I must make a big effort to get along with her and find some way to get on friendlier terms.

Before work had started one morning, I found her sitting on an old chest on the set. I went boldly up to her and said the three or four sentences that I had made up and practised: but no utterance came from her. I began to flounder and grab at anything that came into my head: some sayings of Will Rogers, of Noël – anybody – anything at all, until I came to a wretched end and stopped, pale and panting. After a breathless pause, she slid herself off the chest sideways saying, 'Oh vell, live'sh a pain, anyway.' I knew then that the end was not far off. That evening, as the day's work was drawing to a close, they said, 'You won't mind if Miss Garbo goes home now, will you? You can speak your lines off-screen to the continuity girl all right, can't you?' I decided to trip the end and get it over. 'I'd rather,' I said.

Next day Walter Wanger, the producer, whom I had known and liked in early days in New York, sent for me and said, 'Larry, I want you to know something. We are crazy about you here at MGM, and we want to put you under contract. But it's just that in this particular part . . .' I inconsiderately let him struggle on for a bit and finally told him not to bother, provided I got my dough. 'Why yes, of *course*,' he said. 'Glad to get on to money terms, so much easier than other things.'

Once again I was lucky in my bad luck. The part, even in John Gilbert's hands, was a hopelessly unsuccessful one. Jill and I went for a Hawaiian holiday on Waikiki beach for two weeks to forget about it. Thank God we had both landed a job before we had left London with Jed Harris for *The Green Bay Tree* in New York, a wonderful play by Mordaunt Shairp. Jed Harris had charmed the daylights out of us in London, but in New York he transformed himself, like a chameleon, into the most hurtful, arrogant, venomous little fiend that anyone could meet, let alone be asked to work with – cruel, sadistic, obviously hating us for both our nation and our race. But the ideas behind his sarcastic directions were sound and illuminating; the play, which was a wonderful piece of work, was brilliantly done and sensationally successful for twenty weeks. I know we should have been grateful, but my feelings about him were so scorched with resentment that there was no changing them, and I couldn't ever speak to him again. It was a terrible, poisoning thing. I resolved for the rest of my life never to let this sort of situation arise again, but to find courage somehow to have things out if ever resentment started to boil up like that.

'Where ne'er from France arrived more happier men.' How many times in my life have I found that quotation to be the only way of exactly expressing my feelings? Again I breathed that feeling all the way home, on the ss *Europa*.

Back we went to our lovely house into which we had only just moved when we'd had to tear ourselves away. Here it was, in Cheyne Walk, where Whistler had died – not the beautiful one with the plaque, west of Battersea Bridge, but nearer Chelsea Old Church – and the same stick of bombs that all but demolished the church a decade later obliterated No 74.

The Old Church was eventually rebuilt just as it had been, and the end of the studio that once was Jill's and mine is marked by chance by an exquisite little bronze nude in the centre of a charmingly laid-out garden. It was a beautiful house in an unusual way, with an eccentric, quirky, pre-Raphaelite arrangement of rooms. We had it decorated by Arthur de Lissa, a sweet old puss, slightly pampered in theatre society and a leading light in Fryers, the fashionable decorating firm: duck-egg walls, massive, thick white silk curtains about thirty feet wide and twenty-five feet high, newly carved oak, pickled and limed.

One entered the studio from the river end, through the ample but chic bar. I always thought that in Whistler's last days, crippled with arthritis, this was the place where he would sleep, and then crawl down into his studio, do a touch of painting and crawl back again. Above was a minstrels' gallery with a large, deep-set window overlooking the river; here was caged Tony, our ring-tailed lemur. We put a huge stone fireplace into the studio, a full-size grand piano, massive furniture, and a tapestry on the wall. Oh yes, we were to entertain lavishly. Noël said, 'The trouble with Larry, he has such illusions of grandeur.' But yet, you see, how soon the day o'ercast.

Better than all this was the job I came back for. When in New York, Noël had made me a mighty sweet offer: to play opposite Ina Claire in *Biography*, a high comedy by Sam Behrman. Lovely part, excellent play, wonderful actress.

Ina had made quite a mark in London back in 1913 in *The Girl from Utah*. I had seen her in *Biography* in New York and found her quite stunning in personality, grace, heart and wit. I thought Noël had a good snip here, and I was delighted to be in it.

Towards the end of rehearsals, I found myself wondering what Noël – directing it – was up to; Ina never lacked for speed or sharpness of performance, and here he was hastening her and hastening the play which was a reasonably tranquil thing, not a firecracker like *Private Lives* or *Is Zat So?* Noëlie had always been a termagant about speed, but now he seemed to be getting a bit paranoiac with his tempo. It was as if he wanted to shock the London audience with Ina's speed. It was a pity, in fact it was more than that. The play went for nothing, or very little. It had no run to speak of – four or five weeks – so for the cast, a good one of its time, and for Ina especially, it was a near-tragedy.

It was the first flop that I ever heard of for her – unless you count her marriage to John Gilbert, which was an unkind, empty gesture on his part, taking advantage of a young female's flattered fascination simply in order to parade it in front of Garbo and snap his fingers at her. Garbo, of course, wore a more mocking expression than ever, doing the slow nod and keeping it up pretty steadily, for all the world like an automatic model in a shop window, while poor Gilbert went m-a-a-d and his pretty, sprightly, bubbling young bride couldn't make out what could be the matter. All the other guests at one particularly large ballroom supper-party, which had apparently been selected to stage this drama, enjoyed it keenly. It was fancy dress and Garbo was dressed as Hamlet.

From the ridiculous to the sublime, a lovely job came my way; Gordon Daviot (also known as Josephine Tey) was following up her triumphant *Richard of Bordaux* with another historical play, *Queen of Scots*; Gwen Ffrancon-Davies, who had supported John Gielgud so superbly in the first piece, was now playing Mary Stuart. The leading part of Bothwell, her lover, fell vacant a week before opening as the actor who had been cast 'wasn't happy in the part'. That phrase may seem rather guardedly unspecific, but to his fellows when an actor 'isn't happy with a part' it does not necessarily mean he is miscast or fails glaringly in any particular respect; to us the meaning is clear and exact. The outcome of this was beneficial at least for me; I was not only delighted by the part, but the special drama of coming in at the last moment was an extra fillip to the appetite.

It was a fortunate turn of events for just about all of us in the company. More life long friendships started in that group than, I think, in any other; Gwen, Glen Byam Shaw, Campbell Gullan – these last two and myself formed a threesome we called the Bothwellians, after my character. The two rules that our society boasted were strict. There must have been four scenes in the last act; after the first, Cully would be finished, and his office was to get the bottle, the soda and the glasses ready on the tray. Glen would be off the stage five minutes after scene two; he would pour out the drinks. They would sit talking and staring at them for the four minutes or so that it took me to be through with the third scene (the final scene only involved the Queen and her waiting woman). The pleasure of fulfilment owes much, if not all, to the durance of the waiting upon it. I am sure that the wait before I burst in upon them was to those friends a dedicated vigil. There was only one rule besides this ceremony, and that was always to wear our club tie on any day that any of us had a first night.

Gully died around the beginning of the war, I think. Glen and I steadfastly for the next thirty years or more wore what was left of our ties until they fell apart. Blood red, passionate purple, murky black, whisky yellow and venturesome green – there was something about that tie that made everyone think they ought to know what it was.

It is difficult to keep from gloating over those prizes in friendship; the producer Margaret Webster, Mercia Swinburne, the wife of George Relph, the three Motley girls, those magical designers Percie, Sophie and Elizabeth, besides Glen and Gully; our manager Bronson Albery, a constant friend for years, Herbert Menges, who wrote the music, and wrote the music for everything in the theatre that I was responsible for over the next twenty-five years and last, but the furthest imaginable distance from least, our director, the great John G. There is a special satisfaction, to my mind, in long associations.

Mine with Gielgud continued in 1935 when he invited me to alternate Romeo and Murcutio with him. That year, no less than four jealous juveniles in London all saw themselves in the part of Romeo. It would be unpardonably coy if I did not disclose that the four were John Gielgud, Robert Donat, Ivor Novello and the doubtful character who bears my name. The last three aspirants were all jealously agreed that the first would be the least well cast of us all. But the only one of us who had first call on any London theatre was John Gielgud, by virtue of the happy arrangement he had with his sponsor, Bronson Albery, and the New Theatre. So when he offered me the chance to alternate the roles with him in his production, I grabbed it.

The theatre is replete with emotional legends; it is not surprising that those playing Romeo and Juliet are supposed to present a more stirring partnership if they develop the same passion between themselves as that which they are emulating; some believe that Shakespeare's magic depends on it. After long reflection, I must point out that this is a dangerous notion. It would imply that actual death is necessary to the feigning of it, or at least that physical pain is necessary to give a successful impression of it. Such an idea robs the work of its artfulness as well as its artistry. It is a tempting belief, but a bad principle.

The part of Romeo is difficult to handle because, however much the player may see himself in the role, like Antony it falls short of the glamorous companionship implied by the play's title. Young women have often been heard to express their disappointment in a lover's prowess by the words, 'Oh well, he's certainly no Romeo', indicating a romantic valour that our poor Romeo does not possess. In my own mind I believe that my attitude, passion, poetic realism and Italianate silhouette were all aimed in the right direction. Of later performances I admired Alan Badel's image of the character, and for the ideal of boyish passionate intensity I find it hard to believe that John Stride in Zeffirelli's splendid production can ever have been bettered.

I have always seen myself so vividly as the one and only Romeo that when the sledge-hammer of opprobrium struck its blow from every critic to a man, I was so shocked that it was all I could do to get myself on to the stage for the second performance. While I was making up for this, Bronnie Albery was sweet enough to come into my room, No 3 at the New Theatre, to attempt a few words of sympathy. I quite sincerely offered to give up the part immediately. Peggy Ashcroft, my Juliet, and I had known each other ever since my first term at the Central in 1924, and she was so sweet and tenderly regardful of me and of the hurt she knew I was suffering that I felt strengthened by her support through all the dreadful early performances. I had been judged inadequate in the speaking of the verse, and so incompetent for Shakespeare. From my earliest school performances I had been taught the way I still feel verse should be handled, namely to speak it as if that is the way you speak naturally. Bit by bit and one by one eminent writers began to take some trouble to come to my defence, so that after six weeks, when it came to my turn as Mercutio, I sensed that there was quite a strong tide in my favour. My Mercutio went down, I suppose, very well, but this could never be a compensation for me.

When *Romeo and Juliet* finished in 1936, Richardson and I decided it was about time we entered the managerial lists in our first partnership, with *Bees on the Boat Deck*, which Ralph had got J. B. Priestley to write for us. Capitalised at £2,000, it was split equally between the three of us. No doubt it may seem a little quaint beside modern costs, but for a cast of under ten in a single, if elaborate, setting it was really ample backing. It has always surprised us that it should have only run four weeks, at the Lyric too, an enviable shop window and a perfect-sized theatre. Perhaps we did not do it well enough; perhaps the allegorical similarity to *Heartbreak House* – 'the Boat' was, of course, England – took the bloom off the comedy's freshness.

Fortunately for the restoration of my depleted coffers, Alexander Korda had a most promising and opportune property. Korda, the most brilliant of all Hungarian imports, first attracted attention in England with *The Private Life of Helen of Troy*, which starred his wife. As a result, Charles Laughton had asked him to direct *Henry VIII*, which had scored a huge international success in 1933. He kept a permanent staff of British stars and was to remain in an avuncular role to Vivien and myself.

Fire Over England was a pretty good sort of adventure story by A. E. W. Mason, and I found life to be full of bright promise when Korda told me that as one of his contract players I was to feature in it. It was to be directed by a highly thought-of American, William K. Howard, and produced by Erich Pommer, whom I knew from Beubabelsberg in 1930. We were now in the summer of 1935 and things were just beginning to open up at Denham Studios, all brand-new and very posh after tired-feeling old Isleworth, where I had contributed nothing at all remarkable to two films, *The Conquest of the Air* and *Moscow Nights*. This last was an almost simultaneous remake of a film which looked really rather good when it was in French (even the title *Les Nuits Muscovites* was already better). It contained an imaginatively advanced series of lap-dissolves, all of which were pushed straight into the English picture, which must have been why Korda bought the original. For *Fire Over England* Pommer and Korda showed themselves too much tarred with the Hollywood brush to resist having this thoroughly well-told tale entirely rewritten by the celebrated Clemence Dane. A detail concerning this splendid lady: she started out as Winifred Ashton but chose as a *nom de plume* 'Diana Curtis'. One day she ran into some eminent gentleman (Haggard, Galsworth, Kipling?), who said that neither of her names was effective, and that she should think of something inescapable like Westminster Abbey. She set her mind to the problem and found herself abruptly face to face with another London church, Saint Clement Danes; to her delight, after the obvious minor change, it still possessed the same ring.

I cannot conceal the fact that the completely new story that she produced, which could not even be called a version of the Mason book, neither added point nor made a mark. Alex Korda threw a large muster of his players into it; besides this unestablished film actor, there appeared Flora Robson, Raymond Massey, Tamara Desni, Robert Newton, and – Vivien Leigh.

I first set eyes upon the possessor of this wondrous unimagined beauty on the stage of the Ambassadors Theatre, where she was playing in Ashley Dukes's *The Mask of Virtue*, in which she had attracted considerable attention – though not, at this time, chiefly on account of her promise as an actress. Apart from her looks, which were magical, she possessed beautiful poise; her neck looked almost too fragile to support her head and bore it with a sense of surprise, and something of the pride of the master juggler who can make a brilliant manœuvre appear almost accidental. She also had something else: an attraction of the most perturbing nature I had ever encountered. It may have been the strangely touching spark of dignity in her that enslaved the ardent legion of her admirers.

A short while after this first sighting of her we ran across her – everyone in the profession was bound to meet sometime, in the well-worn run of London spots, and I'm almost sure this particular encounter was in the Savoy Grill lobby. We had taken a charming, smallish place in Burchett's Green, between Maidenhead and Ivor Novello's lovely place in Littlewick Green, and we invited Vivien and her husband for a weekend. Like any first act of the period, isn't it?

One afternoon, I was making up for a matinée of *Romeo* when she popped in to my dressing-room at the New Theatre; it was ostensibly to invite us to something or other; she only stayed a couple of minutes, and then she gave me a soft little kiss on the shoulder and was gone.

I soon began to feel sorry for Jill, indeed to feel pain for her and, of course, guilt. But this thing was as fatefully irresistible for us as for any couple from Siegmund and

Sieglinde to Windsor and Simpson. It sometimes felt almost like an illness, but the remedy was unthinkable; only an early Christian martyr could have faced it. Virtue seemed to work upside-down: love was like an angel, guilt was a dark fiend. At its every surge *Macbeth* would haunt me: 'Then comes my fit again.' It sounds like a Novello musical – 'Rapturous Torment!'

Two years of furtive life, lying life. Sneaky. At first I felt a really worm-like adulterer, slipping in between another man's sheets the studio or theatre dressing-room game blessed by generations of randy actors, but unprotected from sudden intrusion. Then darting, sporadic little hops, covering some mileage, I must say. The night we escaped to Stamford in Lincolnshire is clear in my mind: anywhere odd and unexpected to reduce the likelihood of detection and subsequent joy to the gossip columnists. It was two years before we rewarded ourselves with the selfish relief of confession (we both happened to choose the same night for the event), and our affair became public property.

Vivien's husband struck me as being a dull man, dry, cerebral, without sparkle; I was quite wrong about this. He suffered much more than he should have been required to. He was highly intelligent, clever, but not exciting or outwardly romantic. Later, when provision for love had been sorted out, divorces filed, marriages arranged, respectability hopefully bid for and the scandalous couple returned home for the war effort, we all became friends. We would go to stay with each other and I grew to like Leigh Holman very much.

In 1937 we had started to accept engagements together – *Hamlet* in Elsinore with Vivien playing Ophelia; we could not keep from touching each other, making love almost within Jill's vision. This welding closeness tripped the obvious decision, and two marriages were severed. I suspect this passage may not be pleasant to read. It is, to be honest, a little nauseating to set down.

Artists are supposed to suffer, it is part of their gift. The office of drama is to exercise, possibly to exhaust human emotions. The purpose of comedy is to tickle those emotions into an expression of light relief; of tragedy, to wound them and bring the relief of tears. Disgust and terror are the other points of the compass.

I had plumped for Hamlet for my first Old Vic season in 1937 which I had undertaken with Ralph's moral support ('think it's a very good idea'), having long ago decided that if ever I had the good fortune to lead a season I would start with the big one. For my generation, determined upon realism, the burning question was, of course: 'What makes him what he is?' Two books had recently appeared: Dover Wilson's *What Happens in Hamlet*, and a work on the Oedipus complex by Ernest Jones. Three of us – Tony Guthrie, Peggy Ashcroft and I – went to see Professor Jones.

He had made an exhaustive study of Hamlet from his own professional point of view and was wonderfully enlightening. I have never ceased to think about Hamlet at odd moments, and ever since that meeting I have believed that Hamlet was a prime sufferer from the Oedipus complex – quite unconsciously, of course, as the professor was anxious to stress. He offered an impressive array of symptoms: spectacular mood-swings, cruel treatment of his love, and above all a hopeless inability to pursue the course required of him. The Oedipus complex, therefore, can claim responsibility for a formidable share of all that is wrong with him. There is great pathos in his determined efforts to bring himself to the required boiling point, and in the excuses he finds to shed this responsibility.

Apart from Hamlet's involuntary pusillanimity, there is another important factor in the character-drawing – his weakness for dramatics. This would be reasonable if the dramatics spurred him to action, but unfortunately they help to delay it. It is as if his shows of temperament not only exhaust him but give him relief from his absorption in his purpose – like an actor who, having spent his all in rehearsal, feels it almost redundant to go through with the performance.

After Hamlet came a part obviously designed to demonstrate my staggering versatility – Sir Toby Belch, a performance only remarkable for the weighty encrustations of nose-putty on my face. Then came Henry v.

Until I had learnt to appreciate the part of Henry, I was touched by very little in it. I was intensely shy of a great deal of it, being influenced by the 1930s dislike of all heroism, and I tried to find ways round the problem by playing against the declamatory style and undercutting it; it was hopeless, of course. I went to Ralph with the problem. 'I know he's a boring old scout-master on the face of it,' Ralph said, 'but being Shakespeare he's the exaltation of all scout-masters. He's the cold bath kind, and you have to glory in it.'

Try as I might, I could not stop myself from shying away. The ending to the Crispin speech is a case in point. I took it gravely and quietly at rehearsals until Tony Guthrie could bear it no longer. 'It's too disappointing for your audience, you're taking all the thrill out of the play, and for heaven's sake that's all it's got!'

Somebody told me that when Lewis Waller did 'Once more unto the breach' he had a side-drum roll right through it. I thought I might try that. I did, and it gave me the artificial support that I needed. Alec Guinness, then only twenty-three, put on a masterly make-up and character performance as my 'Uncle of Exeter', and the love scene at the end with Jessica Tandy as Princess Katherine was a delight.

After all this work, Vivien and I gave way utterly to damnèd luxury, as old King Hamlet's ghost described it: eight weeks in France, driving from Boulogne straight down what has since been named *la route gastronomique*. For us it had been mapped out by Charles Laughton with whom Vivien had been making a picture: past Paris to Versailles, then Avalon, Auxerre, Dijon, Beaune, Mâcon, Vienne, Montélimar, straying across the Rhône at Condrieu of the delicious wine; Avignon and straight on down to a rapturous little bay – La Calongue d'Or, peace, anonymity, and an encounter with a very charming 'Monsieur' and a perfect English-speaking 'Monsieur, le cousin de Monsieur'.

Some years after the war I thought I'd go back there, and

I suffered an appalling disappointment. One is told to be careful about returning to places after a war, there can be some shocks. Here in the bay next to Point d'Agay I found that the place had been almost entirely razed to the ground, but what struck me far more forcibly than that was the atmosphere; where there had been such a delightfully happy aura there was now a horrid, haunted misery. I have never fancied myself as possessing psychic instinct, but what I felt was unquestionably real. I made enquiries, and then I knew it wasn't a flight of imagination. Monsieur – I don't know what had been the fate of 'Monsieur le cousin' – but Monsieur had suffered one of those wretched, ghastly happenings of war. Monsieur had been seized at the finish of French hostilities, charged and found guilty of collaboration with the Germans, had his eyes put out and was then killed.

No such hateful episode occurred to blight that idyllic first journey, which allowed the glowing fulfilment of every desire of the wayward lovers, in the pursuit of which we drove westwards along the coast. Hugging the Pyrenees to St Jean-Pierre de Por, we proceeded back slightly north-west to pay a visit to a small country town called Nay, between Pau and Lourdes, from which the last of my Huguenot ancestors escaped to England in 1685.

We came home to find we had missed the London season; never mind, theatres are nakedly public places and we couldn't bear to be seen in public if we could decently avoid it. Time enough when we had to stand up again on the stage, and that was not so far off now; *Macbeth* was looming up in December and I had to steel myself for it, set my shoulders, brace my tights, put on my chain-mail jock-strap and hope for the best. Michel St Denis was to direct it, the Motleys were to do the sets and costumes, George Devine to light it and Judith Anderson to be my Lady Macbeth; and I do not believe there has ever been a more perfect Banquo than Andrew Cruickshank.

This was my first study of Macbeth and I was not an unparalleled success. Without scanning the horizon desperately to see whom I can blame for it, I would say that sharing the pie with me was Michel. We arty lot were at this time going through a phase of avid preoccupation with size; everything had to suggest godlike proportions, and the results could be pretty extraordinary. The audience was given some sort of warning by one's appearance with deliberately mask-like make-up, but appearances, sets, costumes and props were none of them whole-heartedly abstract: it was 'stylised'. I need hardly add that Noël nearly died laughing when he came to see it.

A strange thing – it played to the best houses ever known to date at the Vic. Queen Elizabeth (not to be Queen Mother for some fifteen years yet) paid a visit to see this curious production. I was much encouraged by this as it seemed to indicate that the gossip concerning my private life had not reached far or high yet, but of course that would only be a question of time. There were hints of murmurings from the public, an isolated boo from the gallery, a brick sent through the post with a note saying 'For Olivier's folly'. I was in constant fear that it would suddenly get dangerous, but the houses continued to be full, and though I couldn't help sensing a sullenness among the crowd outside the stage door, which was noticeably smaller than usual, there was no outspoken rudeness or challenge. It did strike me that when there were a few bids for my autograph it was surely in the manner that they would have asked Jack the Ripper for his.

Next, I played Iago, with Ralph as Othello, Curigwen Lewis as Desdemona, Martita Hunt as Emilia, Anthony Quayle as Cassio and Andrew Cruickshank as Roderigo. Tyrone Guthrie directed. You would think that a cast like that was a certainty, but no, most definitely not. No one who had anything to do with it made any contribution that was not a disaster.

There was, I am bound to say, a dichotomy of purpose between Ralph's Othello and my Iago. Tony Guthrie and I were swept away by Professor Jones's contention that Iago was subconsciously in love with Othello and had to destroy him. Unfortunately there was not the slightest chance of Ralph entertaining this idea. I was, however, determined

upon my wicked intentions, in cahoots with Tony; we
constantly watched for occasions when our diagnosis might
be made apparent to the discriminating among an audience, though I must say I have never yet discovered any
means of divulging something that is definitely *subcon-
scious* to any audience, no matter how discerning they may
be. In a reckless moment during rehearsals I threw my arms
round Ralph and kissed him full on the lips. He coolly
disengaged himself from my embrace, patted me gently on
the back of the neck and, more in sorrow than in anger,
murmured, 'There, there now; dear boy; *good* boy . . . .'
Tony and I dropped all secret connivance after that.

I had one more trick up my sleeve; Ralph had to fall to
the ground when Othello, frenzied by Iago's goadings, is
helpless in the clutches of a paroxysm. I would fall beside
him and simulate an orgasm – terri*f*ically daring, wasn't it?
But when the wonderful Athene Seyler came round after a
matinée she said, 'I'm sure I have *no* idea what you were up
to when you threw yourself on the ground beside Ralph.'
So that was the end of that stroke of genius and out it came.
No more shenanigans now: Iago just hated Othello because
he was black, and his superior officer; it was also obvious
that Othello preferred Cassio as his lieutenant because he
was a gentleman and Iago was not.

I think that few who have had experience in the armed
forces can find Iago hard to understand. One only has to
glance round a wardroom table and take note of the ageing,
hard-bitten faces of those passed over. When I was a
two-striper in the Royal Navy, one of my fellow officers was
given a half-stripe more than I and from this favourable
position decided he would amuse himself by taking the
mickey out of me. There was no way I could get back at
him, and resentment began to fester. One evening I suddenly thought of a way: 'Of course; he's married!' Flushing
with horror, I realised – God, I've become Iago.

Munich was upon us, a time of dread. A kind of lugubrious
dress rehearsal for September 1939, the show itself ceased
to threaten for a brief respite; but it was only a postpone-

ment, as between a try-out and a London production.

I got my dearest old friend on the phone one day and asked him, 'Ralphie, be an angel and think a minute for me, there's a friend. Should I go to Hollywood and play Heathcliff in *Wuthering Heights*?' Ralph obligingly thought for a moment and then said, 'Yes. Bit of fame. Good.' For some reason I had the greatest misgivings about the offer; but after that mini-colloquy I didn't have them any more. William Wyler, the most prestigious of Hollywood film directors, had, of course, come over to goose me into it. And when I got to Hollywood my apprehensions returned. I had done one film with Merle Oberon (now Mrs Alex Korda) and liked her reasonably well; but now, as I tried to establish some relationship with both my director and my co-star, I found that my feelings were obstinately lukewarm towards both of them. I was blind with misery at being parted from Vivien, who would have been the perfect Cathy, and I was sure that Merle was lacking in the essential passionate qualities.

Vivien, in company with a myriad of other actresses, had an almost demoniac determination to play Scarlett in *Gone With The Wind*. It should be appreciated, though it isn't easy in retrospect, that the odds against her getting the part would create a whole new scale of betting at Ladbrokes today; but I too nursed the secret ambition for her. This provided a secondary reason for her to sail across and then fly from New York to Clover Field airport; the first was pure, driving, uncontainable, passionate love, which to my joy she shared strongly enough to make the journey as speedily as possible. In the meantime I had a few quiet words with Myron Selznick, indicating to him that there was someone coming over to visit me who might quite possibly be of extraordinary interest to him. He looked knowingly at me and we said no more.

I waited for her crouched in the back of a car a few feet beyond the airport entrance.

The Beverly Hills Hotel in those days was not at all what it is now – it had rather shabby basket furniture, only dismally achieving a colonial style. As in the general run of hotels the world over, if you invested in a suite nobody asked any questions. I took Vivien along to Myron, who studied her, looking from her to me and back with growing interest. I said innocently, '*I* think we ought to take her along to meet David, don't you, Myron?' He nodded slowly, realisation beginning to dawn; his brother, about to launch into production with *GWTW*, had become badly stuck over the casting of Scarlett.

He had put Rhett Butler straight out to the American public for them to cast. The public had responded with several million votes, almost every one citing Clark Gable. Leslie Howard was an obviously popular choice for Ashley Dukes, as indeed was Olivia de Havilland for Melanie. Only Scarlett remained. David had boiled it down to a final choice between three – Bette Davis, Paulette Goddard and Jean Arthur; this provoked endless arguments and much ill-feeling. Davis was universally regarded as exceptional, in fact the best actress, but did not approximate to Margaret Mitchell's description; Goddard was much the closest in looks, but her acting accomplishment was in doubt; Arthur had the advantage of being the darkest horse of the three. I never believed that David had serious intentions towards Joan Crawford. He liked to boost the competitive element.

Myron picked us up in a car that evening and we headed due south down to Culver City where on the old Pathé lot David was burning forty acres of ancient exterior sets for the fire in Atlanta. Three times we saw the horse and buggy drive through the flaming archway of the barn, with the same double for Gable each time but three different types for Scarlett; after the last passage through, a wire was pulled and the roof of the barn fell in a flaming crash. (Flames are obligingly easy things to cut on, so the three Scarletts were readily interchangeable.) The shooting over, no attempt was made to extinguish the fire; and by its light I could just make out the figures of George Cukor, the original director and devoted friend, and David, whom I also knew well from our business differences in 1932.

I looked back at Vivien, her hair giving the perfect

impression of Scarlett's, her cheeks prettily flushed, her lips adorably parted, her green eyes dancing and shining with excitement in the firelight; I said to myself, 'David won't be able to resist that.' I retreated, leaving the field to Myron; David and George were approaching and Myron stepped towards them. He indicated Vivien and said, 'David, meet Scarlett O'Hara.'

David peered very intently at Vivien; Myron made a vague gesture towards me. David threw a 'Hello, Larry' into the air, roughly in my direction. Myron and I were left together, eye to eye and ho to hum. David had drawn Vivien a little way apart from the crowd and was fixing up an immediate test with her, promising to make every allowance for what would naturally be a very imperfect Southern accent. George was with them and was clearly interested too. I could hardly believe what was happening; but there it was.

David took every advantage possible in her contractual negotiations, insisting on a one-way option contract for seven years – seven years is the most that is legally allowed in any American contract on account of an old anti-slavery law. The film was envisaged to take at least six months and he would not move higher than $20,000; this for the movie part of the century was hardly generous, and I said as much to him a bit later. David defended himself stoutly, saying I was unreasonable, and 'I'd be the laughing-stock of all my friends if I paid her any more, an unknown, a discovery, for such an opportunity.'

Wuthering Heights was well finished and I had to think about getting back to some work. It was better not to smudge the career image by hanging around, hoping for a job. *Wuthering Heights* wouldn't make its effect yet awhile, and I was against just continuing to dance attendance, 'announcing her guests and walking the pekingese'; the best thing career-wise would be to get myself a good appearance in the New York theatre, and this was most felicitously provided for me by Miss Katharine Cornell (the top people had a 'Miss' or 'Mr' in front of their names; it was the American equivalent of a knighthood – always 'Mr

George Arliss'). The play this time was *No Time for Comedy* by Sam Behrman, another friend. It was a wild success and I 'besported myself at the organ with more than my usual success' (Handel, on his *Messiah* opening in Dublin).

As rehearsals drew to an end, worrisome news was coming from Hollywood; exhaustion coupled with hysteria due to our harshly testing separation was producing dangerous symptoms, and David got me on the phone and implored me to get out there somehow to use my influence to calm things down, 'if only for a *day*'. How fortunate I was to have such warmly understanding managers as Kit Cornell and Guthrie McClintic; they actually let me off the dress rehearsal in Indianapolis to give me one day to fly there, one day to soothe as much as I possibly could, and the next day to fly direct to Indianapolis and open that night. It was short shrift; very. We opened to 'golden opinions from all sorts of people'; Alexander Woollcott was one of them, and all in all the success was richly rewarding.

Vivien was allowed, while still due for a series of retakes, to leave Hollywood for a few weeks' respite. She was a bit too quick off the mark for me, as I had not finished my engagement by a couple of weeks or so. I was sharing a house with Kit Cornell, Guthrie McClintic, darling Margalo Gillmore, her husband Robert Ross and equally loved John Williams, firmly tried friends in the play with me, as was Robert Flemyng, a constantly welcome visitor. Vivien had perforce to stay and be made most welcome by this precious group. In due course we were on the ss *Majestic* going home. It was sweet, it is always sweet, to be home; we took a fortnight in our adored France. We stopped off at home again to pick up her mama, 'and her mother came too', a sweet, pretty woman, a highly successful beautician named Gertrude Hartley.

Then back to Hollywood where Vivien was quickly involved in her *GWTW* retakes and I, happy with Hitchcock, in *Rebecca*. It seemed no time at all before the unbelievable shock of the war was upon us.

Dougie Fairbanks Jr happened to have taken a yacht for that day and we were part of a delightful party on it; we were just off Catalina, when Chamberlain came on the radio and said what he had to say. Many of us burst into tears at once. Along with most other inhabitants of the earth, we felt blighted right through: careers, lives, hopes. Shortly reaction set in. Doug knew what drink existed for and a consequent hysteria began; my own manifestation of this was a show of frank vulgarity, careering around in a speedboat in and out between the other yachts berthed off the island, declaiming, 'You are finished, all of you; you are relics . . . that's what you are . . . relics!' It was often said at this time that I bore some resemblance to Ronald Colman, with my slight moustache and dark hair. Unfortunately the rumour went round that it was Ronnie himself who had taken this extraordinary turn; it was a shame, for nothing could have been less typical of his habitual dignity or exquisite manners.

There was a general directive to all our countrymen abroad who did not already have a commission or were not within the required age-group to stay put; did we not appreciate that if every Englishman living abroad were to come gallantly dashing home, the public services would have to face an additional population of anything up to half a million extra mouths to feed and extra hands to find employment for? It was a painful situation, and wretchedly embarrassing with the Americans who for once were our not very enthusiastic hosts. Many of them seemed far from certain whose side they were on. There was an enthusiastically pro-German feeling in those areas of the United States containing extensive proportions of German immigrants. Milwaukee, for instance, was largely German-speaking. Whether it would be useful or not, I soon began to feel it would be better for us to go home and take whatever came.

And so the 1930s went limping out, on a note as baleful and grim as a fog-horn on a dark night.

CHAPTER SIX

Call to Arms

I wanted to be married to Vivien before arriving home with her. I couldn't believe that there would be much allowance made for us in the stern situation we were bound to find in England. I was powerless though to fulfil this intention because my divorce could not be made absolute until the next August.

Meantime we could not but be alarmed by the horrid nature of one particularly extravagant rumour that came our way. The danger from air raids of shattered ear-drums in young children caused us to arrange an Atlantic crossing for both the children of our previous marriages; this was not accomplished for a full year owing to an ill turn of fate for which I have only to thank a rash decision of my own. The bad decision was to agree to a suggestion from our dear friend George Cukor: 'If you two kids want to make a little extra money before you go off, why don't you put on and send on the road *Romeo and Juliet*? You could make a fortune in no time at all.' I am ashamed to say that in no time at all our hearts quickened to the idea of making a little splash, not to say a little extra impressive acclaim as Shakespearians, not just film actors; should we survive the war we might wish we had taken advantage of the hour to sow seeds of more potency in the United States than we had had opportunity to do before this time.

Without wasting a second, I rushed the Motleys over to do a quite ravishing lightning job on sets and costumes. I planned the production on the film set in between making shots for *Pride and Prejudice*. I found an excellent cast over there: Alexander Knox for the Friar; Carleton Hobbs for

Capulet; a beautiful actor, Wesley Addy, for Benvolio; Edmund O'Brien for Mercutio; Dame May Whitty for the Nurse; old Ben Webster for Montague – these two were pa and ma to Margaret Webster. The unkindest cut in a pretty lethal collection of criticisms said, 'What the production chiefly lacked was the third member of the Webster family'; Peggy had taken hold of any reputation that New York had to spare for Shakespearian direction as incontrovertibly as had her star, Maurice Evans, in the Shakespearian acting department. A neat vengeance for the old *Beau Geste* days – the idea had not escaped me.

Confessions cannot hope to be halfway complete unless they include the more spectacular examples of the penitent making a really ridiculous fool of himself. As with any Shakespearian production, this one proved onerous, and the heavy responsibility took its toll; the setting up and dress rehearsal time in San Francisco at the Curran Theater did not prove any easier than might have been expected. I don't think *Romeo and Juliet* has ever been a simple play to put on.

At that time the director was still reckoned to be responsible for his own lighting, which usually took a whole night at least. If the director was also playing a leading role it was a gruelling task; he would have to work straight on into the morning clearing up details and do a last runthrough in the afternoon; after that there would only be the first night to face. So, it is not going to be a shocking surprise to learn that I was tired.

From the start of the first show all seemed to be going fairly reasonably, apart from the tiniest *moment d'embarras* when in his first entrance old Ben made a dignified cross to confront me and said, not very quietly, 'Give me me word'; but apart from that all was well until the curtain of the balcony scene, for which I had always made rather a flamboyant sort of finish:

Hence will I to my ghostly father's cell
His help to crave and my dear hap to tell!

and on those last three words, I would turn from the balcony, spin into a run straight at the wall, leap up, placing my hands on the top, pull myself smartly up into a position on the wall fleetingly as if lying along it, give a little bounce with my toes, and take off in a swallow dive to disappear over the other side of the wall.

On this first night in San Francisco, I did not realise that I was, in fact, too exhausted to bring off this manœuvre, and so – round I spin and dash to the wall, leap at it, get my fingers on to the top, miss my footing, hang there helplessly by the fingers, kicking and scratching, gasping, sweating, entirely unable to move in an upward direction. After a century the curtain came down.

The kinder critics resisted the temptation to mention it, the less kind ones all played on the same instrument: '. . . and then, believe it or not, we were required to sit and watch this absurd grotesquerie for an unbelievable prolongation of time, before the merciful stage manager relieved our sights of the painful spectacle . . .', etc. One thing I was sure of, it would be all over Hollywood by make-up time next morning.

Didn't I have augury enough? Oh, no! I swung on into Chicago where the reception was ominously mild. Aha! I thought, what this show lacks is a New York reception and really intelligent, intellectual criticism. I got it. I couldn't believe that such things could be written about me or any human being; for sheer, savage, merciless cruelty I have never seen any judgements to approach those that faced me at breakfast in our New York hotel; our secretary's sobs as she brought in the morning papers told us all. Vivien and I tried hard to comfort each other with the dregs of feelings we had left. It took a next to impossible effort to get up, out and across the road to the Ziegfeld to see what in God's name might be happening at the box office.

As I came within sight of the theatre I saw to my amazement that there were queues all round it; when I got through the crowd in the lobby and squeezed in behind the till, all was speedily made clear. The advance booking had been prodigious, and the queues were composed of all those who had booked wanting their money back. I was proud enough to say, 'Go right ahead, give it to them.'

There was still just enough in advance plus occasional curiosity bookings to keep the thing going with a struggle for four weeks. We were not asked out to supper except by, of all people, the Lunts – just the four of us, rather a grand do with white tie; it was kindly calculated to keep us looking *persona grata*. They kept talking, without cease, about every possible subject in the world, effortlessly avoiding the sore one. I have never known such a supreme example of beautiful manners. I had always adored and worshipped them, God knows, but now I knew I would never know anyone within light years of the quality of their generosity.

We were playing through the New York summer in unequalled conditions of heat and humidity; I had to wear padding, as my legs were thin then; I also had a bit of a tum on me and so had to wear corsets. I had a putty nose on (the Italianate profile), and a thick black wig; period costumes always have to be of a certain weight or they don't hang right, air-conditioning had hardly started to come in yet, and the stage was like an oven. I was drenched. Some audiences are inclined to be tickled by the way Romeo *will* carry on so in the 'banishment scene'; there are few more dreadful fates on the stage than to become aware in a highly emotional scene that the audience is predisposed to laugh. Poor Romeo, he's really stuck with it:

> Wert thou as young as I . . .
> . . . then might'st thou tear thy hair,
> And fall upon the ground *as I do now*
> Taking the measure of an unmade grave.

There's nothing for it but endurance, other than to cut the scene. Going through my head, as this, amid much more of the same, was being joyously greeted with gales of laughter, were these thoughts: 'Here am I, in uttermost misery, sweating, flinging myself painfully around, tearing my soul to bits, and being paid with shrieks of mocking laughter, *and* this pleasure is costing me at least a thousand dollars this afternoon.' We were losing $5,000 a week; the whole enterprise cost $96,000 – all our savings out of *GWTW*, *Wuthering Heights*, *Rebecca* and *Pride and Prejudice*.

The inclination to get the hell home was irresistible. I was fortunate enough to have Duff Cooper for a friend; married to Lady Diana Manners, he was at this time Minister of Information. Telephoning obviously presented some difficulties, especially long distance, but calls to government high-ups went through like silk. I decided 'This deed I'll do before this purpose cool,' and to get him when he was sure to be in his London office. This turned out to be during our matinée at about 4 p.m. The call went straight through from the stage door, of all places. I asked him if there might possibly be a job for me even though I was beyond enlistment age, or any way in which I might be useful in his department. Within a few days came the following cable: 'Think better where you are Korda going there.' A day or two later Alex's voice came over the phone: 'Larry, you know Lady Hamilton?'

'Not imtimately,' I said. 'Wasn't she Admiral Nelson's piece?'

'Right,' he said. 'Arrange meetings with Vivien, Walter Reisch and R. C. Sherriff. I'll come at once.'

Well, the money situation was poignant; how could we return home with nothing? We would be worse than useless. We were living quietly in our old hide-out at Sneden's Landing, opposite Dobb's Ferry. I had been learning to fly, getting some instruction in a small float-plane. I've still got my log book, registering about 250 hours of circles and bumps on the Hudson, while the sands of our *Romeo and Juliet* were running out. As soon as we had made our deals for the film – and Alex treated us both very handsomely – we made our arrangements for the ones most on our consciences to come over; Vivien's little Suzanne in the care of grandmama Gertrude was taken over by relatives in Vancouver, while Jill with my four-year-old Tarquin would be better off in Hollywood where she might pick up some old contacts, and there was reasonable hope of obtaining some film jobs; happily this happened. Vivien and I, by taking home only a modest amount, were able to leave in the hands of those for whom we were responsible enough to keep their bodies and souls together for four or five years.

We found a small house with an egg-shaped pool on Cedarbrook Drive and worked with Alex Korda, Walter Reisch and Bob Sherriff on our script for *Lady Hamilton*. The picture was shot in a small, little-known studio right in the middle of Hollywood, then called the General Services. The work was harmonious throughout; we were all professionals, mutually respectful and efficient. The years of happy association that Vivien, Alex and I had shared were evident in the final result.

Vincent, the youngest of the Korda brothers and artistically the nearest to genius, surpassed himself in his designs, with masterly regard to the all-important aspect of economy. The work was completed in six weeks, including the miraculous model-work – cunningly separated pieces of life-size ship for the close work on the *Victory*. Throughout, I was industriously intent upon completing my flying training in the early mornings and evenings. Alex turned a blind eye to it out of patriotic feeling for his adopted country, knowing very well that if some regrettable accident had occurred any attempt to claim on insurance would have been futile.

Vivien and I married in Santa Barbara on 21 August 1940. We were now free to go just as soon as we had discharged our obligation to this, the last professional commitment we would engage ourselves to for . . . how long? Almost as soon as Alex said 'Cut' on our last shot we were off and away.

Hitler's secret weapon was already gaining a reputation and sailings were not the gay sprees that they had been. If every ship was jam-packed from bilges to crow's-nest sailing from Europe to America, it certainly was not the case in the other direction. We were two of twenty-three passengers on the American ship *Excambion* – not what you would describe as a queen among ocean liners. We endured the most apprehensive voyage I have ever known. The captain, for a start, was a German. Of course, we had no right to assume that he was not loyal to his American citizenship, but we could not rid ourselves of the fear that all was not well.

Our fears were confirmed as the voyage, which was not to England but to Lisbon, proceeded. New Year's Eve, which usually provokes an extra jollity on a sea voyage, was quite nightmarish on this occasion. The toasts on this last evening of 1940 were boisterously made by the captain himself with glass upraised declaiming '*Deutschland über Alles*', and, as the glasses reached most lips, we heard in quietly reverential undertones, '*Heil Hitler.*' We felt far too greatly outnumbered, I'm afraid, to rise bravely to our feet and declaim 'God Save the King' or even 'There'll Always Be an England'. There was a US naval lieutenant at our table, sporting pilot's wings over his handkerchief pocket, to whom I, perhaps foolishly, raised my glass and offered a toast 'To the American and the British naval air services.' To my horror he turned my toast aside and said, 'I prefer "To all pilots trying to get home".'

Over-dramatic as it may well seem now, this constant nightmare was a very real one to us. Some time during the day or night, went our nightmare, we would be aware of an ominous scraping sound against the side of the ship, followed by a sharp rap on our cabin door, through which we would be unceremoniously pulled on to the outside deck, thrust down a rope ladder, to disappear as prisoners-of-war into the waiting 'U' boat. Later, we found the nightmare was not so far-fetched; it had in truth happened a few times, once to someone we knew, who consequently spent the entire war as a prisoner in Germany.

Lisbon, being the capital of a neutral country, was as crammed with spies as a pomegranate is with pips. It was really funny. Furtively, thumb-tips were stuck through lapel button-holes; there was a Mata Hari behind every palm tree, automatically changing over her crossed legs when the right contact, with studied indifference, came to sit casually beside her, so as to present for his inspection the carefully darned message above the inside ankle of the relevant leg. Behind every pillar of the immense lounge – the biggest set in the greatest Grand Hotel show on earth – men would pause, say something in an undertone and move casually on.

I called on the Air Commodore who was Air Attaché at the British Embassy and presented my letter of introduction from Group Captain Adams, our test pilot for American aircraft in the process of manufacture in California. Our Air Commodore in Lisbon was sympathetic and promised to get us on to a plane within two or three days. But drama was not over for us quite yet on this long voyage home. Our windows were, of course, blacked out for a night flight, and about halfway home a fat little uniformed man came bustling out of the flight-deck leaving the door open in his hurry, rewarding us with the sight of the cockpit on fire. Realising his error, he bustled back, closing the door to shut out the uproar from the flight-deck; bundling past us to the tail-end and from there retrieving a fire extinguisher, he dashed up forrard again and disappeared. It transpired that we had not been the victims of enemy action, but that the second pilot, aiming to fire the recognition signal, had pressed the trigger, forgetting to open the window – hence the flames in the cockpit.

We landed at Bristol, properly enough in the middle of an air-raid. Hurrying from the plane to the insufficient shelter of the passengers' lounge, we were accompanied by the only slightly reassuring reply of anti-aircraft guns, still sounding, as I remembered from the First World War, like planks dropping. After a freezing and windy night in an hotel bedroom which had received some previous treatment from the enemy (the outside wall had gone and had been inadequately replaced by a tarpaulin), we struggled, shivering, downstairs to discover what sort of a breakfast we might scrounge. The sweet young waitress explained that the fare was not of the best this morning since 'We had a spot of bother last night.' And so we reached the end of our long journey home: London and Durham Cottage.

Friends rallied round. The Liveseys from down the road, the Millses – John still in the Royal Engineers – Bobby

Douglas and Ralph R., both Fleet Air Arm, which I was going to try for; Roger Furse 'dressed as a seaman' from below decks; my brother Dickie, an officer in the RNVR. Jack Hawkins, in the Royal Welch Fusiliers, kept grinning at me and growling, 'You *are* a silly bugger – *really!*' We followed the universal tendency to keep threatening fears and obsessions at bay by a liberal intake of alcohol, and found ourselves more thrilled to be home than ever before.

I quickly made the right applications to their lordships of the Admiralty, as instructed by Ralph, and was soon summoned to the Mall for an interview and a medical. This done, I was appointed to take a flying test at Lee-on-Solent. We went down to stay with Ralph, who was stationed nearby, and next day Ralph took me for my test in his Lagonda. That night while he was in his bath, his wife Mu told me the next day, she had remarked that I seemed terribly anxious whether I had passed or not. After thoughtfully sponging his face for a moment or two, he had said, 'He'll pass.' Ralph was at this time about to get his half-stripe, and I suspect that he may have had a word with his future colleague, the lieutenant commander in charge of this particular training squadron, a man named Goodyear, who had given both Ralph and me instruction in our early days of flying with the London Aeroplane Club at Hatfield.

I heard from the Admiralty two or three days later that I was to be given a commission and was to report for duty to HMS *Daedalus*, which was the Royal Navy Air Station at Lee-on-Solent, to take a conversion course to service types of aircraft, and proceed from there as appointed. My great dread was that I might be sent to the RNAS in Trinidad, a situation of despairing loneliness, utter boredom, and inevitable separation from Vivien; the dread was exacerbated by the knowledge that all naval appointments were for two years' duration. She was about to star in *The Doctor's Dilemma* at the Haymarket.

It was with a huge sigh of relief that I learnt that I was appointed to HMS *Kestrel*, the RNAS at Worthydown, four miles north of Winchester – a pleasant enough spot, but as an airfield it had been abandoned by the RAF in 1921. In point of fact it consisted of a large hill, sloping away downwards so that much of one side of the perimeter could not be seen from the other, and consequently only a skilful pilot could make a decent three-point landing by putting the machine into a double stall at the last moment before the actual touchdown. I think I may describe myself as a decent pilot.

The Navy's purpose in taking possession of the place from 1939 was to use it as a school for air-gunners. The pilots attached to it were frankly taxi-drivers for these trainee air-gunners, flying them about the sky while they attempted to keep in wireless contact with base. The pilot's role in the exercise was to inform the gunner of his position through the speaking-tube from time to time. The one freedom allowed to the pilot was in his choice of route, supposedly one hour out and one back. This virtually confined one to four hours' flying a day, except for the long, light days of summer when one could get permission for aerobatic practice. Another practice that was encouraged was to jump into the cockpits of all varieties of aircraft new to one and practise 'circuits and bumps'. This increased one's usefulness in being able to transport any type of aircraft to other air-stations all over the country. It also had some entertainment value, at least to me.

I got to know the map of England like the back of my hand. From Winchester one could reach Canterbury to the east, Exeter to the west and Coventry to the north. At no time, of course, was it permitted to fly over the Channel – our aircraft were unarmed and the poor gunner would have been a helpless clay pigeon.

Once I decided to shoot up a friend – a forbidden practice, but fairly generally indulged in – and chose Jeanne de Casalis, who lived a little dangerously near the coast close to Folkestone. I found her house all right, and surely that must be she in the garden? I put myself into a dive straight down at her, to pull out of it, of course, missing the house by a few feet; I climbed quickly to turn and came again from the other side. She was waving at me curiously, as if to push me away. As I climbed in a homeward direction, with surprising suddenness a Spitfire appeared, wing-to-wing on my starboard side; the pilot waggled his wings, I waggled mine back, all in a spirit of friendliness, I thought, and he disappeared as quickly as he had come.

Of course, there was a raid on Folkestone and the pilot was warning me to get the hell out of it, not wanting to see a British plane shot out of the sky, no matter how idiotic the pilot, and of course Jeanne's odd gesticulations had been saying, 'Get away, you damn fool.' It had not occurred to this genius that if I had got the shooting-down that I was asking for, her lovely little farmhouse would most certainly have suffered for my rashness.

I had been very lucky in finding a bungalow only two or three miles from the aerodrome. Uniformed people had a certain swing with the petrol-rationing, especially for motor-cycles. I ran a BMW, and very nice too. Ralph, a motorbike king, was grander with his four-cylinder New Imperial. I still had my pride and joy, my Invicta car, with its chromium entrails bursting through the bonnet. This was only brought out for special occasions, such as picking up Vivien on a Sunday morning from Winchester station. On days of really teeming rain, even such a devoted couple as we were could find the soft top and quickly clouded side-windows too leaky for comfort. When her year's run of *The Doctor's Dilemma* was finished, she came to live nearby for a while at Headbourne Worthy. In these limpid conditions life pursued its uncertain way with quite a lot of happiness in its uncertainty.

After a few months the palpable safety of my service began to make me feel a shirker. My initial reactions to those colleagues who had remained with their profession had been scathing; now I began to feel that my position was hardly superior. They might be doing a more sensible duty in sticking to the jobs they knew, rather than getting into a uniform for the sake of appearances, leaving both the services and the public to an increasingly chill diet of leg-shows and tired-out comedians' gags. Patriotism aside, I had thought, more selfishly, that a complete change of milieu, if I survived, would be better for me as an artist than pursuing the same course that I had followed for nearly twenty years. As it turned out, my real work was obviously considered useful by those in authority, since I was constantly being seconded to the making of propaganda: recruiting speeches for WRNS, and so on. From village hall to Albert Hall, there was hardly a limit to the variety of gatherings that found my supposed eloquence forced upon them, always and without fail ending with 'Once more unto the breach'. The applause with which this was received helped me, and the audience, to feel that the whole discourse had been a success. The BBC was a strong contestant for my services. For some reason this was always a source of particular annoyance to my captain.

It was not long before it became clear that the definitive way out of my uncertainties was a stern one, and I applied through squadron commander and captain to be transferred to operations, whatever the cost might be to Vivien and myself. I had been told that the only operational work allotted to Fleet Air Arm pilots of my age – thirty-four – was to fly 'Walrus'. I had always been fascinated by this strange-looking amphibian. She was a high-wing float bi-plane with the engine in the top plane, its prop facing aft, the fish-tale bow swooped up from the water so that, when skimming along the top of it before take-off or after landing, she looked as though she was travelling back-wards. To embark she was hoist from her special top deck of the ship and craned down to the water. I loved the whole idea.

I was summoned to the Ministry of Information to see Jack Beddington, who was side-kick for the Minister on any question which concerned show-business propaganda. He asked me to undertake two pictures intended to enhance the British cause. One was *The Demi-Paradise*, whose object was to win the British public over to the idea of liking the Russians; hardly an insurmountable task, you would have thought, since Russia had now come into the war heavily on our side. After *Demi-Paradise*, I would be required to make a picture of Shakespeare's *Henry V*. The pull of this play as popular propaganda, I could see, might be far more potent than the first project, and the pull on my artistic ambitions was intoxicating. I explained that I had but recently volunteered to the Admiralty to become operational, and was told that that could always be arranged later. The whole thing was altogether too attractive to resist. It seemed to answer every problem.

Demi-Paradise was amusing to do, Russian accent and all. I had, at first, a Russian lady to teach me this until I began to find my consonants becoming alarmingly, not to say suspiciously, effeminate; I turned to a male Russian, who immediately declared, 'Avreesink see huss tolld you iss alll wrongg,' at which point I decided I might do worse than invent my own Russian accent. I knew the basic principles of it anyway.

The work was very pleasant; Anthony (Piffin) Asquith was the excellent, experienced and very charming director, Tolly de Grunwald was the fine, delightfully friendly (Russian) producer, always helpful and encouraging about my accent; he taught me the correct way of saying that most variously attempted of words, 'Soviet'. It should be 'Suv*yett*'. It was now that I was lucky enough to get to know that most expert team of designers, Paul Sherriff and Carmen Dillon, and plumped immediately for them for *Henry V*, Paul as designer with Carmen as art director. (The title 'art director' represents the person who translates what the 'designer' has scribbled on the back of an envelope into large sets that stand up.)

A further blessing brought by *Demi-Paradise* was that it gave me three nice months of planning *Henry V* in between takes, after work in the evenings, and at weekends, when Paul, Carmen, Roger Furse and I would meet at all possible moments, picking up at once from where we left off. The elusive animal that we were all chasing was, of course, the Style. Paul had drawn some colour sketches of two or three of the sets that would obviously be required. Bless his heart, it was wonderfully helpful that these sketches were so thoroughly wrong; the outside of Harfleur was strikingly effective in the realistic convention in film tradition of slightly forced perspective – and vast, so tall in the right foreground it could hardly have got into a studio, but would have to have been built outside. In sharp perspective the left end of the wall went sleekly down to infinity. Atop the wall, on the right, were two or three upper-half figures, apparently leaning on it and facing out from it towards the cameras. The English Army would have to have been composed of many thousands of men. We got to know each other quickly and well, for it was necessary to be frank at all times, quite pleasantly, but with no trimmings.

'Paul,' I said, 'it's terrific, but too bloody terrific. Harfleur is a small place.'

We all fell to pencilling different ideas on bits of paper.

'You mean like this?'

'How about this?'

'What would you think about that?'

I had drawn a wall, I suppose twenty to thirty feet wide, round castellated towers supporting each side, a church-like Gothic double door in the middle. A few feet, possibly ten, above the top of the door, in the middle of the straight section of crenellated wall, was the top half of what was meant to be the Governor of Harfleur looking down straight ahead of him.

'I *think* that's more what I mean,' I said.

After a minute Carmen said, 'Ooooh, you mean primitive stuff?'

'Well, not quite, I don't think,' I said.

Carmen hastily drew a suggestion of about twenty huge men all crammed together in a boat much too small for them – 'Not forced perspective so much as false perspective, wrong perspective.'

'Well, that's getting warmer,' I said, 'but perhaps it's a little *too* warm – what do you think? A suggestion may be strong for that sort of style, but quite a bit of a compromise. D'you think that would be about all right, or just plain bloody inartistic?'

We agreed that Paul, Carmen and Roger, too, should all get their heads together and do lots of sketches, colour sketches, no matter how rough, but maybe with one indicative detailed element, Roger putting various colours together just to get the feeling of the colour mixtures most right for the period. I had meantime remembered my *Très Riches Heures du Duc de Berri* and they gorged their eyes on the ravishing Missal illustrations of the Limbourg brothers.

And so The Style was found and the shooting script made. Robert Krasker, who was a very brilliant lighting cameraman, frankly never took to the style at all; each time that I showed him a new set he would look at it, shrug and say, 'Looks terribly phoney.' But Bill Wall, the gaffer, did understand it, and some quite unlikely people became fascinated by it.

Dallas Bower, the BBC producer who had originally conceived the idea, took on the character of a fearless tiger, bursting into no matter what ministry, demanding and somehow getting the impossible. We had all realised right away that we would have to be clever or lucky with the exteriors; there was nowhere in England where you could point your camera without there being a pylon or something equally incongruous on the skyline. Our country was too seriously at war to bother with people who craved special allowances or conditions. There seemed to be no horses and no one to ride them. Scotland seemed to be equally forbidding, with no transport or communications or any hope of co-operation for such a civilian exercise as a film, a frivolous thing.

It was Dallas who came up with Eire as a possibility; not too far from studio, office or lab for reasonably quick news on rushes, and telephoning facilities really not bad. All six of us (by this time Reggie Beck, our masterly editor, also from *Demi-Paradise*, had joined us), took the boat across to Dun Laoghaire. There was an extraordinary sense of release on arriving in Ireland. From the first it felt natural to look at people straight and unnervously, eye to eye. I was told they had a charming, if unusual compliment for me – 'Oh, yes, he's a nice enough man, and he's a plain man, too.' I loved their gentle insistence – 'Come on now, be calm, there's noth'n to worry about at all. Relax and take life easy. If it doesn't happen today, it will surely happen tomorrow – sure it will.'

Carmen is Irish and knew her way around and suggested we try Powerscourt in Enniskerry; we got permission from Lord and Lady Powerscourt to visit and inspect their estate. This we found possessed the magic that we craved, and Reggie and I had a great time visualising shot after shot. Lord Powerscourt was persuaded, and from then on was as helpful a host as anyone could possibly be. He even arranged that Dallas, Reggie and I should sleep, most comfortably, in his butler's house, to be as close as possible to the scene of activities.

We scheduled that we should be working in Ireland for eight weeks, which may seem excessive for ten minutes of edited screen time, but the weather conditions in this part of the world are unreliable, and full sunlight was essential for all day exteriors in Technicolor at this time. It was wiser to over-schedule than to under-schedule. Not infrequently my anxious eyes, gazing up into the heavens, could see various layers of cloud approaching my longed-for sun from three different directions.

But as a location, compared to England, it was wonderfully cheap; I was warned by the Irish authorities not to pay my extras over-liberally as this would make things troublesome for the Government, who could not afford wage rates approaching those in England. They suggested that £3 10s. weekly would be generous, and this is what we paid; if they brought and rode their own horses they could be allowed a pound or so more. Of course all the Irish could ride and I would pick out from line-ups those who could double for my principals: the Constable of France, the Dukes of Bourbon and Orleans, the Dauphin. The horses for these had afterwards to be bought or hired and shipped to England for their actor principals. Mine was white – it was named 'Blaunche Kyng' after one of three horses presented to King Henry by the King of Aragon – and that of the Constable needed to be black, with no other blacks close to him ever, for the sake of identification. Familiarity with the horses had to be established by the time our final duel took place, for which the Constable's visor was to be down, as I was not sure of the riding prowess of Leo Genn, later to be so perfect in the part. I changed the real Blaunche for a large polo pony who would react to the slightest alteration of seating angle, leaving both my arms free for sword and shield.

I made one mistake, but only from my own point of view. Apart from the handful of men over which a naval two-striper – wavy stripes at that – can be in authority, I had never been in command of anything like seven hundred men before, and here they were, marshalled in serried ranks before me as I stood on a beer-crate about to address them for the first time. I was aware that the slightest hint of nervousness would spell disaster and that I must now act being confident as I had seldom acted it before. In the process, this was the sort of stuff that issued from me: 'I may sometimes be asking some things of you which might be difficult, perhaps even dangerous, but I want you to know that I shall not be asking anything of you that I shall not be willing at least to try to do myself.'

The warmth and strength of the appluase that greeted this mighty line should have been a warning to me. I was taken literally.

'Look,' I would say, 'you're very gallant on your horse, I want you to shin up this tree and get yourself squatting on that bough, and as this horseman rides under you – leave your stirrups this shot, Paddy – holding firmly with your hands, just push your feet away and hang just for a second and then drop on to Paddy, pull him off his horse and fall easily to the ground. Jack here will ride quickly in and seem to be riding over you – the horse as we know won't touch you . . . quite simple, really?'

My gallant rider looked at me pleasantly but steadily, and as usual it came: 'We'd like to see you do it first, Mr Oliver.'

I sighed with reluctance inwardly and held out my hand for someone to help me up the tree, and half-a-dozen willing hands hoisted me on to the bough, which I suppose was about twenty feet up. (A horse and rider usually measure nine to ten feet in height.) I realised I must get on with it quickly or I might lose my balance altogether. I had imagined that just a little hop and a backward swing on to my hands would be the easiest part, but that little hop was no little matter. Somehow I scraped both feet off backwards, hung for a second and let go. On landing, a tell-tale stab of sharp pain in my right ankle made me clutch desperately on to the tree trunk.

'There, you see?' I gasped out through clenched teeth. 'Easy, really.'

I limped to the other side of the tree gazing upwards, ostensibly looking for alternative branches on other trees. Safely sheltered from my boys, I burst into a shameful fit of tears; but only giving myself a couple of seconds for this luxury, I staggered on round again, singing out, 'There you are. Okay for you now, old chap?'

At one time during these battle sequences I was walking around with a crutch under my right arm, my left in a sling and a plaster bandage right round my face; this last was occasioned as usual by my o'erstepping the modesty of nature. At one point in the battle the French, almost as a *divertissement*, set fire to Henry's camp; I always tried to sketch in this kind if digressive detail by suggestion rather than make a spectacular sequence out of it, saving both working time and screen time. The film was always in danger of being too long, although I had cut the actual text down from its original 3,000 lines to 1,500. Film is a visual medium, it was vital to remember, and we had to be careful to avoid excessive dialogue if we were to succeed in this attempt to put Shakespeare on the screen. The audiences must not be allowed to miss the poetry nor must they be surfeited with it.

So, for the firing of the camp, I tried out a quick shot of a French horseman flinging a lighted torch into a tent, followed by a shot, with smoke in the background now, of the horseman with a companion riding up to a lighted brazier with his spear, tipping it into a gorse bush and catching it alight, then riding towards the camera and passing it closely left. But somehow this bit seemed disappointingly tame. I told the young rider to come as close to the camera as he could; again through the finder I could tell it wasn't very exciting. This time I said, 'Look, boy, aim to hit the camera this time, will you? Your horse will manage to miss it at the last moment.' I watched again through the finder; the horse was looming beautifully large and frighteningly close – and smack! – right into the camera.

The finder hit my upper lip and pierced right through into the gum; the operator had had the sense to dart out of the way and I got the weight of the camera directly on to my right shoulder, fortunately just missing my collar-bone, before it fell on down to the ground on its side, where it lay still grinding. I turned to see the boy, still mounted, quite close to me; had I felt inclined to tears then, it would not have been on account of my own pain but at the sight of the twelve-inch gash straight along the horse's flank, right through its coat and layers of tissue, the lower lip of the wound hanging down a good three inches.

The horse's flank, my lip and gum sewn up, I switched the sling from my left arm to the one in sorer need of it. The scar on my lip has been a disfiguring feature for nigh on forty years now, only useful as a 'distinguishing mark' for passport people. I grow a moustache partly to hide the scar which has formed two other creases one on each side, but, more secretly, to draw attention away from the displeasingly thin hard line of my upper labium, inherited from my father; both these disfiguring features are only of use for playing the harder type of Nazi, only one of which has ever come my way (in *Marathon Man*); or if the period makes moustaches anachronistic then I am stuck with it, *et tant pis*. (No, darling daughter, that doesn't mean 'my aunt is seriously drunk'.)

Apart from the occasional rider being thrown and dragged some yards, there was only one other accident which had an aftermath. All active fighting was done by suggestion, apart from the final blow delivered by me, backhanded with mailed fist to the visored jaw of the Constable, which marked the end of the battle. One horse most unhappily lost his eye; how, it is impossible to guess, since all spear-heads were topped with silver leather-covered wadding, except for close or insert work. He was a favourite of mine, too, a dun – pale buff with black mane and tail (perhaps the origin of the place name Dunstable) – whenever possible kept somewhere in the foreground. He and his rider had to be thanked most warmly for their services and allowed to take up their old life pulling a side-car through the streets of Dublin.

Now whether it was against regulations for a side-car horse to have less than the normal complement of eyes, or whether his owner had failed to fulfil requirements in some other way, this gallant cavalryman found himself up before a magistrate on some charge which concerned his horse. It turned out that this magistrate was either the only man in Ireland who had not heard that a film of *Henry V* had been made in his country, or else rarely ignorant for a magistrate of the reasoning of his poorer countrymen; for when our friend upon being sentenced pleaded, 'Sure and your honour wouldn't take it out on a poor old war-horse that lost his eye fight'n for the Irish in the battle of Ag'ncourt?', this magistrate promptly doubled his sentence.

The rest of the film took about sixteen weeks in Denham Studios. If this seems excessive, it should be remembered that the lighting for Technicolor in those early days was a slow process; in 1943, the shortage of lamps meant that most of them had to be moved and rehung in another position for any reverse or change in angle; and the focus carriage was so limited that even a small group shot was expected to be on one plane across the picture. If in exasperation one dared to break up this line, then only one plane of the group would be sharply in focus.

Although the work was shadowed for me by a sense of my responsibilities, from time to time it also felt most pleasantly creative and I look back on it always with a happy glow. The Technicolor people were nothing if not co-operative, but the technique of trial and error in the printing process demanded limitless patience: 'Too orange, too pink, too orange, too yellow, too blue, too orange; more grey, please, please more grey,' the querulous insistences went interminably on for some weeks. One particularly aggravating result of this business was the likelihood of departures from the established final version; I suppose this has to be the bugbear of any reproductive process, unless one is prepared or able to inspect every copy ever put out for exhibition.

I don't much want to see my own work again and again; one has, after all, in the final editing, run every foot of the thing an unbelievable number of times. But I did once pop into a cinema which was showing *Henry* and was appalled by the poor-looking print, the colour all over the place – and those 'projies' (projectionists') cuts'! When a break occurs in the running of any film in a cinema, there is a white flash and then darkness for the next few seconds, during which the skilful projie speedily rethreads the unviewed part and gets it running again. When that reel is finished and the next one safely on, he then does his best to mend the break, cutting off both broken ends and sticking the new edges together; it is his responsibility to send on each reel in once piece to the next place. But this, of course, is not the end of it; there is now a permanent weakness at this join, and it will break again in the same place, though with luck not at every running. The consequence of these repeated operations is that your film gets to look choppier and choppier and more and more clumsily edited until finally the continuity makes no sense at all. The same fate, of course, is shared by the sound-track.

There was a moment in *Henry* when the relentless advance of the French cavalry was checked by a hail of arrows from the English archers. This was a climax equally contributed to by visual image, sound effect and, above all, musical score – and William Walton's part in the success of the film was unique. (Why he has never achieved any Oscars for this or any of my Shakespeare films must remain a prime example of the miasmically mysterious conclusions reached by the award-giving organisations.) On my visit to the showing of this sequence, to my amazement no arrows appeared on the image. Immediately I could get to a phone I picked it up to express my outraged feelings to

Technicolor; they promised to apply themselves to nothing else until this mystery had been solved, and it seemed no time at all before they rang back. 'We have found the reason for this phenomenon; the arrows were printed on to the lavender, and we don't use it any more.'

The lavender, it must be explained, was a fourth colour; as well as the usual three colours of Technicolor – red, green and blue – the lavender, a dark greyish colour, was added in the belief that it gave extra definition to the edges of all photographed objects, whether human or architectural. This strip of film was therefore very useful for optically graphic details such as these famous arrows – and I describe them as 'famous' because they did indeed make a great impression nearly forty years ago, and have gratifyingly often been referred to since. Like all such trick shots in 1943, we were bulldozed by the fact that not only was the camera we had the only Technicolor one in England, but no quick-cranking gear had yet been evolved. This meant that we had to go back many years to find means to create our effects, for instance in the opening and closing shots of the film – for which grateful acknowledgement must be given to Visscher's perspective elevation of London. A special slow-burning smoke had to be discovered to issue from the miniature chimneys, and the thickest possible oil that could be found was used for the Thames water so that any natural water movement caused by the miniature ship traffic should not be absurdly out of scale.

So these 'arrows', never photographed in flight, had to be composed of the simplest ingredients. One of Korda's geniuses at Denham, Pop Day, drew out a back view of a hefty group of arrows in flight, optically reducing them until they were the right size for the French cavalry about a hundred yards away advancing towards the camera. The also much remarked-on sound of their flight was obtained too by the most elementary means: Sammy Samuel, my general and overall assistant, took a minimum sound crew into a field close to the studio, cut off a long willow switch and swished it past the microphone perhaps a hundred times. Reggie Beck then took this single soundtrack, added closely and multiplied each single swish into a quick crescendo, the diminuendo following immediately in scale, then crash in came Master William's music again, as usual to my intense relief.

CHAPTER SEVEN

Hired and Fired

Before the work on the picture had been finalised I had heard that the dear old Walrus flying-boat had been withdrawn from service in the Fleet Air Arm. There was now no branch of operations for which I was eligible, and to pursue my idea of returning to the Navy to take up taxi-driving trainee air-gunners round the sky again seemed to be really a bit cranky. There were volunteers and to spare for this type of job by now.

I was still in the final stages of fine frame-cutting, revised sound-dubbing and last shades of colour-choosing when I was contacted by old friends Tyrone Guthrie and Ralph Richardson. These two felt deeply that the Old Vic should be redeemed from the extinction into which it had fallen (the old theatre had been bombed and there was no money for touring) in order to answer the growing sense of dissatisfaction with the poor class of entertainment available. Those on leave from services or other war work and even the civilian population were all members of a civilised community and justifiably felt they had the right to the sweets of emotional and intellectual uplift; and we three belonged to the lucky ones who were supposed to be able to do that for people.

So, although the theatre itself was not available, the revival of an Old Vic company came about, with a new (for this century in London) system of nightly changing repertory. The three of us were to be the directors of the theatre company, with John Burrell joining us as a non-acting director fresh from the BBC. He had just scored a great success directing Edith Evans and Robert Donat in Shaw's

Heartbreak House. The governors of the Old Vic, a group of noble as well as intellectual gentlemen, had applied to their lordships of the Admiralty for Ralph and me to be relieved of our duties in order to undertake this work. The speediness and lack of reluctance with which their lordships let us go was positively hurtful; however, we did not spend much time brooding over it and embraced the work with a shamefully careless rapture.

We fell into a little confusion at first, since we were out of practice in theatre management, and came up against this teasing question: Do we get the best company we can muster and then think up the plays to suit them, or do we choose the plays and then look for a suitable company? In our case the matter was already simplified to some extent because we knew what the first play was going to be: it was *Peer Gynt* with Ralph in the title role, directed by Tony Guthrie. This required a large production and a very sizeable cast, so that it should not be difficult to find a repertoire of plays that could be cast from such a wide spectrum of players. In our set-up it was clear that all the plays should suit either Ralph or myself, if possible both of us. We were different enough in both appearance and personality to be good foils for each other, and the partnership became immediately popular with our audiences.

We opened in Manchester with *Arms and the Man* for a warm-up, with Ralph as Bluntschli and myself as Sergius – a part I was not at all keen to do at the outset – with Sybil Thorndike, my own most dearly beloved, and indeed everybody else's, favourite actress; Nicholas (Beau) Hannen, a very valuable, handsome and distinguished actor in his late fifties; our two young leading ladies, Margaret Leighton, whose work we had discovered at Birmingham on a talent-scouting expedition, and Joyce Redman, already established but to develop both to her advantage and to ours; George Relph and Harcourt Williams, both of splendidly ripe character age; and two or three likely enough young sparks.

The receptions were warmly enthusiastic and business could hardly be bettered. We played to a capacity week at the Opera House and actually paid off the costs of that production in the one week; economically but exquisitely set and costumed by Doris Zinkeisen, it had not been expensive. Conscious as we were of being the Old Vic in wartime with a government guarantee only amounting to half our loss, we had to scrimp and save like Lilian Baylis. The materials themselves were for the most part of the cheapest; I remember the sleeves of the rough jerkin under my *Richard III* armour were made of blackout material, as indeed were everybody's, including Sybil's, in the dark forest in *Peer Gynt*; blackout material was reasonably all right for looks, it just didn't feel nice or comfortable to wear.

The day after the opening, Ralph and I took the well-worn walk from the Midland Hotel to the stage door for letters and messages. On the way back Ralph bought the *Guardian*; I must admit I had forgotten about such things as notices. I have said that I was far from happy in the part of Sergius, but I also had a brooding feeling about all my work that first year; I suppose in every partnership one of the parties is apt to feel he has the dirty end of the stick, and I found it impossible to throw off a feeling of grievance. Ralph's package of roles was Peer Gynt, a part acknowledged to be one of singularly great opportunities for any actor; Bluntschli, of the two parts in *Arms and the Man* unquestionably the superior; and Richmond in *Richard III*, a supporting role but the character who deposes Richard by beating him in battle. I suppose you might call him the *jeune premier* of the play; Ralph undertook this in return for my playing the Button Moulder at the end of *Gynt*. It did get to tickle the audience when we each played small parts in support of the other, which was good.

The only other new production we had planned after the first three was *Uncle Vanya*, in which he was to play the name part and I the doctor, Astrov; here again, in my by now thoroughly jaundiced view, the finger seemed to point to him as the more leading of the two of us, and I was despondent about my chances of coming back successfully after years away from the London theatre. I thought grimly

(*Above left*) Macbeth in the Old Vic 1937–8 season. Noël Coward laughed and laughed.

(*Above*) Macbeth at Stratford, 1955. Nöel did not laugh this time.

Hotspur in *Henry iv, Part i*, 1945–6. When the curtain went up on this glamorous pose, a man in the audience behind Johnnie Mills said, 'Here's old Ginger again!'

Richard III with Joyce
Redman as Lady Anne and
Nicholas Hannen as
Buckingham, 1944.

Portrait of Richard III by
Mervyn Peake from the
prompt box at the
Staatsteater in Hamburg.

My first Lear, with Alec Guinness as Fool, 1946.

Shaw's *Caesar and Cleopatra*, 1951.

With Vivien in Shakespeare's *Antony and Cleopatra*, 1951.

Malvolio in *Twelfth Night*, 1955.

The death of Coriolanus, 1959.

Titus Andronicus with Vivien, 1955.

Films and Filming

With Lilian Harvey in my first film, *The Temporary Widow*, made in Neubahbelsberg in 1930.

With Vivien in *Fire Over England* in 1936. It was the first time we worked together.

With Lionel Barrymore in *The Yellow Passport*, 1931, my second Hollywood picture.

Heathcliff with Merle Oberon in *Wuthering Heights* in 1938–9. Wyler, somewhat painfully, taught me respect for the medium.

Maxim de Winter with Joan Fontaine in *Rebecca* by Daphne du Maurier, 1939.

With Greer Garson in *Pride and Prejudice*, 1940. I had given her her first chance in *Golden Arrow* in 1935.

Nelson with Vivien in *Lady Hamilton*, 1941. Alexander Korda kindly arranged for Heathcliff to work with Scarlett and earn enough money to go home.

Henry v, 1943–4. Producer, director and star Laurence Olivier, dialogue Shakespeare. As you will deduce, I am somewhat proud of it.

nlet, 1947. My only moment of courage.

Richard III with Ralph as Buckingham, 1954.

With Jennifer Jones in Dreiser's *Sister Carrie* (1950), my second film with Wyler, twelve years after *Wuthering Heights*.

'My lord, this would not be believ'd in Venice.' Othello striking
Maggie Smith as Desdemona.

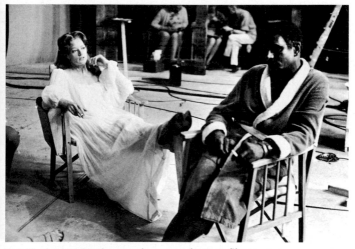

Othello boring Desdemona between shots at Shepperton.

With Marilyn working on *The Prince and the Showgirl*, 1956. Richard Wattis, between us, appreciates the situation.

Directing Joan and Alan Bates in *Three Sisters*, 1969 – in my opinion amongst my best work.

of the lot that had fallen to me; my Big One was to be
Richard III, which was at this time rather a stale cup of tea;
every old actor-manager throughout history had played it
and it bore that sort of stigma. Besides, it had been revived
only eighteen months before by Donald Wolfit with great
popular and critical success. Wolfit was a favourite with his
own formidable public as well as being a critics' pet. I
obviously didn't have any kind of a chance with that one; I
was just not going to be allowed to know the faintest whiff
of success this season.

I looked over Ralph's arm to see what I could of that
notice he was reading, and what hit my eyes made them
smart with displeasure; 'Mr Ralph Richardson is a brilliant
Bluntschli; Mr Laurence Olivier, on the other hand . . .' I
tore my eyes away; Oh God! I really can't go on with this.
I'll go straight back to the Navy. That's the only thing to do.
This was all a huge mistake. I shall do no good to these
people or to myself if I stay on.

John Burrell had directed *Arms and the Man*, and so
Tony Guthrie didn't come to see us until the second night. I
dawdled over the removal of my make-up to give Tony
plenty of time to come to see me, and maybe cheer me with
some advice on my problem. But he didn't come. 'I see,' I
thought, 'I see.' The idea occurred to me to pack up my
make-up there and then, but I felt that might look a bit
hysterical, indeed it might well *be* a bit hysterical. As I was
going down the stairs, Tony, Ralph and John emerged from
the star dressing-room – Sybil's – and so we all came out
together, walked to the corner and turned left under the
canopy. Here Tony left the others and came to say, 'Liked
yer Sergius.' I murmured sulkily, 'Oh, thanks *very* much.'
'Why, don't you like the part?' I looked at him incredulously, 'What?' He looked back at me. 'Don't you love
Sergius?' I almost came to a halt staring up at him. 'Love
that stooge? That inconsiderable . . . God, Tony, if you
weren't so tall I'd hit you, if I could reach you.'

Tony Guthrie in all the shows we had worked in together
had never in my ungrateful memory said anything to me
of a dazzling philosophical nature, but had stuck to

technicalities. But this night, he said something which changed the course of my actor's thinking for the rest of my life. 'Well, of course, if you can't love him you'll never be any good in him, will you?'

And that is the reason for this detailed preamble to the opening of the new Old Vic Theatre Company at the Opera House, Manchester, and of my walk back to the Midland with Tony, and how, under its canopy, I received the richest pearl of advice in my life.

It took me the inside of that week to get on to the idea; by the end of it I loved Sergius as I'd never loved anybody. I loved him for his faults, for his showing off, his absurdity, his bland doltishness. Vivien came up for the Saturday night and was ecstatic about it – probably all the more so because from what I had said she had learnt to expect the worst.

Gynt was our first to open at the New Theatre, and proved to be even more successful than had been anticipated. With Ralph, a Guthrie production, and an orchestra of twenty playing the Grieg score, its drawing-power was tremendous. It was quickly followed by *Arms and the Man* in which everyone's confidence, including my own, had now grown unrecognisably, and that, too, hit the jackpot. I was no longer dismissed with any of your 'on the other hands' – even in *The Times* it was 'towering above them all' that I found myself, by heaven.

But now, yes now . . . the real dread. The company up until now had been buoyantly optimistic, which only increased their gloom about *Richard III*. I had never opened any play with so despondent a company; even John Burrell, our director, could find no heart to cheer us with locker-room talk, and I walked towards my fate as to my grave.

Waiting in the wings by the down-left door, Diana Boddington, my darling stage manager for the next thirty years (she is still at the National), squeezed my hand as the last notes of Herbert Menges's overture went (brass) Pum paPaah pa papa pa Paaaah, into fiddles) Tye tyetye Tyeeeeee. I opened the door with my right hand, turning the ring-handle noisily, limped through and, turning my back to the audience, clicked the lych-bar sharply back into its housing, then slowly turned leftwards to face the audience. A moment of panic at this, which I shook off; after all, what does it matter? I am sunk with it anyway. I'll see if I can enjoy it for as long as they'll let me go on. I started in the thin voice old actors had always put on when they did an imitation of Irving:

> Now is the winter of our discontent
> Made glorious summer by this son of York.

I think the audience must also have been of a mistrustful frame of mind. It may well have been that the apparent hopelessness of our trying to make a success with this play as with the others moved the audience, with English good nature, to something like sympathy. Something caught between us anyway and, like an electric wire, held us together.

I had known cheering before, but I had never known it to be indicative of certain success. My first experience of it was as the curtain fell at the end of the first night of *Ringmaster* (1935), by Keith Winter, at the old Shaftesbury Theatre – still as I write an empty space surrounded by hoardings from wartime bombing. Gilbert Miller, who had put the play on for me and made me a partner, came into my dressing-room and said, 'What are we going to do with all this money we're going to make?' That was on the Monday and it closed that Saturday. So, apart from giving one personally a moment of pleasurable relief, cheers do not necessarily fill one's heart with confidence, I'm afraid; it's better not to kid yourself or let such receptions raise giddy hopes.

Our matinées that season were Thursday, Friday and Saturday. *Richard*'s first night being on a Thursday, our second show was the Friday matinée; I came down to the stage early to feel the atmosphere and – yes, there is was, that sweet smell (it's like seaweed) of success; I moved on in wonderment to Diana's corner; she was smiling, she too had felt what I now felt – there it was, right in the audience, even through the curtain, that unmistakably high expectation. George Relph, my dear, dear friend, came down early for his Clarence entrance to feel the atmosphere too. 'Smell it, Georgie?' He nodded slowly and gravely said, 'Ye-es', in happy reverence for this rare thing. The audience had come in response to some sixth sense; it was in the air, though by no means uniformly expressed by the morning newspapers, that people should come and see – *me*. It was the first time in my twenty-year-old career that I had ever felt anything like it.

Came Herbert's last brass chords, followed by the two bars of high flute and fiddle, and the instant they cut off, bang in came my iron door-handle. As I turned to face them, my heart rose to embrace this communion as to the miraculously soft warmth of a rapturous first night of love. As on the usual cue I turned to make my first move across the stage, I was so aware of being borne by this absurd giddiness that I actually forgot to limp for a step or two before calling myself to order. The evening newspapers were collectively eulogistic in their praises. And so were the Sundays. I took with careful deliberation my step into the flood of that tide in the affairs of men in glad thankfulness.

Thus, despite all gloomy prognoses, *Richard III* hopped up to roost on the same branch as the others to make a record season of three equal smash hits; I think there was no firm favourite among them in public favour, the booking for all three was pretty well balanced. Early in the spring we put on *Uncle Vanya*; this did not, at least in the first season, bask in the same warm approval that we were getting used to and I'm afraid were beginning to expect so, after twenty-one performances, which never seemed quite to click, we put it regretfully but lovingly away, packed cosily in cotton wool with one or two mothballs, and placed it on a nice, warm, tactful shelf.

But it was during this season that I had three astonishing turns of fortune in three different aspects of dramatic art, the first being *Richard*; never before had I known general approbation, expressed equally by my colleagues, the public and the critics. In the middle of the autumn came the beyond-wildest-dreams acclaim for *Henry V*, which established me indisputably as film director-actor-producer; later, in the spring, I was judged successful as director of a stage play, *The Skin of our Teeth* by Thornton Wilder, a favourite both as writer and friend. My joy in this reached its zenith at the brilliant success achieved by Vivien as Sabina. In the face of all critical prejudice, she had now established herself as a stage actress and star of the brightest metal.

At the end of our first season at the New Theatre quite suddenly came VE day and all fighting ceased in Europe. We went, as was our primary duty, to play to the troops still stationed in Europe – memorably at the Flemische Schauspielhaus in Antwerp. Apart from its sublime beauty, as Ralph and I agreed, its wooden interior endowed this theatre with the most miraculous acoustic properties. In keeping with the apparent fate of all such priceless relics, it was torn down some years ago. I have known two London theatres to be torn down almost about my ears: the first was my St James's, after I had for eight years managed, or perhaps more correctly mismanaged it, for the costliness of this tenancy was punitive; almost immediately afterwards came the destruction of the Stoll London Opera House.

We arrived in Antwerp after an arduous tour of *Titus Andronicus* behind the Iron Curtain – Belgrade, Zagreb and Warsaw. Titus was a punishing role and six weeks of the strain brought me to a state of exhaustion which, as I learnt then, must be deleterious to a performing artist. Mrs Minnie Maddern Fiske, American comedienne *par excellence*, decreed that 'You should only play light comedy off the cream of your energies.' I am sure there has never been a light comedian who would not agree, and as my vain boast is that I am every sort of actor, I align myself with this august throng and add my vigorous nod. In tragedy we find it possible, even advantageous to a certain extent, to *use* exhaustion, which seems to add some extra dimension to inspiration; but there is a degree of exhaustion that becomes erosive to the precision of intention. This was the state in which I found myself after the first three weeks of this run at the Stoll, making the last half of the season a long-drawn-out torment to me. Out of anxiety to get on with their job of house-breaking, the builders had started hammering about a bit in various parts of the Stoll roof before we were halfway through our last week, and bits of plaster fell sporadically from the ceiling on either side of the curtain.

Having allowed myself to be thoroughly distracted by the agitation that I always feel when theatres get demolished, I must remember the many glorious examples of theatre architecture which still stand, some of which gave us so much pleasure to work in during this Old Vic tour in 1945. Brussels, Ghent, Hamburg – its Grosse Schauspielhaus upstanding and immune from our RAF bombers which had successfully achieved an impressive shelling-out of their great Opernhaus – that is, of its vast auditorium. The magnificent stage had been entirely protected by its solid iron curtain. With amused admiration we gazed upwards and saw how a far-reaching mind had seen the likelihood that this would be the part of the theatre most likely to stay untouched; for up aloft there was hung in military close order their huge wardrobe – thousands of costumes, densely packed on their hangers, almost ready to wear. Here was the most striking evidence of any we had seen that to the Germans culture was the theatre, second only to music and way before any other of the arts – literature, sculpture, painting. The war had hardly been over a month but already signs of the building priorities were apparent. The situation was indeed enviable to us unwanted English theatre folk.

Finally the Old Vic Theatre Company (for thus we had slightly re-christened ourselves, to make it clear that we were not to be found at the Old Vic again, possibly for some time) had the great honour of playing in the Théâtre Français, making a neat exchange with their company, La Comédie Française, who came to play in our home at the New. Having first played for two weeks at the Marigny exclusively for the troops in *Arms and the Man*, we moved across the Place de la Concorde and Palais Royal into la

Place du Théâtre Français, and gave a repertoire of our first three productions. Here I enjoyed a slight advantage; Ralph, having opened our inaugural production in London, found himself to be closing it in *Peer Gynt*; generously he saw that it was a small advantage and urged me to take the same in Paris with *Richard III*.

First nights in Paris are occasions generally notable for their social significance rather than for much attention to the *chef d'œuvre*. We were prevented from raising the curtain until it was three-quarters of an hour late, as the society élite remained in an obstinately jammed crush in the foyer. Not one couple was willing to make the first foray into the auditorium; all were determined upon making the last entrance.

In keeping with this attitude, there exists close to the stage precincts in the Théâtre Français a large salon where the more intellectual members of Parisian society are apt to collect and take the opportunity to meet the actors. In the interval I retired to my room to mop up a bit (there was a heatwave in Paris), patch up my make-up, sit quietly and possibly go through the curtain speech which I had learnt, or rather been taught, in French. A knock came at the door and I was summoned downstairs '*pour recevoir les compliments*'; I said that I was sorry but I didn't do that. The messenger went on and on in the way only Latin people can. I just sat firmly down and kept shaking my head slowly and repeating, '*Je m'excuse*,' until the wretched man left me alone.

At the end, I wasn't summoned down to a grand salon; '*les compliments*' all brought themselves up to my room and in two or three minutes it was crammed with a jabbering crush of highly excited French-speaking people all shouting apparently charming things at me. Two out of this vast throng, which to me I must say was as exciting as it was excited, turned out to be my great French friends who were not of the theatre: Ginette Spanier and her husband, Paul-Emile (Polly) Seidmann. Ginette was born and brought up by her French father and English mother in Golders Green, but having lived in France for some years

she was now *directrice* of Balmain, the fashionable cour-
turier; her husband was a successful general practitioner.

I number Ginette among my nearest and dearest. The
two of them had a most painful and scarifying war; for the
best of racial reasons they were on the run throughout the
period of the Vichy regime. When they were 'assisting' at
the Paris opening of *Richard*, the first few words of the
opening soliloquy precipitated them into a state of emotion
that lasted the rest of the evening: these were the first
English words they had heard spoken for five years.

Very shortly after, I received the news that Vivien was ill
for the first time with tuberculosis; I couldn't get back for
three weeks. Luckily we had managed to get our housekeeper to come with us from the Fulmer cottage to look
after us at Notley, the glorious abbey which I had bought
earlier that same year. Vivien could stay in bed there and be
visited by the local doctor. When at last I got home, I took
her up to Scotland for a complete change of atmosphere.
We took our little Austin on the train to Stirling and drove
on to Nethey Bridge on the Inver; it was lovely, tranquil;
and peace reigned quite suddenly all over the world, for
hostilities now ceased in the Japanese War. It was hard to
believe that here and now for many people on this earth
there was peace in every part of it for the first time in their
lives; just now, and perhaps for a little while. This holiday
had been a good idea, but on account of it I had missed half
my rehearsal time for the new season and this must now be
remedied by devoting myself to the most concentrated
labour I had ever attempted – Hotspur, Shallow, Oedipus
and Mr Puff in four weeks of clear rehearsals.

It was Tony Guthrie who suggested to us the W. B. Yeats
translation of *Oedipus Rex*. This was very spare, stark and
plain, seemingly anti-poetic, as if in revolt against Gilbert
Murray, whose version was the only one generally acknowledged to be respectable. I liked the Yeats all right, and
thought it might be interesting to deal with material which
prided itself on being plain, but I was filled with gloom at

the prospect of confining myself to quite such a deadly solemn evening.

This fear of frustration made me remember the delight I took in reading Sheridan's *The Critic*. Tony, understandably enough, did not care for the idea since it might detract from his proposed production of *Oedipus*, for which he planned a pretty, dainty-coloured décor, which he reckoned would contrast effectively with the deep tragic theme. I was a little shocked by such subservience to originality and wasn't sure that this might not show a lack of confidence in the author's intentions. Besides, in spite of the shared fiasco of our *Macbeth* eight years previously, I had complete confidence in the undoubted genius of Michel St Denis for this strange beast. I put this to the other two and they agreed.

If Tony was a little miffed by this declaration of independence, he did not show it. Though I have good reason to think that he did have a respect for my work generally, as well as a fondness for me, one would never know of it directly. He seemed to have a wish to prick the bubble of any special success. In due course he took himself to see *Henry V* and came and sat in my dressing-room to tell me so. 'Oh?' I said, hoping perhaps for a word of commendation this time. 'Thought it was vulgar,' he said. He used this expression again when I told him of my plan for the double bill, and yet again when he came to see it. He was always good entertainment, always original, if on occasions wantonly so, but always guarded and reserved, in spite of his brilliant gift of the gab and enviable vocabulary.

I tried to top myself with 'Oedipuff' as the show comprising *Oedipus* and *The Critic* was soon referred to.

When Sibyl (Lady) Colefax, that Queen of hostesses, heard that I was to do Oedipus she immediately gave one of her smallish dinners for eight (at eight) in order to get Professor Maurice Bowra and me together. In this thoughtful habit she had a remarkable usefulness to her ample coterie of friends, who repaid her by calling her 'Coalbox'.

Sophocles would have been the apple of Thespis's eye

had they shared the same generation. Actors are commonly referred to as Thespians, but it seems that Thespis himself was more producer than actor in that he brought to the tradition regnant in the theatre up till then – that of solo recitations at great length of religious eulogies – the idea of a colloquy between two actors, thus instigating The Scene.

The contemporary limitations upon theatre presentation obliged Sophocles to place the action of his story into the mouths of his Messenger and his Chorus. Reality of feelings, though marvellously expressed, disdained factualities, inhabiting realms far above such trivia. Oedipus, when he married his own mother, was given no inkling that he had 'been here before', in spite of her being senior to him by a generation, and Jocasta somehow never seemed to remark to him, 'Honey, do tell me about those gyre marks around your ankles.' All the honours concerning such are the property of the Messenger, scored and accompanied by the Chorus, before being reacted to by the principals, who then decide on suicide, eye-ball removal or whatever.

I enjoyed a long and illuminating talk after Sibyl's dinner with Bowra, who helped me to find the sort of feelings about himself that Oedipus might bring on to the stage, and we hit upon the answer for Oedipus and, indeed, for all Greek tragedians: 'That's it,' he said, 'all you can feel is *Fated*.'

The detail most remarked upon in this performance was the cry Oedipus might give when the whole truth of the Message, in this case conveyed by an old shepherd, is revealed to him. 'Oh, Oh,' is given in most editions. After going through all the vowel sounds, I hit upon 'Er'. This felt more agonised and the originality of it made the audience a ready partner in this feeling. Apart from this, the acting secret lay, as usual, in the timing, which was heightened by the spontaneity contained in the length of the pause before the cry.

Most of us need secondary images to support this sort of intensity of expression. Here, in my case, all the animals that were ever caught in traps came to my aid in all sorts of variations; a favourite instance of this is the ermine who is trapped by salt being scattered upon the hard snow. This the ermine starts to lick, but the cunning mixture holds fast to their tongues, keeping them prisoner though they try to tear themselves free. Trading upon this animal torment helped me to produce a horrifying enough noise. It is, as has been said, next to impossible to produce the effect of great suffering without the actor enduring some degree of it.

The gift of playing in *The Critic*, following immediately upon *Oedipus*, worked like a dream for me. I could really sink myself deep into the Greek tragedy without reservation, secure in the anticipation of the joyous gaiety that was to follow it. I felt I was in for the greatest enjoyment ever allowed me in the work of acting (I was still under the thrall of having directed the film of *Henry V*). My pleasure was indulged for barely a month before a frightening accident occurred. I had worked out an elaborate routine for the finishing of Mr Puff. Anxiously concerned that all was not going as it should up in the flies, waving messages upwards he stepped unwisely across a bar that carried two sizeable cut-out pieces at each end of it. Whereupon, up it came, and catching him in the crutch, took him up into the flies with it. Here I quickly changed over on to a swing-seat, which had a painted cloud on the front of it; down on this, supported by piano wires, at an easy pace sailed Mr Puff, but at a reasonable stepping off distance from the stage a huge explosion blew his cloud hastily up again into the flies. The company on the stage manfully supported these antics with actions of terrified anxiety: 'Where has he got to now?', gazing upwards following Puff's apparent cavortings in various directions at the same time. Meantime, my cloud was brailed off towards the stage right fly-rail, where I inched myself off from my swing-seat on to a rope, which I shinned down to dash downstage to climb a rope-ladder to seize hold of the right-hand half of the divided theatre curtain. In the meantime, my cloud came sailing down, to the general consternation of the company, minus any Mr Puff. The curtains descended finally towards each other with Mr Puff clutching on to the right festoon to be thrown in a somersault between it and the footlights. Needless to say, it was all great fun to do, for me that is; the rest of the company must have felt a bit stoogey.

Then came the occurrence which turned all the fun into terror. It wouldn't have done so for men of sterner stuff, but as must be clear by now, I am a moral and a physical coward. I had got through the routine up to being brailed off on my cloud towards the stage right fly-rail and, keeping my right hand around its piano wire, I inched off my cloud-seat, stretched out and grasped the rope to shin downwards and . . .! The rope moved downwards under the pull from my left hand and – Oh! my Christ! – the thing had not been fastened to the fly grid up top. I continued pulling and screamed at the fly-men to *do* something. The rope slipped through its last few feet and snaked down to the stage floor thirty feet below. I thought desperately of jumping for it, but immediately underneath me was a five-foot groundrow of battleships in full sail, cut out of 3-ply, and I didn't fancy trying that out as a saddle. The fly-boys, only six feet away from me, began to panic: 'It's all right, guvnor, we'll find it. Which line is he on, Bert, for Chrissake? No, surely he's on thirty-eight, in't he? Hang on, guvnor, hang on, we'll find it in a tick.'

I think hanging on with a wire through one's hand and wondering how long before one has to drop is a nightmare common to most of us. After an eternity of the boys arguing and trying one line after another: 'Okay, guvnor, we got you. For Chrissake hold on,' and in full view of the audience, to whom it must have looked to be a singularly ineffectual joke, I was slowly lowered to the stage. Until then the prompt corner had been much too gripped by the situation to think of lowering the curtain.

And that was how my very favourite invention became a living dread for the next six months. After three weeks of the New York season the fates showed me that they were not yet tired of this particular joke. One Saturday matinée I was climbing the rope ladder for the last throw pay-off when whatever it was fastening the top of the ladder to the

stage-side of the curtain broke loose and I was flung down
to the stage. Painfully humiliating, and vice versa.

This 1945–6 season was, I am sure, the one that made our
names and the one to which, years later, people still
referred. It finished in May and off we all went with it to
New York. Here again the reception was as happy as a
marriage-bell. The only consideration that marred it was
the difficulty for Ralph and me of making both ends meet.
We had taken a modest salary by the general standards of
leading players in New York, and the rest of the company,
with admirable restraint, accepted terms which almost
signified that they were willing to go for the trip. But costs
in New York turned out to be a great deal higher than we
had been led to expect. Our people were beginning to get
hungry.

Vivien sweetly came to keep me company and to take
advantage of the complete change of atmosphere and way
of life, and to see old friends for the first time since 1940;
she also used this shining hour to reassure them, as well as
other interested members of the public there, that she was
in fact a great deal stronger, livelier and bonnier than had
been supposed. It was natural for the two of us to stay at the
St Regis; it would have been misunderstood if we had
sought somewhere more economical. ('God, these English
have lost all their standards since the war.' David Selznick
did actually say those very words to us when he came to
Notley for a Sunday lunch a year or so later. *We* thought our
lunch was delicious; didn't remember his *cuisine* in Beverly
Hills being so much to boast about, anyway.)

Our New York season of eight weeks was heralded every
bit as enthusiastically as in London. Ralph was without
any question the most perfect Falstaff in both parts of
Shakespeare's *Henry IV* (each of them one full-length
performance) since these twins were written. I had always
dreamt of his Falstaff, and he succeeded in bettering my
wildest dreams. (With his perfectly sculpted leg-padding,
carefully proportioned enlargement over his front, shoulders and back, the poor love was to sweat clean through the

midsummer heat of New York.) The voice and above all the diction, like a great music-hall comedian, had every consonant hitting the back wall of the pit like a whip-lash; the richness and the detail of his characterisation, the presence, bearing, walk, voice, humanity, wicked love-ableness, the dictionary of the man's humours, the sharp salt of his wit and the sudden blinding sadness of 'Peace, good Doll . . . Do not bid me remember mine end' – it may be guessed that this mighty performance is strongest among my favourites.

I enjoyed a repertoire that must have been more enter-taining for me than for anyone who came to see it. I was Hotspur in *Part I*, not a long role though a stunning example of the line of roles we lump together under the description 'the Shakespeare man'. In *Part II* the small role of Justice Shallow fell to me and I was enchanted with it. Ralph and I found a relationship which I know we both enjoyed and obviously our audiences did too. Shallow only has four scenes, and they are all with Falstaff.

Then came my 'biggy'. The combination of Oedipus and Mr Puff was such a palpable *tour de force*, such a shrill claim on versatility, that I wonder whether Ty was not right – perhaps it was a bit vulgar. (Tony Guthrie had by now declared that he preferred the diminutive of Ty.) I see, it was vulgar, was it? All right then, in that case I'm sorry, very sorry. No – no, I'm not.

When our three launchings had been completed, we turned out attention to our financial problems. We had thought that we should resist all invitations to broadcast; circumstances, however, unhappily dictated otherwise. We recalled all those flattering offers, so loftily turned down, and plunged right in for three Sundays of broadcasting plays that did not belong to our rep at the Century Theatre: *Peer*, *Richard* and *Arms*. It took the load off everybody, except for me. I was still in trouble with my extra financial burden of Vivien and the St Regis.

There had been, naturally enough since *Henry V* opened, some friendly approaches from HMV to record some of it. So I went along to Victor Records, and in an attempt to mix pathos with importance I suggested they might like to arrange for me to make records of excerpts from *Henry V* with William Walton conducting the London Philharmonic in his music. They fell charmingly for the idea, and then waited for the catch in it; having pointed out that the film was to be released in New York very shortly, a detail that struck home nicely, I said that I would very much like to be paid for the job in New York, but, as I was a bit exhausted, do the stuff in London. To my amazement they agreed at once.

Henry V was to open at the City Center on the Monday following our closing Saturday; as well as this excitement I was to be given my very first honorary degree by Tufts College, Massachusetts. There was something delightfully special about being given such a thing by an American university – I remember how delighted Thornton Wilder was about it – and Vivien flew up to Boston with me. Tufts is a college of great charm with a beautiful campus; there is always, for the ones being honoured on these occasions, almost an over-abundance of charm. Articulate scholars talked as if they knew by heart every single job you ever undertook, and admired each as if it had been the work of a combined master of philosophy, art and engineering. A few years later, the classical genius who cited me at Oxford did so in Latin, though he had the thoughtfulness to slip a translation to me as a mememto.

What follows now should be called 'How I came to play King Lear'. Ralph, I must tell you, had a certain very cunning way with him. There were occasions when he wouldn't frankly suggest himself for a part, possibly because he didn't want to risk being talked out of it; in such rare instances he would say nothing, but out of the blue would appear a press announcement that he was going to do *Peer Gynt*, for instance, for the BBC. That was to be regarded as a general 'Hands Off' signal. It was more than natural, having won his listening audience, that he should progress to three-dimensional expression of the same role in some play-house. You may imagine the feelings of his partner, one of whose natural, long-lived ambitions had been to find an opportunity to present himself as Cyrano de Bergerac, upon reading that this golden casque was to be assumed by his friend and partner in service to the BBC.

Once upon a time in the 1920s when the conversation turned as it invariably would to Shakespeare, Ralph had said that if there was one part in the whole of the Shakespearian canon that he yearned for, it was Lear. This must have inhibited me from any thoughts of the part for myself, regarding it always as belonging to Ralph. Touching really, isn't it?

So, at the meeting, John Burrell began: 'Well, whose turn is it; Ralph's, isn't it?' Ralph, with the scrupulous politeness and careful choice of words reserved for meetings, delivered: 'With submission, I venture to suggest that I might be allowed to attempt the part of Cyrano.' 'Fine,' said John, and turned to me. 'What do you think, Larry?' 'Fine,' I said, 'fine.' 'How about you, then?' I managed a fairly well-measured 'I would like to play and produce *King Lear*.' A sidelong glance at Ralph rewarded me with a slight but perceptible start. 'Fine,' he said, 'fine.' 'Well, that's all nice and easily settled,' said John, and we went on to discuss the Priestley play.

Meeting over, Ralph and I walked down as always to the Garrick pub, opposite the Garrick Theatre with the Irving statue standing in between, and ordered the customary half-pints; after the first swallow I turned to Ralph.

'Well,' I said.

'Yes, old fellow?'

'Well, so you want to swap?'

'What, old fellow?'

'You know. Swap . . . *parts*,' I nearly screamed.

'Oh no, no.'

It was quite definite. And that is how it was that I came to play King Lear.

Critical opinion seemed more generally in favour of my performance as actor than as director. This is not strange considering that half the visual effect of the two main interior settings of my *Lear* had to be scrubbed at the dress rehearsal for technical reasons. The costumes however came off successfully as they always did with Roger. He and I worked exclusively together for the next twenty years. Then, when the National started up, it seemed a natural moment for a parting of the ways. The Boys – my associates John Dexter and William Gaskill – were obviously both a little nervous that Roger and I, having been together for so long, would not be adventurous enough, and they naturally wanted to bring in the more modern influences that belonged to their generation. I recognised that it was the proper way to be thinking, but I dreaded telling him. I needn't have worried; Roger had already made his own plans to sell up his little house in Cheyne Row and take his wife to live on a Greek island.

For a little while now, I had been feeling I should be planning another film to companion *Henry V*, and amazingly enough *Hamlet* occurred to me. Ralph was very happy to carry on for the rest of that season by himself, with John Burrell, of course.

In 1947, then, I made a film of *Hamlet*. It could well be left at that, but there are credits; others contributed vitally to it. It was designed entirely by Furse. I chose black-and-white for it rather than colour, to achieve through depth of focus a more majestic, more poetic image, in keeping with the stature of the verse. In one shot Ophelia, in close foreground, sees Hamlet down a long corridor through a mirror, seated 120 feet away; her every hair is in focus and so are his features.

Walton naturally wrote the *Hamlet* music, and Desmond Dickinson photographed it. The cast was remarkable: Basil Sydney as the King, Felix Aylmer as Polonius, Norman Woolland as Horatio, Terence Morgan as Laertes, Peter Cushing as Osric. That beautiful actress Eileen Herlie played the Queen, and a ravishing sixteen-year-old, Jean Simmons, was Ophelia.

It was ancient custom for the most ancient actor-managers to play Hamlet; I am sure Irving was in his sixties before finishing with the part. I was on the cusp of forty. As one of my predecessors is reputed to have said in reply to the earnest question 'Did Hamlet sleep with Ophelia?', 'In my company, always.' His mother Gertrude was probably the elderly character actress in his company – likely enough, his wife. My own arrangements were as different as could be. In 1947 Eileen Herlie, playing my mum, was thirteen years younger than I; it must be a record. I worried not at all whether I would get away with such a major imprudence. 'For goodness sake,' I said, 'it's *Hamlet*.'

It is not always by any means easy to find a way to make something look dangerous without it actually being so. The final dramatic gesture in a film of *Hamlet* seems to require an action spectacular enough to involve such a risk.

The dangers involved in what I had conceived for this moment presented themselves to me in the light of the following five possibilities: I could kill myself; I could damage myself for life; I could hurt myself badly enough to make recovery a lengthy business; I could hurt myself only slightly; or I could get away with it without harm. The odds seemed to me to be quite evenly disposed among these five alternatives.

Bearing in mind that there could be no rehearsal, this reckoning urged upon me sense enough at least to make it the last scene to be shot in the film. I realised that this condition was not going to make things any easier for me, but then nothing was going to be easy in this film anyway – and I had best face up to any growing dreads and keep dismissing them with the likelihood that it might well turn out to be quite easy when the moment came.

That the moment did come is indusputable in the face of cinematic record.

I felt so strongly then that this film was by far the most important work of my life that I regarded the first of the five possibilities with an unworried steadiness that gave me a mild feeling of surprise; but I've always known when to take advantage of something.

The moment arrived and I asked the two acrobats I had engaged for the purpose to show me what they could make of the problem which I had described to them. Somewhat to my disappointment the King stood only two feet out from

Hamlet's taking-off point some fourteen feet above him. I thought 'well, they're showing me various distances'. Hamlet curled slowly over, his hands outstretched straight downwards. His feet finally leaving the platform, his hands landed one on each of the King's shoulders and his feet followed to the floor immediately in front of the King, and there they stood very calmly, and quite still, closely face to face.

'Thanks,' I said. 'Can I see some variations?'

They looked at me as at a really stupid man who could not appreciate what he was asking. I sighed and requested my 'bottom-of-a-strong-man-act' King to stand in his position for me. Not without a tinge of despair, I mounted the platform, from the edge of which I asked my King to move backwards away from me, further, further still. When he was at a distance I thought I could just cover in an outward dive including the decreasing downward journey outwards, I said: 'I am going to say "The point envenomed too! – Then, venom, to thy work," and then I'll jump down on to him there. Okay, roll them. Your lights okay, Desmond? Both cameras rolling?'

The spirit of Jacques Copeau was upon me. I quickly sized up the journey appreciating the two initial obvious dangers. My sword must pass over his left shoulder avoiding his left eye, and I must avoid the right side of his encrusted crown with my right eye. Doesn't matter what happens after that. This shot was entirely for my passage through the air, from my take-off to being about to land on him.

Every conceivable variation of what might lead up to and what might happen on and after the landing I had already shot, had been processed and passed.

'Right, then. "The point envenomed too! – Then, venom, to thy *work*".' Upon that word I was already in the air. In the following second and a half everything worked like a dream – in fact, like the dream I had so often rehearsed to myself. The landing was just right, my King fell back quite beautifully; unbelievingly I scrambled up off his body and was then frightened by his groaning. My weight hitting him under the chin had knocked him out. The one brave moment of my life was over. I looked about for my friends, Tony Bushell and Roger Furse, who slunk out from behind a black velvet hanging – they'd not been able to watch. Editor Reggie Beck had felt bound to see it through. After a few seconds there was a little stunned clapping. I told them all we'd meet for a drink when I'd cleaned off for the last time. As I passed through them, one of the lads muttered to another beside him, 'Good old Larry, he gets on with it.'

Good old Jacques Copeau, say I.

A few months before, during the second season, Ralph, Guthrie and I had been invited to an important meeting by the National Theatre people to discuss some kind of combination of our interests. Ty had prepared us for the meeting, saying that many people considered that there should be a marriage between the two organisations, and perhaps we ought to give it some serious thought. Well, we did. This might be the answer to the questions that we were beginning to ask of ourselves and of each other: what's going to happen to us, and how could we secure the existence of the Old Vic Theatre Company with no theatre of its own? The old theatre roof had been caved in by a bomb. It was no use us pulling the famous company out of the slough of despond for a few years and then letting it plop back again.

About now, Ty, never at the worst of times lacking in sensitivity, began to sense an independent itch in us two boys. One day, at a management meeting between Ty, us two and George Chamberlain, for years the general manager of the Old Vic, somehow the subject surfaced and George said, 'Would you be happier managing the whole thing by yourselves?' We said, 'Yes,' Ty and George together said, 'Right,' and that they would continue to be on hand in case advice was needed at any time. In the meantime Ty was very much a part of the National Theatre approaches.

The chairman of the National Theatre was the Rt Hon.

Oliver Lyttelton, a member of the Churchill shadow cabinet. Also much in evidence was his mother, the Hon. Mrs Lyttelton (one of the prime instigators of the movement, maintaining her interest and proselytising for it over forty to fifty years), Lord Esher, Harley Granville Barker, Dame Sybil, Lewis Casson, Bronson Albery, Lord Lytton, Sir Reginald Row, Ty and we three. Oliver remained the chairman of the NT for the next thirty years. This meeting had been convened for the purpose of solemnising a marriage between the NT and the Old Vic. I suppose they were the groom and we the bride, but I don't think we blushed at all.

On the walk home, Ralph gave me a dazzling example of his gift of prescience. We were just saying how pleased we felt Lilian Baylis would have been by what had been accomplished, when Ralph quite suddenly said, 'Of course, you know, don't you, that all very splendid as it is, it'll be the end of us. You do realise that?' I couldn't believe it. Why? 'Well, I mean it won't be our dear, friendly, semi-amateurish Old Vic any more, it'll be of government interest now with some appointed intendant swell at the top, not our sweet old friendly governors eating out of our hands and doing what we tell them. They're not going to stand for a couple of actors bossing the place around any more. We shall be out, old cockie. But I still think we may have done the right thing.'

Aware of Ralph's insight as I had been for all these years, this floored me. Of course, he must be right. Still, there'd be a few years yet, plenty of time to start up something else. I would do *Hamlet* next year. Ralph and I had come to a good arrangement that out of the next twelve years each of us would give six, either separately or together, to the Vic. We realised that for the most part we would be wise to reckon on operating separately. This tradition of both of us being in everything and going everywhere together was bringing us to a state of exhaustion; and the supporting element in the company was idle half of the time as we had to be in the small-cast plays as well as the large casts, the main body of the company only appearing in the latter.

I had been asked by the British Council to think about a

tour of Australia with Vivien, where we were assured of a tumultuous welcome and an acceptable little package of dough. Two birds could be nicely killed with one stone. I could create a new company for the Vic, using the Australian tour to train it into an acceptably skilled ensemble. I make no apologies for frankly using a great Dominion for this purpose, since there is no way of creating a first-class ensemble except by determinedly playing it in varied rep in all kinds of different conditions.

Perth, where we opened, had not had a visit from a professional theatre company for twelve years; Adelaide, though I fancy better served than this, was paid only the most sporadic and infrequent visits; Hobart, Tasmania – a lovely place with its adorable little theatre, 110 years old in 1948 – was almost always left out by any foreign tour. In these three first places that we visited the audiences were warm and wonderful and the ovations at the end were staggering, even by Old Vic standards; and after the show the public would gather in crowds outside the hotel and applaud and cheer until we had made three or four appearances on the balcony – we began cheekily to call it 'Buck House time' – after which we were allowed to get some supper. (Australian oysters, by the way, are most remarkable.)

As we reached the more sophisticated cities, they seemed to become progressively less enthusiastic, seemingly inclined to sit back as if saying, 'All right, then, show us.' Melbourne gave us our first cool reception, one newspaper saying, 'We have better Richard III's here in Melbourne.' One of my prime duties was to talent-scout, and so I thought, 'That's very promising,' and set out to make enquiries. There turned out to be, after the most diligent enquiries, no professional actors working in Melbourne, and it was hard to believe that amateur groups would have the money required for such ambitious productions.

Sydney not only claimed to be as sophisticated a city as could be found in the civilised world, but wished one to be aware that if it was influenced by anyone it was by America rather than Britain, and so indeed it seemed. Socially, the people of this still new country are quite extraordinary in the generosity of their hospitality. Shortly before leaving home for the Antipodes, we had been to see Danny Kaye in his fabulous one-man show at the Palladium. He asked if we were looking forward to our Australian visit and we admitted to be rather in dread of the ambassadorial aspect of the job. He made me promise that I would not attempt to prepare one speech and that I was to make every public utterance straight off the cuff. 'If you start preparing and learning', he warned, 'you'll have a nervous breakdown in a week.' It was good advice; for grand balls and any big occasion a speech was always expected, but even at small gatherings someone would toast the King in a cup of tea and one was on, replying to the toast apparently on behalf of the King. It was a situation that was apt to get a bit heady at times.

The 1940s were not a tranquil decade for this British subject. Occasionally they danced in nightmare fashion to their own brash Symphonie Fantastique. If the decade's roaring started with bombardment, it continued with the smug victory boasted by the MGM lion; before the end it took on a sneer that at times changed to a whimpering groan.

We were overtired before the Antipodean tour was halfway through. The rep was *The School for Scandal*, *The Skin of our Teeth* and *Richard III*. I soon began to dread *Richard*, particularly the double dose on matinée days. One day my friend Eugene Goossens saw that I was feeling the strain and said, 'How would you like to hear some music – might do you a bit of good. Come to the rehearsal tomorrow, I've got a wonderful artist playing.'

Ginette Neveu must have been one of the most astonishing violinists in the history of instrumentalists. Eugene was conducting his Sydney Symphony Orchestra and Ginette was playing Sibelius Op. 47. I was lifted from my wretched state as if by an archangel. As I sat putting on my make-up for the matinée that afternoon, I felt inspired and blessed. We met her again in Brisbane, where we indulged in those professional sympathies so common between our *métiers*. Ginette, incredibly enough, was playing to a half-empty house and we were seeing gaps in our houses for the first time on the tour.

Only a few months later she was flying to some date in Europe and the aircraft came down in flames. They found her body: she was clutching her violin in her hand.

On a day when I had two shows of *Richard*, a letter arrived from Lord Esher as chairman of the Old Vic Theatre Company, telling me in the brightest, jolliest terms that the Board of Governors, in view of the fact that it was now five years since we had resurrected the Old Vic, had decided that Burrell, Richardson and I must be fired from our jobs as from now. It was so ironical that I was hysterical with laughter. For heaven's sake! Here was I, fourteen thousand miles away from home, right in the middle of building up a splendid new company for the Old Vic. It was so incredible a surprise that, as in a farce, laughter was a reflex action. At this precise time I tore a cartilage in my right knee; my limp in *Richard*, in constantly fatigued conditions, had set up a weakness in the 'straight' leg, and one evening in the dance at the end of *School* it just went. Why is it that in troubled times one's body feels called upon to jump on the bandwagon? But there was something else.

Somehow, somewhere on this tour I knew that Vivien was lost to me. I, half-joking, would say at odd moments after we had got back home, 'I *lorst* you in Australia.'

I suppose I had encouraged it, oh, quite innocently at first. In the normal process of talent-scouting we had heard high praise of this young man's work. He came to see us after a show in Melbourne with his wife. We found them charming and highly intelligent. He invited us to see a production of *Tartuffe* which he was playing and had put on himself. He had developed a way of boiling down the classics to one hour in order to give them to factory-workers during their lunch-breaks. To one such performance we went, and did not notice the hardness of the wooden planks on which we sat. We were watching as brilliant a performance of Tartuffe in as expert a production as could be imagined. We suspected that that clever ballet-dancing wife of his had had something to do with it. I got on to Cecil Tennant, my manager at home, and the managing director of our hundred pound limited liability company, which gloried under the name of L. O. Prods Ltd, to say that we must put this young man, Peter Finch, under contract. (At one time I had three actors under personal contract, as well as Roger Furse. I must have begun to mistake myself for MGM.

We found ourselves flying from Brisbane to New Zealand to play Auckland, Christchurch, Dunedin and Wellington. It was 15 September; we had been in Australia exactly six months. Before leaving New Zealand there had been growing in me a nasty-tasting anticipation of troubled times ahead with the Old Vic governors. I knew that I should have to exert every ounce of my energies to being as helpful as possible in the sorting out of murders most foul, or, at least, problems most fraught. I also knew I should get my knee operated on, and I resolved to save time by having it done before getting on to the boat. It had been increasingly painful and difficult to manage over the last three months and I was beginning to get worried that some permanent damage might set in.

The expert New Zealand surgeon who undertook the job did so only on condition that I woudn't attempt to move without being carried for the first two weeks of the voyage. Four days after the operation he strapped the whole leg in plaster; I was put on to a stretcher, taken to the dockside in an ambulance, and there something happened to me that one literally dreams about. I was placed on a cradle which was hooked on to a cable hawser; and the very same crane that hoisted the heaviest articles on board and lowered them into the hold – Rolls Royces, steam-engines, you name it – now proceeded to pay all its attention to me; up, up and up I soared into the sky, smoothly floating over the side of the ship and gently down, as delicately as if upon an angel's wing; I landed sweetly upon the topmost deck.

Needless to say it was not long before I betrayed my surgeon's commands and took a liberty with the leg, which felt like solid stone; I got out of bed. When I got back in again, I thought, 'I do believe I got away with it', and settled myself comfortably to sleep. Before the god Morpheus had applied his gentle pressure to my 'dormic' nerve, however, something made itself felt just above and on the inside of my patella, and tweekled downwards on its journey of two or so inches and . . . Pain . . . Pain. It was the pain of blood in full flood trying to get out of my knee and through the plaster: I had given myself an absolutely crack-up, first-class contusion. When, after ten days, the ship's doctor sliced down each side of the plaster and lifted off the top half he revealed a remarkable sculpture, its shape determined by the fiercely struggling contusion seeking for *lebensraum*.

It must be seen that such life as I could offer to Vivien at this time was dull in the extreme: there came a moment when I felt driven to have a serious talk with her. I pleaded with her not, please, to make her flirtation with one young man in the company so obvious to the rest of them; I really couldn't see that it was justified that I should be so humiliated. To my great surprise, she took it all very calmly and sweetly; she saw that she had been thoughtless and assured me that I wouldn't have cause for embarrassment any more. That was lovely so far as it went; how far was that, I wondered, though my confidence in the everlasting certainty of our passion was not for shaking yet.

We rehearsed in the ship's dance-room for the rest of the voyage, just as we had the whole of the voyage out. I had worried increasingly that *Skin of our Teeth* might not support a third London season, and had had in the back of my mind a double bill of *Antigone* by Jean Anouilh (this would be the first Anouilh in London), preceded by Chekhov's *The Bear* as a curtain-raiser. So we got some good ground-work done on those two new ones, before facing the two-fold horror lying in wait for us in London: presenting a new six-month season, which was in fact to mark our dismissal from the management of the Old Vic.

On the first morning home, the first obligation was the inevitable press conference. I managed to play any awkward questions fairly safely to leg without getting into too much trouble. Immediately, I plunged in with Ralph and John Burrell. There was only one conclusion that was possible for us to come to, and that was to accept the situation with what dignity we could muster. If they didn't love us, they didn't love us, and they were perfectly within their rights to get rid of us; we none of us lacked for offers and we wouldn't starve like poor Nelly. The idea of a change was not, I think, unwelcome to any of us after five years of such very close partnership that we had felt at times like three horses sharing the same nosebag.

It was a full week before that nitty-gritty meeting with Lord Esher took place. As soon as we sat down I had my ears so effectively pinned back that my head was set reeling. The idea, he explained, was that the three of us having retired gracefully, I should thereupon take over the whole job. My breath recovered, I explained patiently that in my book partners as close as we had been just didn't do things like that to each other, and bowed myself out, only just avoiding falling over backwards down his elegant front steps. Next thing I knew, I was summoned to lunch by a very highly regarded member of the Board, a famous lady economist, Miss Barbara Ward. I explained once more with even greater patience, since I was getting a handsome lunch out of this interview, just what my feelings were.

It was now that Peter Finch arrived from Australia to take up his contract with L. O. Prods. I had his first part all lined up for him. I had secured the treasured services of Dame Edith Evans for the new James Bridie, *Daphne Laureola*, for which I had already taken Wyndham's Theatre. This was very convenient for my purposes with its stage door opposite the back of the New, so close contact was easy, especially during *Antigone* with my helpfully widely-spaced Chorus part. I dare say Sir Charles Wyndham had thought of this when he built them; he already owned the Criterion – quite a tidy little empire for an actor-manager. I was agreeably commended by James Agate for being the first actor-manager to put on plays not merely for his own exploitation but for others, in a private capacity, that is.

So Peter's first appearance in London was in the showy part of the Viennese Lover; Edith was crazy about him, so that was all right. Flushed with beginner's managerial luck and tickled with envy of the Alberys' tidy little empire, before the end of the year I had taken a lease on the St James's; everything seemed to be coming up roses.

But – and please God let that be the most appallingly biggest 'but' in this little lifetime – one day early in spring 'I heard a maid complaining'. I think we must have just finished lunch; I know we were sitting at the table in the small winter-garden of a porch at Durham Cottage and that it was daylight. It came like a small bolt from the blue, like a drop of water, I almost thought my ears had deceived me: 'I don't love you any more.'

I must have looked as stricken as I felt, for she went on, 'There's no one else or anything like that, I mean I still love you but in a different way, sort of, well, like a brother'; she actually used those words. I felt as if I had been told that I had been condemned to death. The central force of my life, my heart in fact, as if by the world's most skilful surgeon, had been removed. It left me agasp but not gasping; it was as if I had been rendered forever still inside, like a fish in a refrigerator. It had always been inconceivable that this great, this glorious passion could ever not exist, like a crowned head after the execution. Some while later a close friend said to me that I should have kicked her out, or upped and outed myself; that I should never have endured in silence such humiliation apparently for the sake of appearances.

The fact was I couldn't move; it would be some time before I could entirely take it in, grasp it, or wholly believe it. My recent knighthood, bestowed just before I set out for Australia, was sacred to me too; I just could not bring myself to offer people such crude disillusionment. I could only keep it bottled up in myself and, as Vivien had suggested, carry on as if nothing had changed. Brother and sister; ho, hum.

Somewhat to my surprise, occasional acts of incest were not discouraged. I supposed I would learn to endure this coldly strange life, so long as I never looked to be happy again. A degree of cynicism did not come amiss. There would still be the lantern of my work, though its flame seemed all but burned out; I would have to find other means of inspiration, this one's throne was empty.

We had opened our rehashed Australian tour at the New Theatre on 20 January 1949 with *School*, the following week *Richard*, and two weeks after that *Antigone* and *The Bear*. The whole thing was blissfully successful and the advance booking soon had us booked out for the next five months – and so to the end of all of us at the New Theatre.

The rest of the year was seized upon by both Vivien and myself to refloat ourselves upon the London tide, almost violently embracing every kind of activity that profession or society could offer. Hard upon our own openings, preparations immediately started for *Daphne*, which opened on 23 March. Australians seemed to be pouring over to the Old Country this year and so we had plenty of return hospitality to give to swell the tide, already high; among my gleanings from down under was a young Englishman who had been working there for the British Council and he, too, arrived now to take up his position with us as permanent secretary to L.O. Prods; his name was Peter Hiley. He soon became familiar with all the business side of our lives.

In much the same single-minded way that Vivien had followed up her impossible ambition to be Scarlett O'Hara, she had now fastened her hopes on the entirely possible Blanche Dubois in *A Streetcar Named Desire*. I was hesitant about this work, owing to my not-quite-dead preoccupation with respectability. Always fortunate in my friendships, I was particularly happy in two of them, with George Devine and Michel St Denis. They scoffed when I brought them my problem, telling me that for an artist my judgements were dangerously warped; that this play contained all the elements most proper to a true tragedy, among them the deadly delivery of a brutal kick in the stomach for the audience. All right, so it was sensational, but what was *King Lear*? Or *Oedipus*? I took this lesson to heart, where it has been ever since. When I took the idea to Binkie Beaumont, suggesting a managerial partnership, I found him extraordinarily amenable. Of course; a Tennessee Williams in London (the fact of a raging New York success does sometimes float across the Atlantic and penetrate our consciousness); Vivien at her height, and the partnership of herself starring with myself directing had already proved to be popular; it did not seem possible for Binkie to lose. He didn't.

When we had finished for the Old Vic, we thought we might have a holiday together before *Streetcar*. Though it would be no honeymoon, we still shared much the same tastes, especially in French *cuisine*, not to mention *le vin*. So we prescribed for ourselves a painting holiday, and took a house in Opio for three weeks or so. We had both read Churchill's book on painting and this had inspired us. He shrewdly explains that anybody can paint, and that the exercise is of exceptional benefit to those whose minds are filled with their work and the worries attendant upon it. When such people decide that they need a holiday, they should take with them some means of charging their minds with something that will push out whatever is obstinately there. The mind needs to be absorbed by something as different as possible from what it is used to being absorbed by. Painting is ideal for this.

It is interesting how seldom life bestows equality of fortune in a man's public and his private life: Ralph has remarked to me once or twice that he never had known a fellow with such extremes of good and bad luck. From 1943 my fortunes seemed to me to be quite wondrous in their goodness, their completeness, their two-fold richness. I would boast to my close friends about this unblushingly and possibly with embarrassing frankness; it seemed ungrateful not to. In 1947 my contentment seemed full to over-brimming; I have everything, I would boast, so much more than anybody could deserve: the love of my life, more perfect than anyone could dream of; my career, after such laborious digging-in, yielding this fantastic harvest; a glorious house in the country; and two things I never asked for, a Rolls-Royce and a knighthood.

The last is not strictly true; you should have heard the screams of fury when Ralph had got his knighthood on the first of the year, before I had. I was not alone in my sense of grievance; my friends, Sibyl Colefax among them, a hostess who was not without influence, flew at Sir Stafford Cripps, who said, 'But, my dear, unfortunately the chap has only been divorced three years and you know the thinking in that regard.' 'It is *not* three years,' she screamed, 'it is seven years at least'; Stafford undertook to do something at once. Arthur Rank, for whom I exclusively produced my films, also rolled up his sleeves and waded into the fray. Deeply fond as I was of Ralph, I was unable to stop the cracked record from grinding round in my head: I've done every bit as much as he has, look how I've carried the flag abroad, New York, the American road, Hollywood pictures and an even fuller record in the classics; *and* there was a little film called *Henry V*. If only we could have been done together, that would have been fine. Fine.

It seemed no time at all before I, too, got that letter. Vivien, who had taken seriously my disapproval of Ralph's fortune, expressed as a matter of principle – 'Artists shouldn't . . .' etc. – said when I showed her the letter, 'Of course you won't take it?' I hedged a bit. So she knew. I very scrupulously told Ralph, of course, and two or three other intimates.

I found myself quite unable to accept my knighthood without writing to Noël Coward, almost as if asking his permission. It was painfully apparent to all his friends that this honour had been withheld from him for years for what we found to be entirely the wrong reasons; but, I asked him, though I knew that it was wrong for any theatre person to accept it before he had, would he, I wondered, be hurt with me beyond repair if I just had not got what it took to turn it down? This provoked from Noëlie the most enchantingly generous letter. Honours tend to beget honours, as any observer kind enough to take note of my recent fortunes would have to admit. I began to report to Noël any likelihood of such turn-ups, which naturally became a joke almost at once; on the spur of one such moment, I put on the usual anguish about how that silly old Auntie Oxford University just would insist on making me a Doctor of Letters – without a hairsbreadth of a pause Noël said, 'Doctor of four letters, I presume.'

On the day that my knighthood was announced, I stalked about Denham Studio, got up in Hamlet's glad rags for the play scene festooned with the blue baldric of the Order of the Elephant, only to·be distinguished from the Garter by hanging across from the right shoulder. People weren't quite sure if I was in costume or if I was always going to be dressed like that from now on.

I started to rehearse *Streetcar* on 29 August 1949, to open on 11 October. I think I can say that I was helpful to Vivien's performance of Blanche; I hit on the practical notion that, as by changing one feature one can create a whole new face, so by the alteration of one major characteristic, not hitherto associated with you, you can become another person with a different personality. I noticed at the first rehearsals, by the reactions among the company, that the unexpected, much deeper, much rougher voice from Vivien had impressed them. I watched, fascinated, the strange new person that grew from this one dominant change of key. I thought, if her critics have one grain of fairness, they will give her credit now for being an actress and not go on forever letting their judgements be distorted by her great beauty and her Hollywood stardom. As it turned out they were not so bad as usual, but clearly reluctant in their approval. Her colleagues and the public were unanimously eulogistic in their praises.

That August, L.O. Prods had opened and closed *Fading Mansion*, a play by Jean Anouilh which I had seen in Paris, where it was called *Roméo et Jeannette*. French into English has always been a problem. In Paris, the audience had been entranced by the young character juvenile who kept repeating, '*Je suis cocu*'; but it's not the biggest joke in English for someone to keep on saying, 'I'm a cuckold,' which is in itself an unfamiliar enough word; and if it be helped out with a more explanatory 'I'm a betrayed husband' it frankly casts a gloom. I had long been convinced that straight French into English, unless freely adapted, will not work. What can be done to imbue the piece with French atmosphere, to make both the people and their milieu seem French and not a funny sort of English? Have everyone talking like zis and like zat?

I came to the conclusion, largely influenced by Emlyn Williams's brilliantly successful translation of *The Late Christopher Bean* to Wales, that some form of Celtic was the answer. Donagh Mcdonagh's transcription of our play into Irish was as perfect as could be. It was the choice of the play that was at fault; the play did not work one hundred per cent in itself.

Through November I was casting Christopher Fry's *Venus Observed* and had a first reading on 7 December. On the eighth (wasn't I the lively little spark, though?) I flew to Philadelphia to see Garson Kanin's try-out of *The Rat Race* (I had put on his first play, *Born Yesterday*, very successfully in London). I found this latest one of Garson's excellent and thought it was bound to be a great hit in New York (wrong this time). Straight back to New York for my real mission, which was to read at the Carnegie Hall the preamble to the United Nations' celebration of its first anniversary. When I told Alfred Lunt how proud I felt that an English actor should have been asked to do such a thing, he saw right through me at once and said, 'And not too bad for Laurence Olivier, eh?' (The preamble, however, was awkward, stiff and porky.)

I got a lucky seat for *South Pacific*, had supper with Thornton Wilder, and got back to Notley on the Monday morning to find Vivien not yet up. This was the twelfth, and I started to rehearse *Venus* on the fifteenth, my first offering at the St James's.

So Vivien and I both saw in the 1950s much loaded down with work. I was determined in this decade to plunge more and more deeply into management, no matter how often I lost my shirt. I had not the faintest inkling of how life would have taken me and shaken me like a rat before the decade closed.

CHAPTER EIGHT

The Feverish Fifties Begin

Venus Observed opened with respectable success on 18 January, and the following month I was rehearsing *The Damascus Blade*, a very promising piece by a new author, Bridget Boland. I put it on as an excellent vehicle for both Johnnie Mills and Peter Finch and sent them to Brighton, Bristol, Glasgow and Edinburgh to try it out. The two boys got cold feet about the play, saying that audiences obviously hated it, and begged me not to bring them into town in it. I didn't like treating the author like that one bit, but I valued Johnnie's friendship too much to refuse.

There was an excellent part for Peter Finch in *Captain Carvallo* by Denis Cannan and, as I was also able to engage the much-coveted interest of Diana Wynyard for this project, I swung into production with it, trying it out in Edinburgh, Bournemouth, Manchester and Oxford (no cold feet this time). Vivien, exhausted from *Streetcar*, went away for two weeks with Alex Korda on his yacht *Elsewhere*.

We realised now that each of us must take rests and short spells away when we could, and that the old good chunky breaks at the same time were going to be difficult unless we worked together. We agreed only to put all our eggs into one basket on rare occasions; one of these would surely be for the Festival of Britain the following year, 1951.

In response to an approach from William Wyler, the great director of *Wuthering Heights*, asking me to consider *Sister Carrie* by Theodore Dreiser as a film with Jennifer Jones and me, I got dug into that wonderful book. On 5 August I closed *Venus* at the St James's and opened

Captain Carvallo there on the ninth; Vivien had already left to film *Streetcar* at Warner's, and now I got on to a plane for New York; on the twelfth I saw *The Consul* and made a deal for it; next day I flew to Los Angeles for *Carrie* at Paramount. In the beginning of September Charley Feldman, a handsome and brilliant agent-producer who should have been a movie star, generously insisted that we take his house in Coldwater Canyon. What should it turn out to be but the lovely one with the egg-shaped pool where we had stayed while we made *Lady Hamilton* in 1941? In a way those were better days. Our love, which amounted to our religion, was still triumphant then, and confident in an eternal future.

We came the long way round home, two of five passengers in a delightful small French freighter, and I am sad to say the voyage was a dismal failure. We were both let down by the extreme boredom of it. As I have already said, we were not exactly a honeymoon couple, and though we needed the rest, the stark reality of our own company plunged us both into deep depression. For the first time, the idea of suicide had its attractions and I found myself more and more drawn to the ship's rail and the fascination of the foam sweeping by. We had never before been made to face the extent to which our lives together had been supported and bolstered up by the companionship of our friends and the glitter of our position.

Arriving at Tilbury on the eighteenth, we stopped at Durham Cottage to pay a courtesy visit to *Top of the Ladder*, which had come on at the St James's in our absence but would be finishing within two weeks. I felt that it had merited an infinitely better reception that it had been given; I still found the play to be an interesting and lovely piece of work; Ty's production of his own work was masterly and Johnnie Mills quite superb. I went next morning to the office to examine the books and form an appreciation of the state of the union. It took very little time to assess that all the dough that I was to have brought home in triumph was already spent. So – we had better start thinking again.

We close partners – Cecil Tennant, my manager until his

death in 1967, Roger Furse, our close friend Tony Bushell, their ladies and the two of us – used whenever possible to take little breaks of a few days all together in Paris, almost always staying at the charmingly atmospheric Hôtel France et Choiseul in the Faubourg St Honoré. This was a perfect way of mixing relaxation with essential business, uninterrupted by social obligations. By this time I had become very friendly with our French colleagues, Madeleine Renaud and her brilliant *homme de théâtre*, Jean-Louis Barrault, whom I first met during our Old Vic visit to Paris in 1945. I now negotiated with him for a visit of his Compagnie Renaud Barrault to the St James's in the autumn of 1951.

Our company was also expanding in other directions; Gian Carlo Menotti brought over his production of his beautiful modern opera, *The Consul*, for which I had taken the Cambridge Theatre. Patricia Neway was a thrilling leading lady, but eight performances a week was too much to ask of any singer and her understudy had to take over one matinée a week. Excellent as she was, the public stayed away unless Pat Neway was singing; again, with too close a budget, one poor house a week sunk me, and we could not afford to struggle on for more than six weeks. But I have always felt proud of it; it was an honourable failure.

As on many a visit to Paris, I fell too hard for the temptations of its *cuisine*, which brought me to my bed for a day or two; but nothing on earth would ever stop me from talking, so no time was wasted. Our five great minds were all pinned fast upon the question of our choice of contribution to the 1951 Festival. We knew we should offer more than a single work or we would look unadventurous. *Caesar and Cleopatra* was an obvious choice; it hadn't been done for years, was a formidable-sized production, and would obviously suit both Vivien and me down to the ground; what to go with it that would be as spectacular a contrast as possible? Roger said, 'You want something that clicks. I'm awfully sorry but there's one thing I can't get out of my mind . . . *Caesar and Cleopatra* and *Antony and Cleopatra*.' I looked quickly at Vivien and saw her looking quite scared, and I must admit that my own immediate reaction was much the same. But it did click. Certainly, it clicked.

Talking quietly to Vivien, having, like her, been through in my mind everything that those bastards might say about her daring the most sacred and exacting of all Shakespeare's female roles, I reminded her of the complete personality change and the formidable technical adjustment that she had made for Blanche Dubois. She must work on some similar technical change; one had to take risks in this job and, after all, the verse was so ravishing that anyone with half an ear would catch it, and the same with the emotional content. And it *would* click. I felt, with Vivien's nervous agreement, that there was absolutely no other choice. The announcement went out and caused the predictable and desired sensation.

The reception given to *Caesar* was fabulous; and since the crowd out front was the same, to a man, on the second night, it was like playing to a house filled with enraptured friends. The feeling was so infectious that even the critics were caught by it. Ivor Brown's headline that Sunday in the *Observer* was:'A Lass Unparalleled'. So, we were home and dry.

Cecil Tennant hadn't waited for this; coming in to see me in my dressing-room on the second night, he suggested that we should run it for six months to put the old theatre back into good fettle, and then take it to New York after a short holiday, as no doubt Vivien would be pretty tired. So our fates were set, signed and sealed for the next twelve months. Living from hand to mouth was, perhaps, more enlivening, but this stable situation was a very welcome change. Our finances demanded some stabilising; they depended on our separate command of high film salaries, which in turn depended on our box-office values, and these were checkable by producers. But together we could think of ourselves as pretty unassailable.

Sizeable as the risk had been in artistic terms, financially it was so giddy a one that it was better not to think about it. The facts were these: our gross capacity at the St James's was £2,600 weekly – grotesquely low as the figure seems in the early 1980s, in 1951 it was very respectable. This was only achieved by my raising the top price of the stalls from 12s.6d., the price for a West End playhouse ever since 1914, to 13s. when I took over the place. The 'Cleopatras' company was large, and though they were not offered Old Vic salaries they accepted some reduction in appreciation of the size of the venture. The production costs were naturally weighty, with two different kinds of sets on the revolve, one basically Egyptian, one Roman, two complete sets of costumes, and the constant change-over costs. Playing every performance to capacity, our weekly profit was a mere £40, at which rate it would have taken us a run of about fifteen years to get back the capital outlay.

How right Cecil was in pressing us to go to New York. At the Ziegfeld we played to more than eight times that figure with a weekly gross of $58,000 for eighteen weeks. All was as well as could be and so much better than we could have dared to hope for – professionally, that is.

A month or so before we had departed, with Cecil, Irina and their four-year-old Victoria on the *Mauretania*, Vivien had, almost imperceptibly at first, begun to develop a kind of behaviour which I had never noticed in her before. She started to be like a slightly frightened daughter; she was inclined to lean close to me and want me to put my arms round her. This gave me a new kind of happiness; it had very little, if anything at all, to do with passion; it seemed a funny little, child-like, clinging need for protection. For the first time in three years she was giving me some sort of happiness by making me feel strong, fatherly; I had become a reliable, comforting teddy bear. Though a little mystifying, it was pleasant. It made me feel good in a way that was entirely new to both of us. I asked her if perhaps she was feeling a wee bit nervous about New York? She only ever gave vaguely troubled, non-committal replies.

We opened at the Ziegfeld on 20 December. The theatre in the festive season in New York is regarded a deal more practically than at home; so far from there being no shows on Christmas Day, there are two. The season carries enough glamour on its own, but together with the sudden blaze of new friends, the generous warmth of old ones and the dazzling glitter of New York success, the reality of our situation was lost in a haze of northern lights.

When we came down from this euphoric state it was with an alarming bump. Vivien became abnormally nervous about our social reputation; should we find ourselves too tired to go to a party, she would avidly plough through every New York newspaper next morning to see if our absence had been noticed. Such unnatural terror was at first difficult to sympathise with until I realised that she had become subject to some strange obsession. True to her habitual generosity, Gertrude Lawrence had given us her apartment for the New York season. It was, needless to say, as chic as could be, but her exquisite taste was a little oppressive: the bedroom was hung in silk with dark grey walls and curtains, a darker grey satin cover for the ample bed, and an even deeper grey carpet. I would come in to find the sitting-room empty; going into the bedroom I would find Vivien sitting on the corner of the bed, wringing her hands and sobbing, in a state of grave distress; I would naturally try desperately to give her some comfort, but for some time she would be inconsolable.

It did not take many repetitions of this to set me searching for a psychiatrist, and I persuaded her to come along with me to see him; she was desperate in her resistance to this for some time before she reluctantly gave in. Her hysterical terror of photographers as we entered and as we left the doctor's was distressingly pathetic.

It has to be frankly admitted between the cousins on each side of the Atlantic that we are kindred in language only. In other respects we are as foreign to each other as are any other two nations. We can sometimes make more precious and enduring friendships among other nationalities than from within our own; but there are certain areas in which we may always feel ourselves irredeemable foreigners. I have felt like that whenever it has been necessary for me to approach American psychiatric medicine. I might be a creature from another planet. Obviously Vivien could make no contact either, for she received suggestions of future appointments with such piteous dread that I could not find the heart to pursue such proposals any further. It was not any personal fear of the doctor, but of what might be the true reasons for her visits to him that she couldn't bear to face.

Throughout her possession by that uncannily evil monster, manic depression, with its deadly, ever-tightening spirals, she retained her own individual canniness – an ability to disguise her true mental condition from almost all except me, for whom she could hardly be expected to take the trouble. By the end of our New York season, she was beginning to rise out of her 'low', but I, in my overwrought state, was in a clamped-teeth, living-from-day-to-day sort of existence. I invited us to Noël's home in Jamaica for a couple of weeks before facing England again.

My need of a real friend was so sore that I went to him after a couple of days in Blue Harbour and told him I very much feared that Vivien was having quite a bad nervous breakdown. 'Nonsense,' he said. 'If anybody's having a nervous breakdown, you are.' Of course, Vivien had got in first. It was back to despair for me, and the well-worn teeth had to be clamped together again. I also had to lie on my front for two days, having been lightly stroked across the shoulders by a stingray's tail while swimming. I am still grateful for the gentle ministrations of Noël's black maids, who periodically laid cool slices of melon, papaya and mango all over my back.

The great excitement of 1951 for us was our meeting and acquaintanceship with our glorious Winston Churchill. The first time we realised that he was honouring us was at a performance of *Caesar and Cleopatra*. In the interval, I was hovering about in my dressing-room, wondering what the great man was thinking of us, when my door opened and that immortal head with the wonderful blue eyes came round it. I was too much taken aback to say anything, but he said at once, 'Oh, I'm so sorry, I was looking for a corner.' Realising his need, I took him back through the outer office, and indicated to him exactly where to go and how to get himself down the stairs again, where there would be someone waiting for him to take him back through the pass-door and into his seat. He always allowed himself the minor extravagance of buying three seats: one for himself, one for his much loved daughter Mary, and one for his hat and coat; I thought this one of the most sensible extravagances I had ever heard of. A little later Mary told me that, returning to his seat and sitting himself next to her, he had said, 'I was looking for a luloo, and who d'you think I ran into? – Juloo.'

After he had been brought to see *Antony and Cleopatra* by Mollie (Duchess of) Buccleuch, who had once invited me to lunch at Drumlanrig with her and the duke when I was playing some date in Scotland, she invited us to sup with him and herself privately; adoring him as of course we already did, we found his sweetly polite, unforced kindness, and the courteous generosity of his conversation an unforgettable example. I had previously found politicians and statesmen to have about them a certain guardedness, obviously caused by a fear of being caught out, which was only detectable in the slightly hooded look around the eyes. The best exemplar of this, who was the object of many years of mildly entertaining observation, was Mr Chifley ('Chiff'), Prime Minister of Australia in 1948. An astute man, who rose from being an engine-driver, he did rather woefully let down this particular visiting citizen from the Old Country. We had been invited to stay with Mr McKell, the Governor General at Canberra, to celebrate Anzac Day and to contribute to the occasion with a speech. We talked over the problems that this presented and Vivien was only too happy to be left with the 'happy to be here' stuff, if I felt the urge to go a bit deeper. I had found my patience much tried at press and public meetings by the constant prefacing of some highly dangerous question with the opener, 'Tell us, Sir Laurence, now that Britain's finished . . .' followed by a wish to know how I would prescribe the dividing-up of what might be left of our departed Empire? The excrutiating trouble I could have got myself into by any attempt to deal with such a question can be very easily imagined; and so I decided to make a bold effort to lay once and for all the hideous ghost that kept howling the unacceptable assumption that Britain was finished. This determination did present some extremely tricky risks of making bad worse instead of better. We were introduced to the Prime Minister as we came into the gathering and, during the drinks with sandwiches before the formalities started, I took the liberty of seeking him out and imploring him for his help and would he have the generous patience, so very nervous and anxious as I was not to say the wrong thing, just to please glance through what I had planned to say, it wouldn't take him more than two minutes? He turned eyes so hooded they were almost shut away from me and said, 'Oh, I would suggest a few impromptu words . . . .' Can any advice from a man in his position to a man in mine have been more dangerous? I have often wondered about it since and was glad I had been told his gallant history as an engine-driver.

If you were speaking to Winston about something, no matter how trivial, those eyes of blue would be fastened on you, bright with intelligent attention, almost as if he was grateful to learn. During *Richard III* I had heard myself being gently accompanied from the third or fourth row; reports came back to me afterwards that he had said every single line in unison with me. When I told him how envious I was of such a wonderful memory, he said, 'Oh, but you – so many myriads of words packed into your brain? It must be a great burden.' I had to admit honestly that three weeks after I had finished playing a part I could not quote a word from it; but he managed with a batsman's skill to glance that to leg and turn it back into another sort of compliment, by courteously nodding in approval of my special gift and saying, 'Aah, that must be a great mercy to you.'

He was obviously most taken with Vivien, and when we went to Sunday lunch at Westerham he gave her one of his paintings; we were assured that this was the only picture of his that he had been known to give away. After lunch poor Christopher Soames was condemned to take us over the model farm with its proud breed of belted Galloways.

There was a highly valuable bull from which was issuing the most distressing sound I have ever heard, a groan of agonised pain and grief; his head was pressed tightly against the wall and his wild eyes rolling. Soames told us he was dangerously mad and had killed a man; and to clean his stall out, a cow in season had to be thrust into the next pen, the iron door between them opened, and only when he was safely about his amorous duties did it clang shut, so that the cleansing of his pen could be carried out.

We returned to the house and found our host, having walked up to the top of his garden to feed his fish, on his way upstairs for his afternoon nap. Nervously giving way to the silly vein of cajolery with which a shy guest will try to seem on more relaxed terms than he feels with his vastly superior host, I spluttered, 'I say, sir, we're frightfully worried about your bull!' He waved this aside, saying, 'Oh, he's all right.' He took a step up; then, as if in forgiveness of my idiocy, he made me a present of a marvellous Churchill-ism, minted on the spur of that moment especially for me. He turned and, placing his hand in a beautiful gesture upon the newel-post of the balusters, he produced, 'And even if . . . he does lead a life of unparalleled dreariness, it is punctuated . . . by moments of intense excitement.'

On another occasion he had asked us to supper at his London house in Hyde Park Gate after *Antony*, for which we both of us had make-up covering most of our bodies; it was hard to clean it off and get out of the theatre quickly, but we both made a tremendous effort – more difficult for Vivien than for me since she had to put on another make-up, I only had to take one off. We made it in record time, but even so it was apparent that our host was a little impatient; it was clearly a trial for him to be kept waiting for his supper.

It was a very full menu for a supper, more like a dinner, necessitating the full complement of accompanying white and red wines, champagne, and port. (Never drink port after champagne; Tony Bushell had a friend in the Welsh Guards whose father had said to him on his twenty-first birthday: 'Three pieces of invaluable advice for you, my boy: nevah hunt south of the Thames, nevah drink port after champagne and nevah have your wife in the morning lest something bettah should turn up during the day.') During the port, at a look from Clemmie the three ladies left the three men. As we three turned to seat ourselves again, I fancied I caught a glimpse of ancient Harrow days as he declared in youthful enthusiasm his appreciation of Vivien: 'By Jove,' he said, 'by Jove, she's a clinker!' He pushed the whisky decanter towards me and, with a slight flutter of dismay at mixing drinks so much, I obediently helped myself: what the hell, I thought, we're *not* only young once. I pushed it on to Soames and reached for the water. Soames passed the decanter to Winston who helped himself and as he reached for the soda syphon, again impelled to that ghastly self-conscious banter, I said: 'Excuse me, sir, but have you ever tried plain water with it? I believe it to be the soda that crawls up the back of our necks the next morning.' 'Oh well,' he said with his usual polite interest, 'if you say so'; and poured the water meekly. Time came for another round and he automatically reached for the soda, and of course I had to remonstrate with him in that accursed would-be waggish tone, 'Oh, sir, you're letting me down.' 'Oh, I'm sure you're quite right; but I think I prefer my little *prangle*!'

On 13 July the first foundation stone of the National Theatre was laid, somewhat inauspiciously in the wrong place, close by the famous Shot Tower which was a familiar landmark. It had ultimately to be removed to make way for the Queen Elizabeth Hall and Purcell Room complex. Many of us suffered a sense of shame that our beloved King George VI's Queen Elizabeth should have been asked to perform this travesty, which she did with such grace. It might also have been observed that she held her bouquet at a delicate little distance from her. To the general onlooker, no doubt it seemed merely a strangely dull-looking little bunch of stuff; some undoubted genius had had the notion that it should be specially composed of all the flowers mentioned by Shakespeare. Apart from a rose, a daffodil, sprigs of rosemary and rue, a daisy, sweet briar, eglantine, luscious woodbine, and a flower de luce, there was a leek, a docken leaf, dogweed, bogwort, virginia creeper (for a vine), a disordered twig, darnel, hemlock and rank fumitory; a freckled cowslip, oxlip, nodding violet, burnet, and green clover as a last desperate bid for sweetness; and then, a rough thistle, a kecksie and a bur; a sprig of willow, a fantastic garland of crowflowers, nettles, daisies and long purples 'that liberal shepherds give a grosser name but our chaste maids do dead men's fingers call them' – as much for their smell as for their appearance, I fear.

Except for playing light comedy to an enraptured audience, acting is not an enjoyable craft. It is interesting certainly, and absorbing almost to a point of mania in its difficulties and problems, but not enjoyable. The intensely suffering characters, which we describe as the Punishing Roles – Lear, Othello, Macbeth, Titus, Oedipus – are not there to be enjoyed any more than a marathon is. However, there is one diary entry in this July of 1951: 'Wed. 2.30 – A[ntony]. Enjoyed performance.' The uniqueness of this entry does much to substantiate the fact that for me at least my contention is not an exaggeration. It seems an endurance test when you are in action, but leaves an aching void in times of rest; perhaps an ox misses his yoke when it is removed from him.

In my career I have been sensitive enough to the need for changes in characteristics as well as direction. I was readily responsive when, towards the end of the London *Cleopatra* season, Peter Brook suggested to me a film of *The Beggar's Opera*. This was exactly the kind of challenge that I dearly love to attempt. As I was about to leave with Vivien in the 'Cleopatras' to New York, I got on to Mary Martin and asked the name of her singing teacher there; she told me it was Helen Cahoon. I went to her two or three times a week all through our New York season; after about ten weeks I thought it would be only wise to have a recording made of myself singing two or three of Macheath's songs in the opera, so that Peter Brook and Arthur Bliss, who was making a new adaptation of the score, would have a chance to talk over my chances.

To my joy, Peter wrote me an ecstatic letter about the record, quoting Bliss as saying, 'It's not only a pleasant sound, but the way he sings the songs is most musician-like.' I was over the moon. I foresaw a great change in my whole life; what was an actor, after all? A poor player that struts and frets his hour upon the stage and then is heard no more; a vagabond no lady of title would dream of allowing her daughter to consider marrying; obviously a cheap sort of person – kissing all those women on the stage!

A strange echo of these old attitudes reached my left ear as I was making my maiden speech in the House of Lords in 1971; I felt it was going quite well, when I caught the unmistakable sound on my left of an ancient, aristocratic tremulousness raised in incomprehension, in accents completely devoid of all consonants: 'Wha hi hi ho-hi hong-how; high ha hu-her-ha hahaw . . .' (What is this going on now, I can't understand at all.) The younger peer sitting next to him was desperate in his efforts to quiet the old relic, to no avail. I blundered on trying to pretend it wasn't happening; 'Ho, huh, wha hor ho a he-oe ih hi . . . Huh?' ('No, but what sort of a fellow is this?') A very quiet whisper from our younger peer, followed by that kind of pause that can only indicate utter incredulity; then – *very* loud – 'Ah-*hac*-ΤΑΑΑΑΑΗ?!?!'

I was above all that sort of thing in that spring of 1952. My life-style was to undergo a greater sea change than ever took place at full fathom five; I was a *musician* now, the most highly inspired of all artists; and what was it a great opera singer got for a performance? And I was to be a miracle mixture of Caruso and Chaliapin!

Well; yes, yes, you may laugh *now*. Hell, even *I* can laugh now.

When King George vi died in February 1952, some friendly Americans arranged for the British who were in New York to hold a memorial service for him in the 'little church around the corner'; this charming title is over-modest, it is a perfectly generously sized and extremely nice church of Episcopalian denomination. Being, I think, the only knight at the moment in New York, I seemed to be generally expected to give a talk from the pulpit; I agreed, of course, and whenever one of the thousand natural daily interruptions occurred would remonstrate, 'Please, I'm thinking about my sermon.'

About my sermon, I can only say that it went down like a dog's dinner, so much so that my congregation besought me to record it. I soon ran out of my own little store of records and have not now a single one that I can lay my hand on. My friend Emlyn Williams got someone at home to send a copy to our bereaved young Queen and her consort; I received a kindly message of courteous royal acknowledgement, but I cannot believe that at that time, so fraught with burdensome considerations, either our monarch or her prince could possibly have found time for attending to such a thing.

I had got Rex Harrison and Lilli Palmer (darling Lill) on at the Century in New York in *Venus Observed* in February, having opened in Philadelphia. I continued the labours on my voice with Helen Cahoon whenever possible. During an interval of *Antony* one evening Vivien and I listened to the Academy Award results and – joy upon joy – she had won her second Oscar for *Streetcar*.

On coming home from New York, we got to Notley as soon as possible, breathing 'Home again' on 23 April 1952. I had a blessed sense of relief that Vivien's condition seemed to have righted itself. I have confessed to a woefully blind spot in communicating with American psychiatrists. I fail, that's all. I am sure that they must have taken some pains to tell me what was wrong with my wife; that her disease was called manic depression and what that meant – a possibly permanent cyclical to-and-fro between the depths of depression and wild, uncontrollable mania. These changes of mood could be irregular, or regular, or increasing in frequency, this last the most dreaded as it almost inevitably led to schizophrenia, which was so far regarded as being incurable. Whether the doctors didn't explain or I didn't understand matters not; the fact is I was quite unprepared for what was in store.

I was recommended a fine singing teacher in London, Mr Cunelli. He had an extremely delicate, light, high tenor voice. Helen had found that my most probable range would be that of a full baritone; so between the two I was caught in a dichotomy of purposes. Nevertheless I thought it best not to shop around for other teachers. Whenever I came for a lesson, Cunelli would be sitting strumming at his piano; he held out his hand to me and we would get on with it. As to most students, the thought occurred to me that if he knew so much, why didn't he made a more paying living at the craft rather than just scratch one by teaching it? The answer is that such teachers really do know how to make the best of the craft, but have never been able to achieve that standard in performance for themselves; but Cunelli really did have an exquisite voice and could use it to great effect. I could not refrain from asking him why he was not a professional singer. His answer gave me a rare, Breughel-like vision of struggling souls, all with some unfortunate disadvantage that forbids them achievement; how lucky, it suddenly struck me anew, how damn lucky to have enough on your side to get through without some over-riding difficulty that made it impossible to fulfil your ambition. He quite simply stood up for the first time before me and, sadly smiling, held out his hands and said, 'You see; I was so small that whenever I came on to the stage the audience could not stop from laughing.'

CHAPTER NINE

La Fièvre Recule Pour Mieux Sauter

Our production team for *The Beggar's Opera* was as follows: Peter Brook was the director, Denis Cannan wrote the original screenplay, Christopher Fry was a sort of dialogue-sorcerer and 'atmos-illuminator', George Wakhevitch did the sets and costumes, and Arthur Bliss was the musical arranger and stern critic, sometimes disconcertingly so for this his chief male voice.

The weakness in this set-up was basic. Herbert Wilcox invited me to join him as co-producer, even offering me first billing. We both felt that as this was to be Peter Brook's first picture it would be wise to have a strong producer for him to answer to, should things seem to be going wrong. But the position of a director who has less authority than his leading man is a rotten one, and poor Peter had an utterly miserable experience. Actor and director should understand the importance of their partnership, in which the word of the director should be recognised as being the final one, except on some matter of conscience for which the actor is prepared to take public blame.

There is at present a tendency for famous players to produce and direct their own pictures. If they are prepared to take on the entire responsibility, this is OK. But if they enlist a stooge director to whom they can hand out blame for technical errors, and who is supposed to relate well both to the actor, who is supposed to accept his direction, and to the same man, the producer, who can give him orders, I say forget it, it spells disaster.

The script was finished in mid-June and I went south to

join Vivien on Alex's *Elsewhere* for a week; Vivien seemed well and I returned untroubled to the normal preparatory stages of rehearsing. Stanley Holloway was playing Peacham, and George Devine, as good at acting as at theatre-creating, was Lockit. Stanley and I were the only two who did our own singing; the rest were all dubbed by first-class British singers, both Peter Brook and Arthur Bliss insisting on the sound being critically unassailable. This seemed reasonable, but it had the effect of making me sound inferior to the rest of the cast. The main point of the enterprise was supposed to be that I was now a singing actor. The fact that I was not known to be a singer would cast doubts, while possibly promoting some curiosity. But the unhappy result was that the sounds that I made were not up to the general standard of the music. I had begged my two partners to think again about using professional singers. The voices of almost all in the acting cast were good enough to pass muster; it might not be a musical event but it would be all of a pattern, and the unpretentious can sometimes have its own special charm. I maintained that in the final analysis this would be better for the film itself, but failed wretchedly to carry the day.

There is little satisfaction in being right in prognosticating a failure when it happens to be one's own. I just hope and pray that my personal flop in *The Beggar's Opera* will be the worst that I shall ever disenjoy.

There was near the end of the job, in sharp relief, an unforgettably divine experience. In company with Susana and Willie Walton, Elisabeth Schwarzkopf and Walter Legge, I was enraptured by two evenings of the Philharmonia Orchestra playing Brahms, conducted by Toscanini. After the second glorious concert we took the world's greatest conductor out to supper. In vain did we try to express our feelings to him, but could only stammer like gagged idolaters. Our great guest, I may say, was not much help on this stultified occasion; not even playing with his food, with his daughter's anxious eye upon him, he could only keep tapping upon the edge of the table with the middle finger of his right hand, declaring again and again,

'The orchestra played well . . . The orchestra played well . . .'

For a while I had had a small but growing sense of worry. Vivien, who had always chosen her work carefully and wisely, had recently become enthusiastic about an idea for a job which I felt to be a most unwise choice – an undistinguished melodrama to be located in Ceylon, and shot at the end of January 1953.

The producers had suggested that I might consider taking the male lead opposite her in the film; Vivien asked, was I sure I wouldn't like to? It was a safe enough question, I realised, knowing as she did that not only was I against the project, but also that I had ahead of me the sixteen weeks needed by any producer for editing, post-synching, scoring, dubbing, final colour-matching, titling and negative cutting of *The Beggar's Opera*. When, almost without pause, she said that in that case none other than Peter Finch would be her leading man, the penny dropped, and it dropped with the knell of a high-pitched chapel bell.

I was allowed on to the tarmac at the airport, and as the plane began to move gently forward they both looked back at me through the window, Peter making a gallant effort to look the assuringly protective friend, and she, with a little smile of infinite sweetness, blowing me a sad little kiss.

I turned away and drove back to London in a state of nothingness, to pick up the relatively light cudgels of finishing off a picture. I saw to things at home, my beloved Notley, which I have sometimes accused myself of loving to excess; I nursed an obsessive, possessive love for it which at times made me feel guilty. It is inhuman, immoral to love a thing more than people, work, intellect, art, my dead, my friends. I felt I had become an eccentric who, having had the love of his life extracted like some rotten tooth, turns all his affections to his dog, or some collecting hobby. Notley Abbey had been founded and built by Walter Giffard, Earl of Buckingham, during the reign of Henry II, 'in order that the souls of the King, his Queen Eleanor of Aquitaine, his own soul and those of all his own family might be prayed for in perpetuity'. What a wonderfully simple way of bargaining with God!

Two weeks of comparative peace served to give me time with my loved friends again – always there, ready to talk or stay mute, as need be. I remember Alex Korda chuckling when he recalled our recent three-way discussion concerning Vivien's future; avuncular as always to both of us, there was still some ancient contractual tie between Vivien and him. 'Forgive me, dear Larry, but I nearly had to laugh when I asked her who was to be her leading man and she said, "Peter Finch", in that incredibly off-handed way – I mean, really! It was the only truly bad performance I've ever seen her give.'

It seemed hardly two minutes before my peace was shattered. To give my St James's Theatre a slight face-lift, I had thought of encouraging companies from abroad to think of it as a home from home; so that apart from a few welcoming functions and first-night parties, my responsibilities in that part of my work, at least, should not be harrowed by whatever extra demands Vivien's state of health might make of me. The second week of February found me in Paris looking over the work of the Comédie Française. Poor darling Ginette Spanier, my beloved friend, how she suffered; she was not all that fond of French theatre anyway, and night after night of French classics – well, I didn't find it all that much of a thrill myself; but she soldiered along with me, an act of purest friendship if ever there was one.

This first crusade was cut into very sharply after two days. Irving Asher, a friend of long standing and the producer in Ceylon, called Cecil Tennant in a state of great panic; Vivien's conduct was making the work on the film quite impossible. She showed no vestige of her habitual discipline and was impossible to reason with – could Larry for Chrissakes come over and do something? I was anxious to see the state of the union for myself, and so, knowing the hopelessness of my quest, I got limply on to a Comet and flew from Paris as directly as you then could: Rome, Beirut, Bahrain and into Colombo.

Vivien met me at the airport, which dismayed me a bit because I was sure that she should have been in front of the cameras. She was all for stopping off at a 'rest house', a name so delightfully vague that its sense of accommodation would seem to be limitless; she was insistent upon needing a little drink and a relax, but I said that we should really get her back to work as soon as we could, since we surely didn't want to worry them unnecessarily. This was met with a blaze of rage that surprised even me; in the unhappy colloquy that followed I thought ruefully of the wretched waste of time, effort and money that I had been a party to. It was a long drive, but at last we got to the hotel in Kandy.

I found there that Peter Finch was very much in charge, being the only person at this time who had any kind of influence upon Vivien; to do him justice he used that influence as best he could in the film's interests, but the governing factor of the situation was that the two of them were helplessly lost in the floodtide of the all-consuming passion to which, for the first time, they were giving enthusiastic licence. Sweet little Ethel, Vivien's maid, upset and distracted with terror, told me that so far they had not been to bed but had lain together all night in the open on the hillsides.

I could find no blame in my heart for Peter – was he not simply doing what I had done to her first husband seventeen years ago? I found it pretty old-fashioned to work up any extra feelings of outrage on account of my being his boss from whom he had been able to glean a very nice career, thank you; besides, I had always liked him, and in the strangest of ways, just then, the utter confusion of the mess in which we found ourselves seemed to dispel hostility.

The humiliation of hanging around in Ceylon would have been quite enough to send me packing without any special application of common sense. My 'mission' had been as futile as any fool would have known that it would be. I'd arrived on Tuesday, the 17th, and having expressed my regrets to Asher and wished him all the luck that he needed – which was a super-abundance of it – I got myself on to a plane early on the Friday morning and was in Paris on the Saturday afternoon. I went straight on home the next day as I had music sessions for *The Beggar's Opera* from the Monday; and so, on with the motley. My situation did not really bear any more thinking about and I managed to insulate my feelings in a soft coat of numbness. Vivien and the film unit started shooting in Hollywood on 4 March, and on the same day my beloved brother was married, for the third and last time, at the Marylebone registry office to an angelic girl, Hester, with whom we still keep in close contact, although Dickie died more than twenty years ago now.

As soon as I had completed most of my work, I suddenly had to get away, right away, even from England; I called up Susana and Willie Walton in Ischia and asked them to let me stay with them for a little while. Wonderful friends that they are, they could sense something was wrong and told me to come at once.

When I arrived at their Casa Cirillo on the Via Cesotta, the first of the many in which they have lived on this magical island, there was a telegram for me. My heart sank and with reason; it was from Cecil, telling me to meet someone called Peter Moore in Naples on Friday morning and be prepared to return immediately. At 6.15 next morning I was on the boat back to Naples, and I shall never forget the colour of the sky: blanketed all over with turbulent cloud, it was dark red; yes, it was ominous all right.

At the dock a pleasantly correct young gent approached me with his hand extended and said, 'Moore.'

I took his hand and, ever the little copy-cat, said, 'Olivier.' Then, 'I am sure it's something wrong with my wife, could you please tell me what it is?'

'Nervous breakdown,' he said.

The ten o'clock train from Naples got into Rome an hour later, and the Comet left for London at 1.20 p.m. I did some very necessary phoning at Durham Cottage. Thank God our dear GP, Dr Armando Childe, was at home. Owing to the mental sickness of someone else close to me, I knew about the great Dr Freudenberg, head of the Netherne Hospital in Coulsdon, and so was able to do a quick bit of programming with Armando. Then Cecil and I took off from Heathrow, touching down at Idlewild at 8.55 New York time. Danny Kaye met us and gave us the latest overall picture. He took us to the Sherry Netherland, fed us, fixed us with some rooms, and I had a massage and a sleep before taking off again to Los Angeles at 12.30, that Saturday midnight. I can't help smiling when I see that I noted in the little memo-panel in my diary at the end of that week: 'Cattle off upper pasture into new acre. Sulphate great field. Harrow and lime orchard.' I wonder what it would have taken to get Notley completely out of my mind?

Sylvia Kaye, Danny's wife, a close and understanding friend with an intelligent viewpoint, was the first person we saw. Then it was the turn of the psychiatrists, brought in by our inestimably valuable friends David Niven and Stewart Granger (whom I think of as Jimmy Stewart, his real name, which had already been made famous by another actor, forcing him to invent Stewart Granger).

Next was the encounter with Vivien, more dreaded than any other in my life. She had her own house, of course, to live in while making her picture; Cecil and I were staying at David Niven's. David had told me a great deal; I had learnt how he and Stewart Granger had been hearing of goings-on of the most sinister kind. An old flame of hers from the days before she and I had met – his name was John – had taken up residence in the house with her; barking mad himself, he would lord it about the house, draped in long tunics and togas of towelling, taking the most obvious advantages of her being *non compos mentis* and thereby exacerbating her condition. Niven and Jimmy had decided that the rumours were worrying enough to warrant a forced inspection; having got inside the door, their horrified eyes gazed upwards to see Vivien balancing quite naked upon the baluster rail of the landing. John appeared from the shadows, making the mistake of adopting a truculent manner; my two gallant friends took firm hold of him and made it clear that if ever he attempted to re-enter the house he would be made to feel exceedingly sorry for it.

When I arrived at this house I was told I would find her

outside on an upstairs balcony; stepping gently on to this, I saw her. She was leaning with her elbows upon the railing and her face in her hands. I called her softly and she looked up at me. It was as if her eyes were misted over, all grey-green-blue; only the tiniest pin-prick of a pupil was discernible. I said, 'Hello, darling', and when she spoke to me it was in the tone of halting, dream-like amazement that people in the theatre use for mad scenes when they can't think of anything better. My instinctive reaction was that she was putting it on. I took her very gently in my arms, not able for the life of me to think of anything to ask beyond did she think perhaps there was something the matter with her? She turned away from the railing towards the wall and with the wonderment of a first communion said, 'I'm in love.' I asked very gently, 'who with, darling?' Then – approaching the Most High – 'Pe-ter . . . Fi-i-inch.' Where the hell was he by the way, I wondered.

Next day Cecil and I went to see the Paramount people, and no big motion picture firm could possibly have been more kind, understanding, or so generously sympathetic in such circumstances, with not one hint of justifiable grievance or complaint. So we had no problems other than logistic ones. Again the American top-brass authorities were marvellously helpful, cutting through their own red tape with realistic abandon. 'People are in trouble, then help them' seems to be an American motto as cardinal as '*Unum in Pluribus*'.

There were already two nurses in residence at Vivien's house; that Tuesday morning she complained to me that in the night she had been woken, strapped up and wrapped in sheets of cold water. Horrified by this, I told the nurses they had some explaining to do to me. This they did. The most vitally important thing for her condition, they pointed out, was sleep; this was unusually difficult in her case as she exercised an extraordinary will-power in her resistance to succumbing to even the strongest advisable drugs; so, having sedated her all they dared, they had recourse to this crude way of inducing sleep. It did not take long for her body-warmth to warm the wet sheets and, in the process, sleep would overtake her. They would then remove the wet sheets, dry her gently and wrap her again in warm, dry bedclothes, and she would remain asleep for the rest of the night.

Then came the big consultation with Drs Grotjohn, Greenson and Macdonald. Of these, Dr Grotjohn was reputed to be the big white chief. The others I was beginning to know quite well: Macdonald was a kindly general practitioner of good reputation; Greenson was the psychiatrist I felt most trust in. The big maestro Dr Grotjohn made one pronouncement in his mid-European accent at which I nearly laughed out loud: 'She must go to her home,' he was saying. 'You must take her there immediately; it is what she needs, she will recover there wonderfully quickly.' Warming to his subject, he continued with increasing fervour, 'She wants her mo-o-ther!' Now Gertrude adored Vivien, but on Vivien's side I would say there had been no great feeling of need for her mother since she stopped breast-feeding; and in these present circumstances, she would as soon have knocked her mother out as listen to her. This is not an unkind exaggeration. Some time later at home she gave way to a fit of fury with poor Gertrude and tore her breast, hurting her badly; Gertrude forgave her at once and never mentioned it again.

Cecil had, for a spell, a more calming effect on Vivien than did I; thank God somebody did. But it was impossible for me ever to be too far away, so I tried to sleep on one bed and Cecil in his clothes on Vivien's with his arms round her. I think there is nothing in the world so precious as truly selfless friendship; I am aware that this is not an original thought, but if it can do nothing else this book must register this gift as the richest in my unfairly rich cake of a life.

If there was one thing of which Vivien was terrified it was needles, hypodermics of any sort; but the time came when she had to be put out and got on to the plane. Our new nurse appeared with what seemed to be an unusually large needle and a hefty container filled with liquid; Vivien saw them and made a desperate attempt to escape. To my horror I saw that the nurse was enjoying it; she was waggling the syringe in her hand and there was a glint in her eye. But there was no time for anything; Danny Kaye and I threw ourselves on top of Vivien and held her down. Vivien fought us with the utmost ferocity as the needle went in, biting and scratching Danny and me, screaming appalling abuse at both of us, with particular attention to my erotic impulses; it seemed an eternity before she went limp and Danny and I were able to let go of her, both shattered and exhausted. That night, back in England, she was safe in Netherne Hospital.

Vivien's Pa and Ma came to dine with me at Durham Cottage. When I had told them the whole wretched tale, I remembered I had to ask them if there had ever been any insanity in either of their families. Ernest, nearly splitting a gut with outrage, almost shouted, 'Good God, *no*.' I had, by this time, very little patience with those who would insist on making such a distinction between mental and physical illness, and barely managed to bite back, 'Well, you have now.'

Next day I went down to Notley, and slept and slept. (What a wonderful gift that was; a life-saver. Thirty years later I look back with envy; but life and one's ways of adjusting and dealing with it change all the time.)

Then I left the others to start the sound-mixing on *The Beggar's Opera*, and went with Willie Walton to Ischia. Dr Freudenberg had assured me that he had every hope of putting her to sleep for three weeks, but of course . . . Talking to Gertrude at one time about her daughter, she had told me that when Vivien was tiny her lack of need for sleep was phenomenal. She told me that she stopped worrying about it after a bit, settling for the simple thought that her daughter was just 'not a sleepy baby'. My God, I thought, what a title for a book about Vivien.

It would be most ungrateful to declare that the price of fame is too damned high, because it does have great and wonderful conveniences occasionally, witness our escape from Hollywood; but there are other equally poignant situations when you're just not allowed to get away with it. On the boat with Willie from Naples, a lady asked me for my autograph and I signed the damn thing without thinking. I hadn't appreciated that, though I had been allowed to get through all that had happened over the past ten days with such apparent smoothness, the news value of it had not eluded the humblest organ of the entire world press, every detail having been carefully noted and reported with utmost relish every day. It had never occurred to me or to my friends to look at a newspaper throughout this horrific time.

I soon wished I had cut my hand off before giving that one autograph on the boat from Naples. Within three days there wasn't a soul on the island who didn't know that I was there; poor Susana and William made ceaseless denials in response to ceaseless hammerings on their front or back doors; if we wanted to go out I had to lie on the floor in the back of their Bentley covered with a rug. The intense vulnerability of my situation – a wife in a mental home and I obviously on the run – had made me the object of unusual press interest, and the island was quickly covered with *giornalisti* on swarms of Vespas. My darling friends would not hear of me simply getting the hell out and going home; but after another day of it William said, 'It may seem an absurd solution but I really think we'd stand a better chance on the mainland. The Bentley can go pretty quick and if we stick to unlikely places and choose our routes carefully enough . . .'

The Bentley was perched grotesquely on the steepest part of the stern of what had been a sailing-ship; we followed in a small fishing-boat. Up at four, we spun straight across the country to Bari; went all the way down the east coast through Puglia to the end of the Appian Way at Brindisi, under the 'arch of the foot' to Taranto ('Is it not strange . . . . That from Tarentum and Brundisium/He could so quickly cut the Ionian sea' *Antony and Cleopatra*, III, vii); and round 'the toe' to Reggio di Calabria; by boat to Messina and Taormina; by ferry back to Reggio; then the long, long drive up the coast road to Paestum, Salerno, Amalfi and Ravello. Here John Huston, whom I knew from his writing days on *Wuthering Heights*, was directing a film in the piazza.

There happened on this trip one of those reverses that can still bring a little smile in memory. In spite of a heavy disguise, a few days' growth on my face, dark glasses, a beret, one of William's jackets that fitted me not at all, as I emerged from our hotel in Lecce, a young fisherman pointed me out to his friends and said, 'Lavrenche Olivaire.' It was not all that amazing; if you're not known in Italy, you're not known anywhere.

The last treat on this excursion was to be in Naples. We took a couple of rooms in a hotel; our evening clothes, which had accompanied us on our eccentric journey, were pressed, our heads were trimmed, and off we drove to the San Carlo opera house for a rapturous evening sharing *Il creposcolo degli Dei*. It had been directed with much originality by Wieland and Wolfgang Wagner, grandsons of the immortal composer. During this, the Bentley was again being hoisted to its precarious height on the old sailing ship's stern for the trip back to Ischia.

The next morning, back on the island, Susana came into my room with a telegram in her hand. 'Oh, Larry darling, you're beginning to be so much better, I do pray this is not what I'm afraid it is.' It was from Cecil; 'Awakening imminent come back quick.' Surprisingly I managed to get Armando on the phone, and was in London the following evening.

I found Vivien in an altogether changed condition, in the London Clinic. She found it impossible to understand why I had not been waiting at her bedside for her first stirring while still at Netherne. I had, of course, been over-anxious to believe that Freudenberg would not allow her to waken before he was satisfied that the cure could continue at the rhythm required. We were none of us sufficiently trained in the extra wariness always needed to keep up with one who was 'not a sleepy baby'. I blamed myself and I still do for not being more alive to my duties, no matter how painful or how mortally sick of them I was. It was typical of Noël Coward to be as thoughtful as I had been self-removing, and he had had placed by her bed all the things that girls would most like to find by them at such a waking – flowers, Christian Dior perfume, toilet water, powder, the lot; Vivien never ceased to appreciate this thoughtfulness.

Of course I knew that she had been given shock treatment, many applications of it. Freudenberg explained to me now what the future was likely to hold; a permanent though not rhythmically regular series of the downs and ups associated with manic depression. There was as yet no known cure for this condition, which in some cases cured itself spontaneously; but it was much more probable that the sickness was a permanency. The great thing was to keep it under reasonable control. This could be best achieved by riding through the depressive stage, then watching very carefully the interim period of apparent normality and at the very first sign of the 'up' to take the patient, by force if necessary, to be put under the briefest anaesthesia so that the lightning passage of current could be shot from one temple to the other. The patient would wake to a state of calm normality.

There was one aspect of this treatment which did cause me some anxiety. There is no question that by now such side-effects will have been greatly, if not entirely, ironed out. I have not happened on any companion experiences with which to compare notes, but the reservations in my mind were concerned with slight but noticeable personality changes. I can only describe them by saying that she was not, now that she had been given the treatment, the same girl that I had fallen in love with. I have said that some four years before this her feelings for me had changed and that she had told me so; but now it was not so much a question of her feelings as my own. In so far as she was no longer the person I had loved, I loved her that much less. She was now more of a stranger to me than I could ever have imagined possible. Something had happened to her, very hard to describe, but unquestionably evident. However much her feelings for me might have changed, I had never been able to believe that the same could happen to mine.

She was released from hospital and advised to keep to

her bed at Notley as much as possible for a time. This she seemed quite willing to do. We used those old spots on her lung as cover. It was now mid-April, and apart from my foreign seasons at the St James's my own career seemed to have come to a halt as well as hers.

As 1951 had called for some special effort, so, by heaven, did 1953; for this was Coronation Year in Britain, and that it should be the last of such for a very long time was everybody's prayer. For now we had a lovely young Queen, the first to assume the throne for a hundred years; Elizabeth, Anne, Victoria – they had all ruled over great periods in our country and we all felt that we had a gift of special significance.

We were not, in our particular actor-management, in the very finest fettle for this sort of programming, and we were going to be pushed to improve on those 'Cleopatras'. Our minds raced through the list of current playwrights and we felt a bit dim at the prospects; we did not think of Terence Rattigan because it seemed certain that, were there something in that gold-mine, we would have heard about it.

A few nights later we met Terry Rattigan at a party. I remember taking him to one side and asking him if, by any chance, he might have something in the oven for Puss and me for this very special year? He looked at me interestedly and said, 'Why, is she . . . er . . .?' I assured him I was quite certain that by the autumn she would be in full health and strength again. He then said that, as a matter of fact, yes he did have something that might suit us very well indeed. I read *The Sleeping Prince* and passed it on to Vivien within two hours of receiving it. As far as being a Coronation play was concerned, it hardly left anything to be desired. As a play? Well, it suffered from a dichotomy of interests.

This, we know, is not necessarily dangerous to a play; it may well, in fact, provide the tension for many that are famously successful. In this light comedy the romantic interest was intended to be provided by the Prince Regent of Carpathia and the Chorus Girl; but in order to contra-spice the predictability of such a tale, our author introduces another character, a brilliantly successful role, played with brilliant success by Martita Hunt. To the dazzling Grand Duchess our author awards a whole cartload of sympathy by making this character, who knows that her marriage to the Prince Regent had been arranged for the usual royal reasons, uncommonly accommodating. She not only condones but appears quite kindly disposed to the wayward life that her husband leads. Whether or not she had herself fallen for the charms of his previous mistresses in the way she was now obliged to need not and had better not concern us; in Hollywood terms, she just has to fall for Vivien Leigh, or whoever.

After five weeks on the road, our much delayed opening took place on 5 November. *The Sleeping Prince* ran for thirty-five weeks at the Phoenix; not a smash hit after the first three or four months, but respectable enough. There was always that duality (English for dichotomy) in the play, that was generally felt to detract from a hundred per cent acceptability of the work. If ever one was to make a film of it, a concentrated attention to this problem would obviously be crucial when fashioning the script.

In August 1954 we were preparing for the film of *Richard III*. Tony Bushell had been scouting hard for a possible Bosworth Field (the real one in Leicestershire is cunningly twice intersected by a railway and a canal). He thought of Spain; this, difficult as it may be to believe since it has for twenty-five years proved the most popular film location for the industry, was actually the first time it had been thought of.

Bearing strongly in mind the characteristics and colouring of Leicestershire, he went to pay homage to the Spanish military hierarchy for advice; their immediate response was that the finest battle scenes could undoubtedly be found in the south, in Andalusia. Tony's automatic reply was, 'Ah, thank you, but is it green?' Oh yes, certainly it was green, he was assured. His mind full of doubts, he travelled quickly south to find that, yes, it was green all right, but shade was provided by impenetrable cactus. He tried the areas round the Escorial and there the terrain was certainly very promising; his only worry was still the colour, but he thought it might be worth my making the trip to have a look-see, and it was. Admittedly the grass was of the palest silver, but the assurances were strong that it was always green in September; just in case the autumn that year should prove to be extraordinarily late, we concentrated our attentions upon terrain of the most marshy nature.

I thought enviously of the money-no-object attitude of the more luxurious Hollywood pictures and of their natural resources, their birthright from the very infancy of movies – California. How quick were those early boys to find the place where they had God-given light for more than twelve hours a day, 360 days in the year, as well as every known type of landscape from snow to desert, from arid plains to spectacular mountains and everything in between. I had cause on my Spanish location to remember their Yorkshire moors for *Wuthering Heights*, and how a huge shadow was painted by an aircraft spraying oil over a vast acreage; how conveniently might I have given the same treatment with green paint over a few square miles round the Escorial!

Our location work in that month of September 1954 was followed by thirteen weeks in Shepperton Studios. I adored every moment of the picture's making and have always felt quite happy about the result – with the exception of one pretty important element, the battle sequence. Somehow, after *Henry V*, I couldn't find another battle in me and even that one, which did seem to come off, was littered with petty larcenies from our Master of All, Eisenstein. I could only show as well as I could the happenings, as history tells us they took place on that day on Bosworth Field, with the usual hideous problem of trying to make 500 men look like 60,000 – this time on a wide screen, not that little hider of wicked secrets, the now longed-for 66 × 33.

I also had Alex Korda on the phone, breathing hotly down my neck every night, 'Larry, you must cut, you know? You ruin me, you know.' When I showed Carol Reed an early screening he said, 'Why on earth didn't you invent some Shakespearian-sounding lines to help the audience understand better what was going on? "Go to thy furthest westest with the utmostest speedest!" I bet you've done it before, often.' He was right, I had, but here when it was most essential I went and got all prim and orthodox. Infuriating. I fear that when they occasionally revive it, out of some misguided respect it is always shown in its full-length version, though I actually prefer it cut, particularly the battle sequence. So Alex was right after all: so much cheaper to leave it off the negative at the outset than on the cutting-room floor. As usual, William Walton's music was a life-saver.

During a weekend at Notley in the summer of 1954, Vivien and I had promised Glen Byam Shaw that we would gladly 'assist' at his tenth season as director of the Shakespeare Memorial Theatre at Stratford-upon-Avon – *Twelfth Night* as Viola and Malvolio, and *Macbeth*: as Sybil Thorndike always said, 'You must be married to play the Macbeths.' Finally, as an innovation, the never-performed *Titus Andronicus*, with Vivien as Lavinia and myself in the punishing role.

All started merry as a marriage-bell. It was lovely to be with Glennie again and with Johnnie Gielgud as our director; though, as twenty years before in *Romeo*, he did not always agree with what I was trying to do, we had enough mutual fondness and respect to recognise that perfect agreement in matters of characterisation would never be ours, not in this world; and so peaceful co-operation was possible. He still had the disconcerting habit of changing moves at every single rehearsal; of course a director has the right to change his mind, but after almost four weeks and with the opening night looming closer, I began to be nervous that the occasion would be a shambles, with an utterly confused company knowing neither the timing nor the placing of the moves. Noël Coward once said that the only real use of a director was to stop the actors from bumping into each other; at the rate our *Twelfth Night* was going our first performance would have been more like a game of Blind Man's Buff than anything else.

Sensing disaster, I had to talk to Glen and explain that

none of us had yet been allowed to do the same things two days running. He asked John Gielgud to join us, and at the risk of hurting his feelings I asked him to leave the company at the point we had got to and let us go over and over it for a couple of days until we knew the moves well enough to do a run-through without a stop; then at least he himself would be able to see his own mistakes if there were any, and if he needed to make more changes he could make as many as he chose, since we would at least know what we were changing *from*. I'm afraid he was a bit hurt by the suggestion that he should quit his own rehearsals, but for the sake of avoiding a disaster I had to be firm and insist. At the end of the two days we were able to offer him a clean run-through. As I suspected, he did not find that he had to alter that much, and he recognised that I had respected his production and, as I had promised, made not a single change in it.

Well, we got by without any shambles and were allowed to feel pleasantly successful; there was a newspaper strike which meant that we were free from worries concerning the critical faculty for the first two or three weeks; and then, out they came. I was chiefly upset because, in spite of her Cleopatra in which she had carried all before her, the critics chose to revive the old prejudices that Vivien was not acceptable in Shakespeare.

The severe critic gains respect by being feared and his approval is much coveted; in order to win such prestige the quality of his writing has to be immaculate. This lends distinction and authority to his opinions. Most nations can boast a leading light among theatre critics; at the time of which I write, the one flicking a duster over his clothes and sleeking down his hair to mount the stairs to this rickety throne (all thrones are rickety) was Ken Tynan. His destructive weapons were deadly, strengthened by the scintillating quality of his writing. His praise was equally impressive, but rarer, of course, because bitchiness is the journalist's handiest tool. Having made his mark in the *Spectator*, he was now seated where St John Ervine, followed by Ivor Brown, had so long held sway, on the *Observer*. Following him, though quite a way behind, came

John Barber on the *Daily Express*, whose owner, Lord Beaverbrook, was reputed to have instructed his entertainments writers: 'Make a star or break a star, I'm not interested in anything in between.'

Besides their whipping boys, critics sometimes show marked favouritisms. I found myself thus favoured by a few for a time, which, though it fed my ego, was destructive to any professional partnership, particularly a marriage; the puissant few don't like their favourites to have favourites, and for some months our critics had turned cruelly upon Vivien, whose illness seemed to sharpen their knives, Tynan referring to her dismissively as 'his stricken lady'. She was hard-working and self-critical, and had addressed herself to the study of variety, breadth of scale and colour in vocal tone under the guidance of none other than John Gielgud, with an occasional practical hint from me. Tynan described the result as 'dazzling monotony'; the judgement was blatantly prejudiced. The production, to my great relief, rewarded Johnnie G. with truckloads of laurels; my Malvolio was received with much controversy, as I knew it would be.

Macbeth was to be directed by Glen Byam Shaw; I was both pleased and challenged by the chance to have another bash at this impossible monster. I had just turned thirty the previous time I had tried it at the Vic. As the work fell round me like a cloak, one thing struck me: it is obvious that experience of acting is predominantly valuable, but experience of life too has special gifts to offer. I was now forty-eight, in the plenitude, as one kind writer said, of my powers. I don't think my memory flatters me if I hear in my mind – from critics, public and, above all in significance, from colleagues and loved and admired friends – the opinion summed up for me by Terry Rattigan: 'Yes, at last, the definitive Macbeth.'

I had at that time, most importantly of all, lungs like organ-bellows, vocal power and range that no infection could seemingly affect, and bodily expression balanced by a technique that could control all physical expressiveness from dead stillness to an almost acrobatic agility; my performances were apt to have, if anything, too much vitality. Romeo forgotten or forgiven, I was now described as a Shakespearian actor; whether I had won them round, which I liked to think, or whether I had unconsciously and imperceptibly adapted myself to be more in line with their requirements, which I did *not* like to think, who is to say? I had now a Shakespeare-trained intellect, and had come to terms with the verse-speaking problem by reaching the truth behind the text *through* the verse – never ignoring it, never singing it (natural speech is essential), but working in harmony with the inherent fabric, rhythm, beat, with full awareness of all the poetic values and nuances. ('Hates himself, doesn't he?' All right, I can hear you, reader dear.)

The lack of positive response to her Viola should have spelt out for us the tenor of the critics' attitude to Vivien for the whole season; but without optimism we would, most of us, never even have sought a second job. So we continued to sail into the wind. Tynan was, grudgingly, less dismissive of Vivien as Lady M. I told him long afterwards how old-fashioned I thought he was, knowing how that word would appall him, to imagine that only Mrs Siddons or her modern equivalent could possibly play Lady M. I also told him that he had been directly responsible for at least one of Vivien's nervous breakdowns. His attitude towards her as an artist, in combination with that of one or two others of his tribe, had made me extra watchful over her; she was managing to keep herself steady, but I could see what a strain it was. Soon after rehearsals started for *Titus*, the crash came.

I was already tired by the work that we were doing, and now with this thing upon me I could not imagine how I was going to be able to manage Titus, an enormous part that nobody knew anything about. The familiar trials and tribulations started up again – Vivien entertaining anybody and everybody far into the night, mostly younger members of the company who hadn't the *nous* to see that anything was strange and were just flattered to bits to be asked. As usual I felt responsible and never dared to leave. With luck the kids would be tired by three, or I would make no effort to conceal how tired I was, and, having got rid of them, I could persuade her to bed and put my head on the pillow with a sigh of relief – until I learnt to know the rhythm. At 5 a.m. sharp she would be up like a lark and busying herself all over, in or out of the house. I could never allow her to wander too far from my sight outside: in the front, fast cars would blind down at any hour of the day or night, and the River Avon ran through the bottom of the garden. With only two hours of sleep, how in God's name had I any hope of committing to memory the unfamiliar myriad of words in this huge part?

I felt a growing sense of desperation, more intense than anything I had yet known. Glen had engaged Peter Brook, no less, to direct this dangerous piece and was particularly anxious that it should come off with the brilliance that nobody believed was possible.

One afternoon I persuaded Vivien to let me drive her down to Coulsdon to see Dr Freudenberg; she was not too difficult to persuade, but she had a trick up her sleeve. When we had been ushered in to see the doctor in whom I had more faith than any other upon this earth, God help me if she didn't put on the most devastatingly convincing performance of a calm, sane, normal woman, not even aggrieved to have been brought all this way: poor Larry, he's over-anxious, that's all; it's easy to understand when you think of all the terrible dances I have led him, but, you see, I've never really been or felt better.

To my horror, I saw that she had hoodwinked even Freudenberg. He took me outside; my heart rose, but he said that he could not see that she was in need of electric shock treatment, and that in these circumstances such treatment could be highly dangerous. My hopes fell in shattered fragments. I couldn't do anything, I couldn't say anything. I was expecting a blasting storm of abuse all the way home but she kept up this silent calm, looking out at the views and even falling asleep. The only thing that I could think – and it was not a very enlivening thought – was that I might get as mad as she and be taken away and locked up. As for Vivien, she gave a really splendid party that night and I didn't even get my usual two hours. I was drained of everything and didn't know how I would manage to drag myself through any more of those rehearsals.

What happens in cases like this is an extraordinary act of mercy from the God of Artists; the work takes hold and takes over. I am fortunate in that, however unexciting or even distasteful a role may seem to me at first, with the first glimmer of invention or imagination I become lost in the magical wonder of being in its grip; one is barely conscious of the process by which one pours oneself into it and it into oneself. After the first reading I began to be aware of the rare possibilities and unusual effects that the role might offer.

Titus Andronicus is one of the very earliest of Shakespeare's plays and there is evidence that it was his first box-office smash hit. This is no doubt a sad reflection on the public taste prevalent in the Globe audiences at the time. But here it was: a Shakespearian problem in pure mathematics, and if ever there was a master-interpreter of its symbols his name would be Peter Brook, who had not only the genius for the job but also the generosity to make me a partner in his thinking. Vivien was in a fairly normal state but, not uncharacteristically, there was a slight feeling of irresponsibility about her, like a spoilt woman a bit bored with things. She seemed unable to enter into, let alone explore, the character or the problems of Lavinia; and as these were predominantly problems of the finding and the transmitting of reality, she just gave the impression that the part was beyond her; this was palpably absurd. I think Peter thought it best to leave well alone.

The rest of his production was masterly in the extreme and was duly hailed as such in the 'critiques', as the Edwardians used to call them. But for the first time I felt bound to agree with Tynan when he wrote of the scene in which Lavinia must be raped by the two appalling brothers on top of the body of her murdered husband, that Vivien expressed nothing more vivid than that 'she would have preferred Dunlopillo'. From now on for the next five years, it was as if she had just lost touch with her craft.

Notley is exactly halfway between London and Stratford. I managed to survive by sleeping every spare minute, either snatching nights at Notley (Peter Finch was in residence at Stratford, so I was safe from that quarter), or more frequently in my theatre dressing-room (rather like some old actor who can't pay his rent). I regulated my own time with care – so many hours of memorising, and so many of sleep. In Stratford life was more of a social whirl than I had ever known it, and somehow, despite its areas of quaking emptiness, life seemed dazzlingly full. Something drove me to what are frequently called acts of folly – a few, a very few escapades in matters of love. Apart from natural desire and sickness with my situation, I was also aware of an impulse of rebellion, due to what? *Amour propre*? A post-menopausal flare-up that had to make some statement and hear the last echo of itself?

A strange and unexpectedly beautiful thing was once said to me by a gardener in California. There was a bit of garden with the path up to our front door; on each side of this there were six orange trees in two rows of three. All were in splendid condition except for one little tree on the end at the right. It was a quarter the size of the others, all of which were in full leaf and full blossom and full fruit all at the same time, as is the habit of this wonderful citrus; this particular one, besides being stunted, had not a leaf on it. But it was covered in small oranges. I pointed this out to my gardener friend, and asked, 'Why?' He replied, 'Well, you see, it knows it's going to die; and it's making a last desperate attempt to reproduce itself.'

What a lexicon of menopausal excuses can find support in that limpid little pronouncement.

Before phrases like 'Women have been kind' should occur, let me say that these tender venturings into the blessed unction of sex were gifts to me – acts of purest kindness, with some love, warm understanding, and strongly laced, no doubt, with pity. They pursued their kindly, sporadic, unenvious courses through 1956 and 1957; their effect was first to give me a slight sense of displacement and then an equable detachment from the obstinate grasp of the single, if tattered, standard I held for Vivien, as I believed for ever.

CHAPTER TEN

The Prince and the Showgirl

The first word came to Cecil Tennant from Warners, I think, that Marilyn Monroe's company, run by Milton Green, her stills photographer, would be very interested in filming *The Sleeping Prince*, and that she would like me to produce and direct her in it. So Terry Rattigan, Cecil and I buzzed over to New York for the great meeting. We called on her in her apartment on Sutton Place for some jubilant conviviality.

There were two entirely unrelated sides to Marilyn. You would not be far out if you described her as a schizoid; the two people that she was could hardly have been more different. Her three visitors on this first meeting were a little the worse for wear by the time she vouchsafed her presence, as she had kept us waiting an hour, ably and liberally refreshing ourselves at the assiduous hands of Milton Green. Eventually I went boldly to her door and said, 'Marilyn, for the love of God come in to us, we're dying of anxiety!' She came in. She had us all on the floor at her feet in a second. I have no memory of a single word that was uttered, except that all was as convivial and jubilant as could be.

The evening wore on to its self-congratulatory close; everyone was making their departure when Marilyn, in the small voice she sometimes used to good effect, gently piped: 'Just a minute; shouldn't somebody say something about an agreement?' By George, the girl was right; we arranged for a purely business meeting in the morning, and I was then to take her to lunch at the '21' Club.

By the end of the day one thing was clear to me: I was

going to fall most shatteringly in love with Marilyn, and *what* was going to happen? There was no question about it, it was inescapable, or so I thought; she was so adorable, so witty, such incredible fun and more physically attractive than anyone I could have imagined, apart from herself on the screen. I went home like a lamb reprieved from the slaughter just for now, but next time . . . Wow! For the first time now it threatened to be 'poor Vivien'! (Almost twenty years ago it had been 'poor Jill'.)

Vivien had taken being passed over for the role she had created really very sweetly, considering that in telling her I had chosen to be clumsily truculent. After all, it *was* her part, even if she did know that she had not been wildly successful in it at the Phoenix, and that the dazzling heights of fame that Marilyn had achieved were unchallengeable; but that is something that is never easy to accept, and she behaved with attractive understanding and shrugged it all off beautifully. I was grateful and relieved to find no cause for anxiety in that direction.

The day of the great arrival dawned, and Marilyn was wafted onto this blessed plot in the illustrious charge of her new husband, Arthur Miller, a playwright both respected and popular; and so we were under starter's orders. I had arranged that we should have two weeks or so rehearsals before starting the cameras rolling, so that strangeness could wear off and we should all feel at home with each other. So many years at the job made it hard to believe that this might be impossible but, by God, it was.

We started off with two days of press conferences. I had said last thing the night before, being already disturbed, that her famous reputation for unpunctuality somewhat belied the strict professionalism that I seemed to discern in the technique supporting her dazzling spontaneity. It sent up a host of question marks about the as yet undiscovered complexities of her make-up. She had been pretty good at the huge press conference in New York, during which, making a gesture, her shoulder-strap had broken, and one and all took it to be a gag; now I said, 'Marilyn dear,' I said, 'please, pretty please, we cannot be late tomorrow, we *cannot*, they will take it very unkindly and half of them will be expecting it, so do me a favour and disappoint them, *please*.'

She promised, and was one whole hour late. I don't think I've ever known such embarrassment. I filled in as best I could, answering personal questions about my self. My attitude to the giving of interviews was well known, so they had me where they wanted me for once; but interest was petering out a bit by the time she showed up. For the first twenty minutes all the questions started 'Why are you late?' The way she handled this difficult situation was an object lesson in charm, and in no time at all she had got this vast ballroomful of people nestling cosily in the hollow of her hand. To give her a chance, I spontaneously declared that since many of the questions could not be heard by more than a few, I would take the liberty of repeating each question, thus making her answers more intelligible (and incidentally gaining for Marilyn a few more seconds to think out the answer).

She would always do exactly what was asked of her by any stills photographer. I marvelled at first at this show of discipline and thought it augured well; my reaction only a few weeks later would have been, 'Well of course – a model.' I think that wherever she gleaned that particular training it taught her more about acting than did Lee Strasberg; my opinion of his school is that it did more harm than good to his students and that his influence on the American theatre was harmfully misapplied. Deliberately anti-technical, his Method offered instead an all-consuming passion for reality, and if you did not feel attuned to exactly the right images that would make you believe that you were actually *it* and *it* was actually going on, you might as well forget about the scene altogether. Our young American actors felt an aching void where there should have been some training or grounding from which they could leap or fly. In the ten years since the war there had been very little repertory training; Stanislavsky, upon whose philosophy Strasberg's Actors' Studio was founded, was much in the mode in England at the time when we were in rep in the 1920s. It was a gift we could take advantage of but not be obsessed by.

I went along to Strasberg's Studio on two occasions early in 1958, when *The Entertainer* was on in New York. On each occasion his judgements lengthened into a homily which, absolutely off the cuff as it was, mounted into an outpouring of spontaneous wise saws, all unthought out and probably unexpressed before, and therefore dangerously unreliable as information; but he was off, mounting into the skies of his own sudden visions. He was the revivalist minister of pure naturalism. The phrase 'natural behaviourism' would have a different meaning dialectically and, to some of us, would lend that redeeming mite more technicality.

He was giving an unduly severe stream of criticism to one young man who seemed to me to have some sort of a natural gift, and at the end of the session I ventured to say as much; obviously only used to obsequious adulation, Strasberg waved me aside as an ignoramus, saying, 'Aw, naw-naw-naw, he has many problems.' More gently, I put it to him that removing any shred of confidence the boy might have wasn't likely to help many of them: 'Aw, naw-naw-naw.'

Only a very little time before the picture started was I told that Lee Strasberg's wife Paula 'always came along with Marilyn'. This alarmed me considerably as I had rarely found that coaches were helpful. Philosophically I clung to the thought, 'Oh, well, perhaps she may bring out the better of those two halves.' Marilyn was not used to rehearsing and obviously had no taste for it. She proclaimed this by her appearance – hair pulled back under a scarf, bad skin with no make-up, very dark glasses and an overly subdued manner, which I failed dismally to find the means to enliven. I just prayed that that miracle between the lens and the celluloid would happen for me, as I knew very well it must have done for half a dozen of my colleagues on the West Coast. I managed to contact two of them, Billy Wilder (who incidentally once said it had been like working with

Hitler) and Josh Logan; they commiserated with me cheerfully (their labours over) and said yes, it was hell, but that I would be getting a pleasant surprise when it was all over. When Paula arrived, I called off rehearsals for two days in order to go over and over the part, teaching *her* the way of it, so that she could then teach Marilyn. Pride was a luxury I coudn't afford. Paula seemed willing to co-operate with every scrap of timing and whatever inflections or stress she thought Marilyn could cope with, 'and make her feel it was her idea, you know what I mean?'

The truth came to light with uncanny speed: Paula knew nothing, she was no actress, no director, no teacher, no adviser – except in Marilyn's eyes, for she had one talent: she could butter Marilyn up. On one car journey I heard Paula play an innings in this, her special ploy, which pinned my ears back as I sat in the front with the two of them in the back. 'My dear, you really must recognise your own potential, you haven't even yet any idea of the importance of your position in the world, you are the greatest sex symbol in human memory, everybody knows and recognises that and you should too, it's a duty which you owe to yourself and to the world, it's ungrateful not to accept it. You are the greatest woman of your time, the greatest human being of your time; of any time, you name it; you can't think of anybody, I mean – no, not even Jesus – except you're more popular.' Incredible as that must seem, it is no exaggeration; and it went on in unremitting supply for a good hour, with Marilyn swallowing every word.

This was Paula's unique gift to the art of acting, or rather the artful success of Marilyn's career, out of which the Strasbergs stood to make much capital. This was what, I realised in growing alarm, I was stuck with.

Nevertheless, I refused to treat Marilyn as a special case – I had too much pride in my trade – and would at all times treat her as a grown-up artist of merit, which in a sense she was. Her manner to me got steadily ruder and more insolent; whenever I patiently laboured to make her understand an indication for some reading, business or timing she would listen with ill-disguised impatience, and when I had finished would turn to Paula and petulantly demand, 'Wasseee mean?' A very short way into the filming, my humiliation had reached depths I would not have believed possible.

There was one relief from it; during the coronation sequence there was no dialogue except what was laid on to the effects soundtrack later; and so there was no need to go into long explanations before each take, and I could risk side-of-camera directions; to my intense relief she accepted these like a lamb. 'Do a little curtsey as the King passes, watch for when Dickie Wattis bows by your side, I'll say when to rise; now try to look up to your right where the altar is; now look back questioningly at Dickie; he'll hand you an open prayer-book for you to follow; now look up and try to find the Regent towards the altar, find him, but of course he won't look at you, so, a wee bit disappointed, follow in the prayer-book a little while, feel moved by the music' – I had a massive selection of records, but she would have nothing but the Londonderry Air, which had perforce to go on for the whole day; the poor unit nearly went round the bend with it – 'Now, catch sight of that stained glass window, it's the most beautiful picture you can imagine; let some tears well into your eyes, Marilyn . . . .'

As if by magic, submissive and scrupulously obedient, she followed every instruction exactly and at once and, what is most important, quite perfectly. I had cause to reflect once more, this time with gratitude, 'Of course, she's a model.'

I had run a closed set, admitting no one who was not actually involved in the work, nobody that was even related to anyone of the press, sad to say thereby making enemies of many whom I had thought of as my friends in that profession. But the press of the entire world was screaming and tearing to get in; the set would have been a shambles. Besides these practical reasons, I had some more theoretical convictions of my own.

I had taken note of the fact that a few weeks after her wedding to Prince Rainier, Princess Grace (Kelly) was presented in a film production of Molnar's *The Swan*.

There seemed to be no reason in the world why this should not have been a prodigious box-office success – unless one takes into consideration the fact that for months before her wedding the wealth of romance that surrounded this event ensured that her picture, together with some story or anecdote, would appear in almost every newspaper that could be bought. I believe the public was surfeited with the sight of her name in print, even with her beautiful features and, I am afraid, with her story, in fact anything that could be associated with her for some little time to come.

This taught me to be wary about Marilyn's promotion. If success has a limit then so has the publicity which, it is claimed, brings it about. This thought prompted me to soft-pedal. But in spite of the most elaborate precautions there were leaks galore, all to do with the unhappy atmosphere on the set, with wildly exaggerated tales of screaming rows – *faute de mieux* our journalists did not lack for invention.

In the last shooting days, I was allowed one petty triumph in the Prince's first saunter down the chorus line backstage. It was fixed that her shoulder-strap should break as she made her first curtsey, to echo our first big press call in New York. It was fine, but Marilyn took it into her head that her breast had showed itself. 'Nooooh, Marilyn,' I said, 'Nooooh,' and called in the boys on the rails as witnesses. The message came back, 'They say they weren't looking at Miss Monroe, they were watching Sir Laurence.' Knowing the intensity of their appraising curiosity for the first few days of the work, this complete lack of interest was an object lesson in something or other.

The last word on Marilyn belongs to Irina Baronova, Cecil's wife, who had been watching quietly with her Russian intuitiveness from the darkness off the set:

She has a quite unconscious but basic resistance to acting. She loves to show herself, loves to be a star, loves all the success side of it. But to be an actress is something she does not want at all. They were wrong to try to make one of her. Her wit, her adorable charm, her sex appeal, her bewitching personality – are all part of *her*, not necessarily to be associated with any art or talent.

After the script had all been shot, I had feelings of vague disquiet. As a producer I was entirely satisfied with the picture, which was to be called *The Prince and the Showgirl*; as an actor, shamelessly unashamed of myself; but as a director, I wished I had got better stuff out of Marilyn. Other directors had, and it lay uneasily on my conscience that I had not. I began to admit to myself that I had not achieved greater perfection because I had shirked the probability of more rows. I asked Marilyn to see the picture run and to bring her husband, Arthur Miller, with her, after which would they please come and talk to me? They agreed and I talked to them sincerely and frankly. If she and Arthur found that they were entirely satisfied, then, God knew, I would be only too happy to leave it at that. They both agreed there was room for improvement, but what could be done now it was over? I told them that if Marilyn would undertake to contribute to a better atmosphere between us, discipline herself to absolute punctuality, accept my word when I passed something as okay and not insist on take after take more than was necessary, I would be willing to re-shoot certain scenes. I would guarantee to get the work done in two days, but in no circumstances would I undertake more to help Marilyn. For once I had the other side by the short and curlies, and they knew they had to agree.

The first morning made my heart sink, a sensation I was getting profoundly sick of; we had spent the whole time trying to inject a scintillating spirit into the scene of our first meeting. I had never dreamed up such a variety of expressions, examples, illustrations, images to help inspire the essential wit and sparkle needed to make a lively start to a picture from which a great deal would be expected. Marilyn made her inevitable way towards Paula, who said, 'Honey, just think of Coca Cola and Frankie Sinatra!' I suppose that might have been the Actors' Studio approach. God! Don't tell me they would have been right and I wrong throughout this whole thing? Needless to say, it worked; enough to make a man cut his throat, enough for this man, anyway.

The day of the great farewell dawned. It had been agreed that whatever our personal feelings might be, a great act must be put on at the airport; our own crews were careful to take the right pictures of the right-looking embraces which assumed the right intensity of passion for any two great lovers of history: Marilyn and me kissing, Vivien and Arthur kissing, Vivien and Marilyn kissing, me and Arthur kissing – it deceived no one. An absurd show, the press called it, who did we think we were kidding? *L'envoi*.

Going home, I thought of all the excitement when the first news of the approaching partnership broke; how Josh Logan had declared it 'the most exciting combination since black and white'. I thought incredulously of our first meeting, and how I had feared falling in love with her. Some weeks later I had to go across the water to show the film to Jack Warner.

Milton Green grabbed hold of me and said, 'Howbout a stills session tomorrow, huh?'

'By myself?'

'Oh no, with Marilyn of course.'

'*Oh no*, Milton, *no, no, no,* you'll not get me with that dame again!'

'Oh, hell, she won't be that way t'morrow, you'll see. You won't recognise her, she'll be marvellous like she used to be. Besides, we want the picture t'make money, don' we? We've had no promotion at all.'

It was as he said; he provided delicious caviar sandwiches, drinks of all kinds, the lushest music. He knew how to lay it on; after all, he'd managed to persuade Marilyn to sign up with him and form their own company – strictly business: his own wife was extremely attractive and intelligent.

Two years or so ago a couple of my Hollywood friends, as a sort of joke after a dinner-party, ran this twenty-five-year-old picture for me on their library projection machine. I was a bit embarrassed as I didn't know how long it might be before the joke would begin to get a bit tired; however, the picture ran through, much to my surprise. At the finish everyone was clamorous in their praises; how such enchantment could have been poorly received defied imagination; I was as good as could be, and Marilyn! Marilyn was quite wonderful, the best of all. So.

What do you know?

PART THREE

CHAPTER ELEVEN

Sea Change

Up to now I had not really known whose side I was on about the National Theatre; I had been serving on something called the Building Committee, which was composed of an ill-assorted *mélange* of ancient managers, one or two actors, Johnnie Gielgud and me. Hardly any meetings were called. I recall being struck by one element that amazed me: there was no director and no theatre designer on this panel. There were supporters for two or three already existing possible buildings: in favour of which I had already spoken in 1937/8 at the Old Vic, from its stage, chiefly I think in order to bring a smile of approval to Lilian Baylis's sad, half-paralysed old lips; Stratford, already a shrine, only occasionally seen for short seasons in London and with only two seasons in its home-quarters; and then – but did I believe that institutional theatres were really a good thing anyway? They were reputed to develop an unimaginative, uncreative, sepulchral sort of an atmosphere. There had been constant resurgences of enthusiasm for more than a hundred years which had died off for lack of support.

In 1956, I had been invited by the noble Lords Esher and Chandos (Oliver Lyttelton), to join them as a trustee. As it was frankly explained to me by Lionel Esher, they felt that they lacked glamour: 'You're to be our picture postcard.' Well, I was flattered, and it would certainly help me to determine my own feelings about the whole rather important question. Up to this time the idea of the National Theatre had enjoyed little more significance than that of a good cause.

As the most efficient and experienced candidate in the

running, Kenneth Rae, whose life had been devoted to the more splendid theatrical causes, was the obvious choice for the job of secretary. These three were now joined by me. Esher seldom attended meetings. He was a very active member of the House of Lords, besides being an eminent lawyer. He had created the Esher Standard Contract, which was the most popular one used between managers and actors, so his theatrical interest were self-evident.

The Royal Court Theatre opened that year (1956) under the enlightened management of George Devine, whom I had held in close affection for more than twenty years. I dutifully went to see *Look Back in Anger* and, I blush to confess, felt disappointed in it; somehow my disappointment made me disappointed in myself, so when Arthur Miller expressed an interest I was glad to take him to it with Marilyn. After the first act, Arthur turned to me and said, 'God, Larry, you're wrong, this is great stuff'; by this time I had begun to see that it was and was beginning to kick myself for my lack of perception.

I was starting to script the film of *Macbeth* and took Tarquin, my son by my first marriage, up to Scotland with me to prospect for locations for a couple of weeks. I felt it was time I made a real effort to form some proper relationship with him. He was at Oxford now and doing me proud as an oarsman; that spring he had stroked Christ Church in the Torpids and three nights out of the four had bumped the three top boats, St Peter's Hall, Merton and Magdalen, gaining the Head of the River. But apart from showing us our differences, our holiday can't be said to have succeeded in drawing us very much together. We were an embarrassment to each other – I to him because I had upped and gallantly left his mother with him when he was only ten months old, he to me because of the unquenchable guilt that would not leave me, even after twenty years. Only in the last few years have we found untroubled contentment in each other's company and real enthusiasm for it.

Soon after, I went round to see John Osborne to congratulate him on his remarkable character performance in *Cards of Identity*; at the same time I congratulated him on

Look Back and boldly asked him if he might ever think of writing a play with me in mind. The humility with which he took this suggestion surprised me; he kept asking me if I really meant it. I was feeling frustrated by the boredom of my own career, and my personal life was a tiresome tease to me.

Meantime I went to see *The Country Wife* and was entranced by the Margery Pinchwife of Miss Joan Plowright, whose very name was enough to make me think thoughts of love. Vivien and I went round to see George, who sent for the 'young people' to meet us in his room. I had eyes for no one but Joan, whose smile at this first meeting had more than a hint of mockery about it; I divined that I stood for everything that the young generation at the Royal Court would find most objectionable, and everything that was most odious to a girl of this generation of actors who had come from North Lincs. I was titled, necessarily self-satisfied, pompous, patronising, having obviously come to visit in a spirit of condescension – I could see it all. It preyed on my mind and, thinking I suppose along the lines of 'if you can't beat 'em, join 'em', I got on to George and asked him if he really thought that that young man John Osborne might be serious about a play for me. I was off on one of my running-away escapades to New York again, ostensibly to see some show for possible presentation, and George said he would airmail any bits of typescript to my hotel. In an amazingly short time the first act of *The Entertainer* arrived; the minute I had read it I phoned George and said I would accept the part on the first act alone.

The reason for this haste was not exactly pure; more and more my impulses were to create a condition of detachment from my marriage, and a sharp change in the direction in my career might help to form such a wedge. I rushed through the music and the dubbing for *The Prince*, talking to George, John Osborne and Tony Richardson, who was to direct *The Entertainer*, as often as possible. By mid-March John Osborne was taking me to all the few remaining music-halls to study form, often with Tony and John

Addison, our composer. I was being taught a tap-dance by an expert, Honor Blair; we rehearsed through the last half of March and opened at the Royal Court on 10 April, playing to capacity for four and a half little weeks.

I had an understanding with Glen Byam Shaw that I would undertake a European tour of *Titus Andronicus* through May and June 1957; *Titus* joined festivals in Paris, Venice and Vienna (Burgtheater), Belgrade, Zagreb and up to Warsaw. It was the first tour to play behind the Iron Curtain. As in the 1955 Stratford season, this play seemed to have the worst possible effect upon Vivien. Her dreaded illness always seemed to add mercilessly to my troubles just when my work was at its most exhausting. From time to time during this anxious period of our lives, I would put a last desperate arrow into my bow and, as at the end of Lady Chatterley, try 'fucking' our love back into existence; it was successful. My prowess, so often failing from nervous prematurity of ejaculation, had gained, through the practice given to me by my gently, kindly, patiently bestowed few love affairs, a calmly confident strength; these last-throw ventures worked as they had not done since our radiant passion had been extinguished as by a candle-snuffer in 1949. It was successful up to a point, but not to the extent that I was hoping for. Had I not been made so aware by her bodily reactions that it was not all self-deception on my part, I would have suspected it. She would avoid any sustained pursuit, shying away like a young pony, and absenting herself in the company of some other person or persons; it made me think of early silent movie coquetry. I was almost happier spending an evening in the company of Tony Quayle and a couple of other friendly spirits. I have often fallen gratefully into the warming change of male company, and never more so than at this time.

Just in case I should not have enough to do, I was presenting the Elizabethan Company from Australia in *Summer of the Seventeenth Doll* at the New Theatre and later Lesley Storm's *Roar Like a Dove* at the Phoenix, both of which, thank God, were wonderful successes. In Paris on 22 May, Monsieur Julian, the owner of the Théâtre Sarah

Bernhardt, brought a huge birthday cake on to the stage
with fifty candles burning upon it. My lungs were in good
shape and out they all went in one breath; I think that
fetched more applause from the French than the performance. On to Venice, Vienna, Belgrade; the only way we
could manage more than two shows in Zagreb was to give
one at 3 p.m., one at 8 p.m. on Saturday and one at noon on
the Sunday; and then off to Warsaw, getting back in time
for the opening of *The Prince and the Showgirl* at the
Warner to which Noël Coward accompanied me and, thank
God, loved it.

For the past few weeks the St James's Theatre had been
threatened with closure. The roof had been shifted by the
bombing in the 1940s; it was an old theatre, built in 1820,
and a fire hazard. It could not be licensed by the London
County Council any longer unless £250,000 were spent to
make it safe; as its capacity was barely 800 there was
no hope of finding an investor who was that charitably
inclined.

Vivien decided to make the saving of it the great mission
of her life, and fired the council of Equity into organising a
mammoth march, starting at the theatre and proceeding to
the large space at the back of St Martin-in-the-Fields,
where gallant speeches were made. I, of course, knew that
the efforts were quite futile, and Equity did too. But I
seemed to be stuck with going along with the ludicrous
farce; I was in a helpless situation, neither able to have an
open confrontation with Vivien on such an issue, nor to
look unwilling to march to save my own theatre. I just had
to allow myself to be swung along with the tide.

My constant pusillanimity was dictated by my fear of
aggravating her illness. She fought vigorously against any
plan for public separation – what was the matter with the
way we were? Well, nothing really, and no, I didn't want to
live with anybody else; I had to take great care not to stir up
an hysterical condition which could switch so easily into
mania. Meanwhile the seed had been sown.

We had moved out of Durham Cottage when we went to
Stratford, for no better reason that that we were a little

tired of it, so now we took the Waltons' house in Lowndes Place for two years. Very soon I found myself wishing increasingly strongly to form a union with someone to whom I had been growingly attracted for a few months. One day Vivien asked me suddenly if I was in love with this girl; I admitted that I was. She was sympathetic about it, to my intense relief. 'How marvellous for you,' I remember her saying, 'and how marvellous for her.'

I thought perhaps I had got away with it without serious results; but in a lightning two or three days she had taken off again into a sky-high phase of scaring proportions. It fed itself, as had the fit at Stratford, by the determination to allow me no sleep. One night, almost against my will, I drifted off; seeing this, in her manic state she slipped out of bed, fetched a wet face-cloth and started to slash me across the eyes with it. Enraged as I was and as she intended me to be, I got out of the bed and went quickly down the passage into the study-bedroom that William used for his music, and just in time managed to shut and lock the door. She immediately started hammering on it; she was obviously prepared to keep it up all night.

Something snapped in my brain – I know I must have read that phrase, but it'll do fine. I remember what followed exactly, but if I had to answer for it I would not be able to tell a judge what my intentions were. I threw open the door, grabbed her wrist, pulled her along the passage, pushed open her door and with all my strength – it must be true that in all-possessing rage it is doubled – hurled her halfway across the room to the bed. Before hitting the bed she struck the outside corner of her left eyebrow on the corner of her marble bedside table-top, opening up a wound half an inch from her temple and half an inch from her eye. I realised with horror that each of us was quite capable of murdering or causing death to the other. I must get out and quickly. I had already taken a furnished room in a mews across the road as an escape-hatch. I went to see Vivien quite early next morning to see how things were and found Mary Mills already there dressing her wound. She looked up at me with horrified reproach.

After six years of contending with the anguishes of this disease, my whole nature was in revolt against further voluntary torture. By degrees, calculated so as not to exacerbate her condition, the break must be made. At least her animal inclinations were finding their own ways of sorting themselves out.

What a life-saving relief is concentrated work. My new love was naturally and sensibly coming to the conclusion that the fruition of her love for me was altogether too mixed a blessing. Her mother wrote a letter which I had to see was really very sweet; beyond the normal hen-clucking over her chick, she was asking me to think fairly and clearly of the sort of life I was expecting her daughter to share with me. I wrote to her and in honesty had to thank her for making clear to me the extent to which I had allowed myself to indulge my selfishly shallow way of thinking. We parted and remain on the friendliest terms.

It was obvious from the success at the Court that the potential of *The Entertainer* had hardly been scratched; George Devine and I took the Palace from Emile Littler for an eight-week season. I lacked the necessary confidence to engage it for longer, but after three weeks or so I asked Emile if we could extend it; he undertook, if we went on the road for four weeks, to let me have the Palace again for seven more after that. I was more than happy to fall in with this arrangement and we played Glasgow, Edinburgh, Oxford and the Brighton Hippodrome, scene of my first music-hall sketch with Ruby Miller in 1925.

There was a feeling of full-circle about this which grew rapidly more intense when Joan Plowright, now playing daughter Jean, and I fell in love. It was in the last three days of the tour and, owing to a previous engagement to play *The Chairs* and *The Lesson* by Ionesco at the Phoenix in New York, Joan had to leave us. So our union began with proper regard for theatre discipline – after three euphoric days in Brighton, which doubtless influenced our choice of domicile when we were to return home with our eldest on the way in mid-1961. Joan went to New York and I was to continue *The Entertainer* at the Palace with Geraldine McEwan taking her place as Jean. It was 1958, and in February Vivien started to rehearse *Pour Lucrèce* by Jean Giraudoux, Christopher Fry's version of which was called *Duel of Angels*. It was an excellent, strong piece and Vivien made a glittering success in it. She had now become an actress of the first rank, richly developed in all the strengths – bearing, composure, vocal power, technique and magnetism. Her Paola was to cement her unique position on both sides of the Atlantic. Meantime *The Entertainer*, Joan having rejoined it, opened in Boston at the Shubert for ten days and then in New York at the Royale, originally for an eight-week season though we extended for another four weeks – not so much to rake in the shekels as because I couldn't bear to say farewell to the part I loved doing so much. Meanwhile, after a six-week try-out, Vivien opened very splendidly at the Apollo in London.

On these terms, a life of sorts might have seemed possible and even tolerable for one who had struck fifty, and who might in all decency have devoted his remaining years to a partner, burying selfish thinking. But as will have been gathered by now, selfishness is almost like a gift with me. There is a fund of friendly argument always pouring into the fancied artistic ear – that sophisticated wisdom put into John Tanner's mouth by Shaw in the first act of *Man and Superman*: artists must be selfish, it is in fact their duty; ambition was not given to a man for nothing, it can be of service to mankind. All the advice of friends, particularly if it is convincingly realistic, serves to reassure the selfish. Cynicism is also marvellously helpful stuff.

My diaries bear evidence of determined encroachments on my resolve; Vivien departs, Vivien back; Peter away, Peter back (this was evidence of another encroachment from another quarter). One or two other more casual affairs came into and vanished from her life. After the Stratford nightmare was over at the end of 1955 Vivien came gently down from the manic phase; and depressions seemed not to exist now. Lilli (Palmer), one of my two great European women friends, the beauty and purity of whose friendship has never been marred by romantic intrusion, asked why in God's name I had never given Vivien a child; that would surely be the natural answer to our problems, and would transform her life and remake her as a person. Everything suddenly made sense; I talked to the doctors about it and they did not seem discouraging.

When spring was flowing into summer and her pregnancy was reaching its third month, that wounding miscarriage came about. Our doctor prescribed that another child must be started at once, as soon as was admissible after the necessary curettage. Vivien had given every sign of being thrilled by the approach of motherhood, part of Notley was in full-scale replanning for the happy future, and yet, and yet; for some reason I couldn't make out, Vivien was quietly but firmly resistant to the idea of trying again, and I knew somehow that it would never happen now. Perhaps it was all for the best.

So for Christmas 1956 we had decided to go to the south of Spain, our dearly loved friends Ginette and 'Polly' Seidmann coming with us. The two of us were embarrassingly quarrelsome most of the time, and the poor Seidmanns had a miserable holiday.

By the end of a four-week tour with *The Entertainer* (in the middle of the Palace run) I was finding that in Joan 'here every flower was united'. My relationship with her brought a new kind of headiness in its rapture – nothing exotic, rather a strangely natural kinship, and more powerful than anything that I could remember. We could foresee nothing; we had no notion of what might or could happen. She understood enough of my situation to recognise that we were both helpless.

I got hold of George Devine, who showed at once the depth of his love for both of us; he also understood the intensity of our difficulties, knowing very well that Vivien was 'hysterical' as he called it. He had a rented room, furnished, in Walpole Street for which he would let us have a key.

* * *

To business matters now for which in *my* book, from long years of habit, private matters, no matter how precious, must always give way. My great ambition to make my fourth Shakespeare film was still uppermost. I was not used to promoting my own films and missed Alex Korda sadly in every way since his death in 1956. I made arrangements to see two of the Rothschilds in the beginning of June; I had sounded out the clothing trade when in New York. Not too despondent when none of these responded favourably, I got to know of other sources of backing. I was only asking for £400,000 – a fifth less than any of my other three Shakespeares. I could get the 'front' money; Sam Spiegel was offering me £260,000 for this, but nobody was tempted by the idea of putting forward the vital 'end money'. Rank, the first man I tried, since the three others had all made money for him, refused on the grounds that the bank rate had gone up to seven per cent. Sounds funny now, but it didn't then.

The more immediate business for me, however, was the prior commitment to play General Burgoyne, with Burt Lancaster and Kirk Douglas, in the film of *The Devil's Disciple*. Wonderful part though it is, I came up against a severe personal difficulty. The heart-wrenchings, the guilt, the longing, the romantic joy and the tortured conscience of the past few months had taken a toll on me, which not only cowed my spirit but impaired my efficiency. I just couldn't seem to handle the normal problems of acting any more. I was irritatingly not 'with it'. I gave way to the unattractive habit of getting everyone's names mixed up; the least fortunate of these mistakes was always with Burt – the *boss*, for God's sake! Every time I addressed him as Kirk, he would look at me straight and steely steady and say quietly, 'Burt.' I could only stammer that I was afraid I must be having a nervous breakdown. I have thought ever since that my excuse must have been very close to the truth.

I was awful in the part, as dull as ditchwater, you wouldn't think anyone could be with that pearl among parts. After three or four weeks Hecht sent for me; he

Plays and Players

With James Dale in *The Green Bay Tree*, a brilliant first play by Mordaunt Shairp, as successful in London as here in New York, 1933–4.

The famous breakfast scene in *Private Lives* with Adrianne Allen, Noël and Gertie. Me struggling with 'The man with the clob foot'.

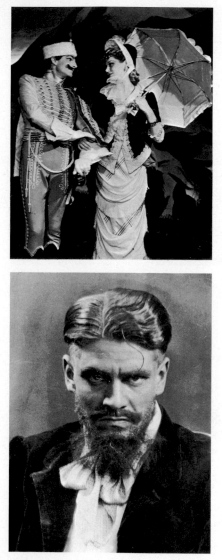

Sergius with Margaret Leigh in *Arms and the Man*, 1944.

Uncle Vanya in 1927.

ov in *Uncle Vanya*
Margaret Leighton
Ralph Richardson,

ov again at
hester, 1962.

Oedipus Rex.

The Critic.

...ith Vivien in 1948: *The
...hool for Scandal* (*right*) and
...e Skin of Our Teeth*.

Chorus in *Antigone*, the first Anouilh play produced in London, 1949.

With Daphne Newton, Vivien and Martita Hunt in *The Sleeping Princ*
1953.

With Brenda de Banzie and Joan Osborne's *The Entertainer*, which we played in 1957 and filmed in 1959.

Archie Rice.

With Alan Webb in Ionesco's
Rhinoceros, 1960.

Henry II in Anouilh's *Becket* with
Arthur Kennedy in the title role,
1962.

Halvard Solness in *The Master
Builder*, 1964. The beginning of th
terrors.

Family and Friends

The beginning and end of my war: Lieutenant (A) RNVR, 1942 (*left*), and with Ralph on an ENSA tour in 1945.

Knighted with Malcolm Sargent
(the King had been warned about
my Hamlet hair).

With William Walton at Notley,
1953.

With Marilyn and Terry Rattigan, 1956.

Night of a Hundred Stars at the London Palladium: (*above*) rehearsing 'I guess I'll have to change my plan' with Jack Buchanan – Jack worked with me twenty hours for the two-minute number; (*above right*) 'Three Juvenile Delinquents' with Johnnie Mills and Danny Kaye; (*right*) zipping up Kenneth More.

The day of the last wedding ever.

Father fetching kids from school.

Joan enveloped by Richard, Tamsin and Julie-Kate, 1967.

really was a thoroughly nice little man, and gave me an instruction which set me off into uncontrollably hysterical giggles. 'Larry,' he said, 'we want you to put more Mr Puff into your General Burgoyne.' I can't remember having such a miserable time in a job ever. I never heard one word about how the film was eventually received around the world. Somehow I never enquired.

I undertook my first English television play, *John Gabriel Borkman*, and had that to work on, still staying odd nights with friends. A car belonging to one of us had been left in Florence, so I emptily decided to go down to fetch it, taking a strange route, via Ischia – to see the Waltons, who, I found, were away. A neighbour, a great friend of theirs whom I knew quite well, called out from an upstairs window and offered to put me up. Lydia Cassati was an extremely kind, respected and respectable lady with whom there was no question of a romantic adventure. My interests were entirely preoccupied in the heart, soul and lap of one I was proud to call 'my Joan'. After three days' rest at Lydia's, I went on to Florence where I picked up the abandoned car, and so northwards via Portofino up through my adored France, stopping for a meal in Orange so delicious that it caused me to weep.

From Paris, staying with the Seidmanns in Avenue Marceau, I sat down and wrote a letter to Vivien that I hoped would make the situation clear and straighten out our futures – without avail. I had supper with her on her birthday, 5 November – the last of the sentimental occasions. I was able to talk calmly to her, lying that there was no question of anyone else in my life, I just knew that our relationship must come to an end. I said we should take advantage of the six months' separation that was forced on us by my approaching departure to Hollywood for *Spartacus* with Kirk Douglas to learn to accept the situation.

I was staying much with friends – two nights here, four nights there. I sound like the most grasping scrounger that ever was, and only hope that it didn't seem to be as bad as that to the friends concerned. Soon I was to rent a sitting-room, bedroom and bathroom from Roger Furse for a couple of years. On the run again, I was off to New York for a television version of *The Moon and Sixpence*, Maugham's masterpiece. I had gone to the Lunts for dinner the first evening, but on the second I was on my way back home, for my dearest brother Dickie had died of leukaemia, less than five months after the diagnosis.

He had told me that he wished to be buried at sea; the remarkable Peter Hiley, my great fixer of fixers, made a lightning arrangement with the Royal Navy, who provided a small mine-layer, HMS *Sheraton*, to carry his body out to sea and slide it down into the waters between Fishbourne Abbey and Stokes Bay. The young two-striper lieutenant RN captain managed the little ceremony with impressive dignity and thoughtfully gave me the chart which he had marked exactly for me. My sister Sybille, Dickie's widow Hester, Vivien and I returned to Notley for the night. To avoid awkwardness, I left the three girls at the house and went to sleep in Dickie and Hester's cottage, Notley Mead, so named by George Devine.

Next morning I drove to London to face a busy afternoon, and met Joanie in the evening. We knew there was little likelihood of our seeing each other again for about six months, and sharing a perfect trust we were not afraid of that; but it is a long Lent that lasts till Whitsun. Vivien phoned me late that night from a party and, through sobs which rather confused the issue, said she had fallen in love – and gave me his name, Jack Merivale. Jack had joined our Romeo company in 1941 and had come over with the Canadians for the war. I could only think, well, time will tell.

I was back at the Algonquin and in the welcoming arms of David Susskind, my producer, and his admirably skilful director, Bob Mulligan, to whom I took a great liking. The script of *The Moon and Sixpence* was excellent and the part offered glorious opportunities, so at least I was going to be happy in my work. Starting on 6 December, we were shooting on the twentieth. I had never known such wildly long hours: Saturday, Sunday, all day and all Monday night until 7 a.m.

I went on to Los Angeles for *Spartacus*; but it was actually eight weeks before I found myself dressed, made-up with applied classical-shaped nose, coiffeured and ready to portray the part of Marcus Crassus, which, God knows, I'd had time enough to learn. It was a good job that Joan and I had made up our minds to a long parting of our ways, for Joanie was busy with *Hook, Line and Sinker* with Robert Morley. There was nothing for me but to wait to be called and enjoy the rich company of my Hollywood friendships.

It was pleasant to be with Peter Ustinov, Charles Laughton and my darling Jeannie Simmons again, and considering the weighty subject the work on *Spartacus* went by pleasantly enough under the direction of Stanley Kubrick, hitherto little known. Luckily I was sharing a house with Roger and Inez Furse: Roger was doing the costumes for the film.

In the five months of enforced romantic starvation separated by the six thousand miles between Hollywood and London in 1959, Joan and I could only communicate by letter, which indeed we did daily. Telephone calls, for every reason at this time, had to be rare treats.

Our letters were frank and unsparing in their recognition of the dangerous implications of Vivien's situation. This at all times threatened some much dreaded and possibly violent tragedy. But there was no possibility of stifling the hopes that insistently sang in our hearts – the knowledge of what, with patience, a more joyful future must surely bring to both of us.

I finished *Spartacus* on 4 June. A few days later I was in Stratford, rehearsing *Coriolanus*, which opened on 7 July with Edith Evans as Volunia, Harry Andrews as Menenius, Anthony Nicholls as Tullus Aufidius, Albert Finney as First Citizen, Mary Ure as Virgilia and Vanessa Redgrave as Valeria; we were directed by Peter Hall. In late September we started the film of *The Entertainer* at Morecambe Bay, so I was dodging between there and Stratford for a couple of months.

There is a comforting theory that if a knee or an ankle-joint is warmed up with exercise you are in far less danger of a sprain. I had been doing a whole day of Archie Rice tap-dancing for Tony Richardson's cameras, and at seven o'clock we were through and I was tired out, when Tony asked if I could bear to do one more take. I sighed and said okay and went right into it; I was feeling glad we were doing it once more, as it was going great guns, when – snap went my old cartilage. It hadn't happened for ten years, and, God knows, my knee was warmed up; there was no accounting for it.

It turned out to be a great nuisance. The next day I was to do two shows of *Coriolanus*, but I had to be confined to bed; so a promising baby of an understudy named Albert Finney went on for me. I met Alby in the wings when I was back and congratulated him on the lovely things I'd heard about his performance, to which he replied: 'Well, after all, it's much less tiring than the First Citizen.' I bade fond farewells to both Coriolanus and Archie Rice at the end of November.

Joanie and I decided to take a complete break, and George Devine asked Michel St Denis for advice on where he thought Larry '*et un tel*' might find peace and quiet somewhere in France. Michel knew perfectly well who was meant, but we had all of us learnt through many testing years to be mighty cagey on the phone, and so 'Aaah, Larry *et un tel*?' said our old friend (Joan had been an ace student at the Old Vic Theatre School which we the directors had thought up in the early days of the Old Vic's resurrection in 1945; it was run by a threesome, Michel St Denis, George Devine and Glen Byam Shaw), and advised us to go to a darling little place called Les Bouleaux (The Birches) in a small village called Seine Port, not far from Paris. We could walk at peace along the river; Joanie was learning to drive and had plenty of practice through the forest of Fontaine-bleau; I had long learnt to hire a car with French number-plates, thereby attracting no kind of attention. And so back into the loving arms of the Seidmanns in Paris and then overnight home.

CHAPTER TWELVE

The Start of the Sixties

By the end of March 1960, Joanie and I were rehearsing together for Ionesco's *Rhinoceros* for the Royal Court, to open on 28 April. One Monday morning there was a grievous wrench in the death of George Relph; he and Mercia had been such devotedly close friends for so many years that it was hard to grasp. We had a flat in Eaton Square where I was living while Vivien was in New York, and I insisted that Mercia come and share it to find relief from the relentless reminders of her loss.

In mid-May there was a National Theatre meeting with Chandos, and two days later another with the proposed architect, so things were beginning to get lively. From across the Atlantic came a flash that was altogether too lively; Vivien had told a press reporter that I was in love with Joan Plowright and that she was intending to give me a divorce so that we could get married. At that time divorce procedure was very different from what it is today; what Vivien had done could have been regarded as collusion, which meant that no divorce would be allowed. Nicholas Hannen and Athene Seyler told me that that action on the part of one of their partners had prevented them from getting married for more than thirty years. Jack Merivale, who was with Vivien in New York, asked her what made her do it, and she declared she couldn't remember saying it.

The effect on the world press was like an explosion; the whole of the road outside my flat was crammed with photographers and reporters. It was quite scarifying to look out of my front window. I did the only possible thing; I sent down an extremely polite note by my secretary, to be read aloud. I said in it that I would make no statement whatsoever and begged them to believe it, as I could not bear them to wait all day and spoil their weekend. I had no reason to leave the building as there was no performance, it being Sunday. The scene outside the house was on television that night and the cameras all zoomed in upon my letter, read by a voice-over. I was jostled and shrilly questioned coming out of my stage-door for a few nights, and sometimes a sturdy pressman would plant himself firmly between me and my car door. Nothing more dangerous happened, but one was constantly apprehensive.

As soon as the dread news broke I persuaded George Devine that the two of us together would embarrass the hell out of the audiences, and that he must take Joan out of the show. George demurred, saying he wasn't quite sure that that would be professional behaviour; I argued that there was a time for idealism, but that this was, above all, a time for practicality; would he feel idealism had been better served if Joan got badly hurt by a missile from the hand of some 'idealistic' lunatic? Of all the days in the year this happened to be my birthday, and that evening Joan, Mercia and I were alone at dinner in the flat. At the end of it our Portuguese lady brought in a birthday cake with one candle burning in the middle of it: 'One,' we all muttered, and Mercia said, 'That's for the one you'll never forget.'

Monica Evans, Joan's understudy, played out the run at the Royal Court. It was our good fortune that Maggie Smith, brilliant and brimful of promise as she already was, should have been both free and willing to take over Joan's part when, on 8 June, we transferred to the Strand Theatre, where we enjoyed eight weeks at capacity.

John Clements came with Katie Hammond to see the show, and they were commiserating with me afterwards about the terrible drubbing I was getting from the press when he suddenly offered me their house in Brighton for July. It was such a blissful idea that I could hardly believe my ears; and as soon as they had taken off for Capri we moved in to No 7 Royal Crescent, with what is known as unseemly haste.

Joan had opened *Roots* by Arnold Wesker in Coventry, while I was filming *Spartacus* in 1959; *Roots* had come to the Royal Court and was revived there again on 28 June 1960. In it she made one of 'those successes'; I'd been allowed into the dress rehearsal by George Devine, and was knocked right off my feet by her performance. For characterisation, for technique, observation, application and study – the result of which was work almost miraculous in its richness – she earned an unlooked-for blessing: unstinting acclaim, both critical and general. Over the years this has found expression in a collection of coveted awards: for *A Taste of Honey* she won a 'Tony' as Best Actress in 1960 and the New York Drama Critics Award in 1961; in 1963 her Saint Joan received the *Evening Standard* Award; in 1976 her role in *The Bed Before Yesterday* won the Variety Club Award; and in 1978 the Society of West End Theatre chose her as Best Actress in a new play, *Filumena*. Perhaps most treasured of all was a CBE in 1970.

From the last half of 1960 onwards life took on a pattern which, if it were not for my unbelieving gratefulness, might read like a steady crescendo of happiness and success, in danger of becoming tedious in its concern to avoid boastfulness on the one hand and a blasé nonchalance on the other.

The 1st August 1960 took us to Paris, where we started with a day's shopping spree with Ginette at Maison Balmain; then straight down the loved old route south. Coming back, instead of following the Rhône straight on up towards Condrieu and Vienne, for the first time I tried turning left at Mâcon and proceeded to saunter towards the Loire through the Charolais countryside, the most beautiful that I know in the world. On the 11th we were both back in London, and the following day Joanie left for New York to rehearse *A Taste of Honey*; she went on to Los Angeles to open at the Biltmore on 6 September.

A week after she had gone, I had packed up at the flat and three days later it was my turn to take flight to New York, to rehearse the name part in Peter Glenville's production of *Becket*, with Anthony Quinn as Henry II. I had been flattered into playing the title role by Peter saying, 'But my dear Larry, if you played the King, who on earth would I get to play the Archbishop?' To my shame, and increasingly to my chagrin, I fell for the flattery like a lamb for the slaughter.

We rehearsed where we were to play, at the St James, a pretty good sort of house for New York. (Forgive the patronising tone of that; but to a London theatre person New York theatres are all over-wide, with very shallow stages; the reason is that they were usually built back to back, and in order to gain the maximum gross the auditorium had to be stretched sideways.) At the end of the first week, I left New York to catch a glimpse of Joan in John and Mary Mills's house in Beverly Hills. I saw *A Taste of Honey* the next night and was thrilled with her. Joan opened at the New York Lyceum on Tuesday 4 October; I opened the next night at the St James. The best thing about these two engagements for us was the coincidental timing of them.

The 8th of November was election night, and the hair's-breadth race between the two contestants will long be remembered. No one believed that a Catholic could ever actually become President. We English visitors, being mostly given to Democratic thinking, were rooting for John F. Kennedy. It could be said it was none of our business, except for the fact that more and more does it seem to become so.

As a known 'alien' actor I was invited to take part in the Gala the night before the inauguration of the President. They had given me a homily by the nineteenth-century English statesman, John Bright, expressing the opinion that it was infinitely preferable for a president to represent the leadership of a country than for a king to do so; sympathetic as this sentiment would have undoubtedly been to the occasion, it would not have become the proposed speaker very handsomely, as he had thirteen years previously been only too proud to be honoured by his sovereign with the title of 'Knight Bachelor' – never a quainter description than in my case. I offered to write my own speech of welcome on behalf of my country; Frankie Sinatra, to whom had fallen the job of organising the performers at this ceremony, agreed to this. Sidney Poitier was another objector; he had been given a very corny coon's act to do, which he justifiably felt suited neither the occasion nor him.

I wrote the speech for the Washington Gala ten days ahead, as I wanted to have it well-prepared and in plenty of time. When the day came there was a devastating blizzard in Washington; it took me four and a half hours in a taxi to get from the Alban Towers Hotel to the Armoury where the show was to be. There could be no rehearsal, and the lighting had to be improvised during the show; everyone, audience and entertainers, arrived at least two hours late. It started at 10.30 and finished at 1.45 a.m. There was a magnificent party afterwards at Paul Young's restaurant where the feeling of relaxation was enhanced by relief that all was over and had gone brilliantly well. Everyone apart from the entertainers, who had no time, was superbly dressed, the Kennedy brothers all in white ties; I had a dark suit anyway and had thought to grab a black bow tie and stuff it into my pocket.

Joseph Kennedy, the father of the family, was not a popular figure in England, since at the beginning of the war, when he was American ambassador to the Court of St James, he was known to have advised Washington to forget about England as she hadn't a hope. He now chose to make himself known to me and, as if trying to make amends for the past, persisted in trying to be excessively charming, in the course of which he asked casually, 'Have you met Jack?' I murmured that I couldn't have expected such an honour. He grabbed me by the arm and very irritatingly slapped the President on the back and said, 'Jack, meet Mr Olivier!'

Here I was given a lightning insight into the salient characteristics of the new President: he was a brilliant man of heroic looks, rare charm, *and* he was the smartest cookie that I had ever had the privilege of confronting. On this introduction he darted his father a look that would have killed a less insensitive man and, turning quickly to me, said, 'Sir Laurence, I'm so pleased that you are here and I thank you for your fine speech, which I understand you wrote yourself.' How any man in his position, at this particular moment of his life, could be so firmly on the button as to remember foreign titles seemed to me quite incredible: a smart cookie indeed.

Our decree nisi came through on 2 December, which meant that provided Vivien committed no act of moral turpitude that would invalidate her claim to divorce me, there should be nothing to stop the decree absolute from coming across to us in about three months' time. The decree absolute came through on 3 March. We knew the press would be extra watchful and we wanted to avoid fuss if possible; there was no need for hurry, so we let things cool off for a couple of weeks and gave our great friend and lawyer, Arnold Weissberger, plenty of time to make arrangements. We had practice runs for the purpose, I am afraid, of foxing the press. Joan would have a date with our friend Angela Lansbury, who was playing her mother in *A Taste of Honey*; I would be seen to go out with one of my friends, Tony Quinn or Dickie Burton. We would sup at the usual places, even sometimes risking the two parties joining up, but we would always leave separately, going into our respective friends' houses by the front door, then straight out through the back and into our separately waiting cars. Often we were pursued by the press as far as our friends' home, but never further.

After our shows on the evening of 16 March we met up by our separate routes at Josh and Nedda Logan's house in Connecticut. Nedda, who had guessed what was afoot, had left a glorious bouquet in our room. Early the next morning Arnold picked us up and took us to collect the licence. We were both, of course, desperate not to be recognised when the forms were filled in.

'Name?' the little old lady asked.

'Laurence Olivier,' with a gulp.

'Profession?'

'Actor.'

'Are you?' she said. 'How very nice.'

On to Wilton, Connecticut, where we were married by a judge as unsuspecting as the little old lady until, halfway through the proceedings, the penny obviously dropped and his manner became slightly strangled.

We had to rush back to New York as I had a rehearsal at the theatre. 'Sorry to be late, chaps,' I said as I bustled in, 'but you don't get married every day.' We had a party that night. Next morning it was a matter of some patriotic pride to us that the first mention of what had happened should appear in our London *Times*.

As soon as I was back from the Gala in Washington, I was told that *Becket* would be likely to finish at the end of March; it had not yet recovered its investment and couldn't go on. There was no sign of Joan's play fading and so I decided to be a little hero – at least with New York managements. I went to see David Merrick and said that I didn't like the feeling that with my name billed above the title the play should lose money. Might he get his money back if he sent me on the road for six weeks or so? When he recovered from his surprise at the offer, he thought and said yes, if he could choose the theatre company; so I left him with it, having stipulated that he recast the part of Becket and that I should play the King.

At the end of March I checked into the Boston Ritz and opened my first performance as Henry II at the Colonial, with that lovely actor Arthur (Johnnie) Kennedy playing Becket. On to Washington, Detroit and Toronto – where Merrick cleaned up; I was at first dismayed by the size of the O'Keefe Center with its capacity of 3,500, but we broke the record of the theatre for a straight play, and I found ten per cent of that gross quite acceptable, thank you. Merrick was so delighted by the success of the tour that after Philadelphia he took the Hudson in New York for three weeks so that my Henry II could be seen in the big city, where they packed it out even after our previous run. While playing that little season, I rehearsed the television play of *The Power and the Glory*, Graham Greene's wonderful story.

It was during this doubling up of work that I made an

interesting discovery. I was in my middle fifties now, and I found that an aging artist can find a parallel for himself in the characteristics of aging wine. A strong young wine will last pretty well after it has been opened; it can still be quite drinkable for two or three or more days if respectfully corked up or decanted. This length of life will be progressively reduced with the years, until at a certain age the wine requires to be drunk within a minimum time after it has been opened, as its character, although enriched by age, seems almost to evaporate in contact with the air.

This particular day I had been working very concentratedly on Greene's Mexican priest, and in the afternoon run-through the cast took fire; one after another we all caught that rare and inspiring spiritual communion which makes us all living parts of a living whole. It was a wonderful experience and took from us everything that we had. When it was finished we were quite exhausted, and that evening trying to play my thrilling part I missed everything all the way down the line. My judgement and my sense of discretion had left me.

Halfway through the evening I understood what had happened to me; I had, that afternoon, done all the acting that I was capable of in one day. I thought back enviously to my youthful days in rep, when I could rehearse all day and play at night, acting at full vigour for twenty-four hours a day if necessary. And here it was; this was age. I was depleted of power, just like the wine. I couldn't expect to do as well or maintain my ability ever again over such long hours as in the past.

A couple of days after the last Saturday of *Becket*, we started shooting *The Power and the Glory*. The going was fantastically tough. When it was over, I went straight to bed in our cabin on the *Queen Elizabeth* and slept for two nights and two days. Disembarking at Southampton, we were met by Cecil Tennant and Peter Hiley and drove straight to Brighton. Most of the structural alterations had been completed at No 4, but there were still six months of decoration and furnishing to be got through. Joan was four months pregnant with our first child and was causing great and unwelcome interest from press photographers.

But before anything I owed a courtesy visit to Mr Evershed Martin. Leslie Evershed Martin, leading optician in Chichester, town councillor and late mayor of this city, was remarkable beyond these distinctions for being the founder of the Chichester Festival Theatre. He had written to me at Tyrone Guthrie's suggestion to offer me the directorship of this theatre earlier in the year. Joanie and I did not have to spend many hours examining the pros and cons; it was obvious that it was one hell of a marvellous idea and a brilliant answer to my eternally nagging question, What can I find that would be a change? So without prevarication I accepted the offer. It would be the first time that I had actually started a theatre; companies, yes; theatres, no.

After our first lunch we were both impatient to visit the site in Oaklands Park. It was a fine site; a good flat area of about five or six acres, I guessed, with a slope rising gracefully up to a skyline about six hundred yards to the north and an attractive group of trees halfway up the hill. In the clear space in which we stood were six eight-inch drain-pipes perpendicularly stuck into the ground, marking the six points of the hexagon which was to be the outline of the theatre; there could be no better, cleaner, more economical shape for a single-walled auditorium, whether in the round or with a three-sided audience, as was to be the case here. Leslie had sent me photographs of the architect's models when he first wrote to me, so I was already familiar with the general scheme. How lucky can you be? In mere gratitude I was bound to keep gloating upon my wonderful fortune: a new home life and an entirely new profession, at my time of life.

The second half of 1961 was to be enjoyably taken up with the cheerful bustle of preparations: for our baby, for our home and now for our theatre. For the first of these we had immediate need for conferences with the medical department; our Brighton GP was Dr Fitzgerald (Fitz) Frazer and our highly recommended gynaecologist/ accoucheur Kenneth Mackenzie (three zeds in two names gave extra confidence). I don't remember press photographers ever being more avidly persistent than those multitudinous knockers on the door and hiders behind pillar-boxes who wished to record Joan's condition on film. Joan had a natural resistance to this; in desperation we begged David Niven to let us stay with Hjordis and him at their house in the south of France, just so that no one would know where we were for a bit.

Well, I suppose St Jean Cap Ferrat is not a place where a camera has never been seen, and it did not take long before lenses were trained through our bathroom window from the next-door house. There are circumstances in which guests, however loved, cannot be quite as welcome as they might be. We moved out and on to the only really quiet place I have ever found in that part of the world; the Millses came to join us and it was all as jolly as can be.

Home again, where the press mercifully seemed to have forgotten us. My play-reading scanned every author from Webster to Wodehouse. The 23 November saw the topping out of the Chichester Festival Theatre, and on 1 December Joanie went into her nursing home. Her contractions started at 5 p.m. the next evening, and our son was born at 1.20 on the morning of Sunday 3 December.

It's hard now to recollect how much I wanted a girl, I was so blissfully happy with what I'd got. Joan never would admit to any preference for boy or girl; but when I held the infant close to her and said, 'You've got a son,' the joy in the croon that came from her told me which, all along, her hope had been. I felt so blest in her happiness that I never thought about a daughter again – until the next time. I had managed to get the house all ready for her when she brought her baby home a week later. I then had to leave her there in the skilled hands of nanny, cook and maid to start the film of *Term of Trial* in Dublin.

By dint of spending more hours travelling than at home, I managed to snatch a little time with my family every weekend. It had been established that it would be safe for the baby to travel with his mother and nanny to Dublin when he was six weeks old, so my peregrinations ceased then and I moved from my hotel out to a charming house belonging to a highly respected judge, Lanagan O'Keefe, in Ballybrack. Here the whole family joined up together on Friday 12 January and enjoyed a lovely life together for the next six weeks.

It was the worst luck imaginable that the announcement of my directorship of the National Theatre should have leaked just two days before the opening of the first Chichester season. Knowing well what the consequences of such a leak would mean, I though, 'An enemy hath done this.' An announcement of that sort was bound to provoke comments of the most harsh, snide and merciless kind: is one to think that a man who makes this sort of choice/error of judgement/wild statement/childish mistake (I could go on) is *really* to be considered the best choice for the director of the National Theatre of Great Britain? Gone is the hope of charitable welcome. Once more it is gritting-of-the-teeth time.

Early on in the Chichester planning I had decided that, at the risk of looking self-centred or bossy, I would undertake the first three productions myself, in order to give myself a fairly comprehensive course in the various uses to which that stage and theatre could be put. In my long stint of play-reading I had been searching for a repertoire which, though familiar in general, might not be too predicable in particular. *The Chances* by the Duke of Buckingham, though an obvious choice for such a theatre, was certainly not familiar to this generation. I felt very touched by Ford's *The Broken Heart*, equally unknown, a tragedy of shamed honour. But the choice of *Uncle Vanya* for that stage frankly drew hoots of laughter from the wise-guys. I was not disturbed by this; I was by now confident that any work of worth could be as good in this kind of playhouse, though differently no doubt, as in any other; not that anyone had agreed with me yet, of course. That word 'yet' had a dismal and a muffled knell for me just then; the critics had fairly roasted what had been offered them so far, and what had been confidently forecast for *Uncle Vanya* was total extinction.

The company being what it was, uniquely fine, it soldiered gallantly on as if for all the world we had as much chance with *Uncle Vanya* as any average first night. I was unspeakably grateful to them for their exemplary behaviour, but my own heart was full of lead. I was about to do worse than irreparable harm to my career; I was about to sink this brave little theatre venture into eternal oblivion. Those distrusting, suspecting, scathing barrackers would have been proved forever right. When I popped in to see the girls (two Joans, Plowright and Greenwood) to wish them luck, my Joanie and I looked across at each other with the faint smile of condemned people. We knew.

When the house lights dimmed out, I nipped up the staircase from the dressing-room basement to take my position downstage right on the two steps up on to the stage. It was the first and only time I can ever remember living through such a moment without apprehension or nervousness of any kind; there was no uncertainty about our fate which could induce such a state. I felt sure they wouldn't boo it off in the middle, the cast was too superlatively good; there was Michael Redgrave, the definitively perfect Vanya of all time; and Sybil Thorndike and Lewis Casson, the most respected couple in any theatre ever. No, they wouldn't boo it off. As for me, Astrov was a very favourite part of mine; I might as well enjoy it. 'There, drink it, my dear,' came a voice from behind me; I turned to Sybil, who was handing the glass of tea to me, and looked into those eyes. She had her own very special gift with them; just when the occasion demanded it, she could pour trust into you; it was like a message from God.

We were all staggered by the incredible success of *Uncle Vanya*. It was Joan's glowingly triumphant Sonia that prompted numberless people who had seen it to write or phone and demand that she should be seen as Saint Joan; it was very happy for me that my own personal wish for her should be so strongly supported by so many strangers as well as friends. I think her Beatie Bryant in *Roots* first put the idea into people's heads. With this *Uncle Vanya*, for the first time, the theatre began to win some grunts of approval; even members of the National Theatre Board began to melt. Among these an implacable opponent of the conception of the Chichester theatre, much to my surprise, was Henry Moore; when another board member was defending it by referring to *Uncle Vanya*, Henry snorted and said, 'That's not fair, that production would be all right in Liverpool Street Station.' At the risk of seeming merely to boast, I quote that as a quick measure of the general regard that we had won for ourselves in spite of despairing prognoses.

On 22 July 1962 our son was christened Richard Kerr in the Bishop's Chapel in Chichester Cathedral; the first of these two names was given at my request because it was what my beloved brother was always known by, though his name was not Richard but Gerard Dacres, and it was from the second of these that the diminutive 'Dickie' was arrived at.

The season finished on 8 September. I deliberately kept the seasons on the short side at the beginning; in the first place, so as not to make it too tough for the leading players to fit us in to their busy schedules – at a reduced salary – and secondly, in case we should be stuck with one disaster which would absorb all our hoped-for profits. When the place had made its name and its seasons became recognised as a yearly English summer event, then one might afford to stretch one's wings a bit.

The day after the finish, Joan and I were out like lights for our usual precious three weeks in France; we came back to multitudinous interviews, meetings, visits to reps, and a thorough exploration of the West End and shows on the road. There were two main boards connected with the proposed National Theatre: the National Theatre Board, the final authority for all theatre, programming and company business (my position made me the servant of this board), and the South Bank Board, in close touch with all ideas, plans and suggestions for the building of the National Theatre, and the instigator of many of them. I was a member of this board, having graduated to it from my chairmanship of our little old Building Committee. Its

membership comprised Norman Marshall, co-chairman
with me on the insistence of Lord Cottesloe; the designers
Roger Furse, Jocelyn Herbert, Sean Kenny and Tanya
Moiseiwitsch; the directors Michael Benthall, Michael
Elliott, Peter Hall, Peter Brook, George Devine and
Michel St Denis; for the National Theatre, Stephen Arlen,
Frank Dunlop, John Dexter, William Gaskill and Richard
Pilbrow (technical adviser), with Kenneth Tynan 'in
attendance'. Eighteen in all, fully recognised authorities on
theatre government. I was the only actor.

Our chief assignment was the choice of the designer of
the National Theatre itself. Our problem was that apart
from the architects who had designed the Chichester
theatre, Powell and Moya, and Elidir Davies, who was
responsible for the Welsh National Arts Theatre Centre in
Cardiff (both admirable conceptions for their purposes),
there was no one alive who had designed a theatre of such
international importance in a capital city. It was a hazardous game to pick out an architect who only *might* have the
stature for such a job, as with a fly-fishing rod. Late one
night, when our committee were getting seized up in frustration, I had one of my rare brainwaves. The chairman of
our committee was Sir Robert Mathews, the chairman of
the Royal Institute of British Architects. 'Instead of inviting an open competition for a single winner,' I said, 'which
we know can cause difficulties, why not make it a competition for, say, the best twenty entrants to be judged by the
R.I.B.A.; then we of this committee will interview carefully every single one of those twenty.'

All this was done. Five of our committee were to be
operative in these final interviews: Peter Brook, George
Devine, Michael Benthall, Michael Elliott and myself were
chosen. We diligently questioned every candidate, some of
whom had achieved impressive eminence; they all seemed
to find some extra security by bringing with them a largish
entourage. Denys Lasdun made an immediate impression
by coming in unaccompanied and sitting entirely alone on
the other side of the table. We had much admired the
striking illustrations of his work that we had seen. He

seemed to carry within him a quiet conviction; he said things like, 'I imagine the supremely vital element in such a building to be the spiritual content of it.' Of course we all fell like a hod of bricks for that one. When we asked if he could agree that our committee might be of some small assistance in an advisory capacity, he declared that he would welcome any comments of any kind that we might care to make and that the relationship should surely be regarded as a partnership. He was the one for us all right.

Early in October I had a letter from, of all people in the world, Kenneth Tynan. He frankly acknowledged that I must have been bitterly infuriated by everything that he had written against my interests over the past year, and particularly in regard to the Chichester season, but said that his admiration for me was intact and his enthusiasm for the National Theatre with me at the head of it was unbounded. He was writing to beg me to fulfil his dearest desire and award to him the post of my dramaturge.

I was utterly flabbergasted and scoffingly passed the letter to Joanie, saying, 'What do you think of that for the coolest sauce?' While she was reading I started to concoct in my mind the most withering reply that could be contrived. 'Well,' I said, my pen poised, 'how shall we slaughter the little bastard?' She looked thoughtful and finally said, 'You know, you might do worse. If you think it over calmly enough, you can see the advantages; it would be an extremely surprising choice from you. I think if people have any doubts about you for the job, they come from the fear that you might be too set in your ways and your theatre thinking. People are praying that their National Theatre will be something not in the old mould, but something more daring, new, surprising, glistening. We may have our own reasons for hating this fellow but if you could bring yourself to have him he would immediately dispel all those doubts and everyone would be surprised and relieved that you were able to forget the past and turn up such a trick. They would look at you with a new eye; all the younger generation would rejoice.'

I have been at some pains to reproduce this conversation

as nearly as I can; I want very much to show the reader the sort of leavening value that Joan's advice almost always had for me. There were, though rarely, times when her opinions were as much dictated by prejudice as anyone else's, and at those times I would have to go straight for whatever I truthfully believed was right.

It may be asked why I just couldn't do that anyway, but I had to consider the views of my associates (and, God knows, Joan should be accounted one of them), otherwise why have associates? This was not after all a private theatre venture, it belonged to the nation; and as in the case of a king or a prime minister, the public's belief in a governor is fortified by the quality of the advice around the throne. I used occasionally to try to reason with authority that it would be right for Joan to be a director – look at Helli Weigel with Bertolt Brecht, Maxine Elliott, Katharine Cornell in New York, our own Lena Ashwell, and for heaven's sake what about a dainty blossom called Lilian Baylis? But no, they said; in this case it would not do. One day, if good sense should ever prevail, Joan will make a superb director of a theatre company.

I found myself getting stale with my mind so continuously poring over similar problems and, during a lull when we had gone as far as we could for the moment, I read a play and said to Joan I would like to do it; she'd read it and said, 'Why not?' It was a comedy set in a Birmingham suburb called *Semi-Detached* by a talented new author, David Turner.

Stephen Arlen was a close friend and wonderful partner to me – he was sharing the administrative directorship of the National, with the same appointment for Sadler's Wells. One day in 1962 he and I were taking Ken Tynan out for a 'let's talk turkey' lunch at the Savoy. *Semi-Detached* had thoroughly established itself as a flop and it was obvious that everybody hated me in it. I asked Ken why. 'It is a comedy,' he said, 'which fulfils a perfectly proper purpose, that of making the audience hate themselves; you can't expect them to love you for that.' Stephen asked Ken if he was really convinced in his belief in a National

Theatre. Ken nodded towards me and said, 'With him there, oh yes.'

Early that autumn, I was sitting in my London office in Hamilton Place, wracking my brains for some trumpet call of an idea for the opening, when I was brought word that Peter O'Toole wanted to see me. In came Peter at the appointed hour and brought his agent in with him. He told me that he wished very much to play Hamlet for a short season in the West End some time in the following year and would I direct him in it? I said no, I wasn't available for the West End just then, but if he would like his Hamlet to be the opening number for the National Theatre in October I could fix that; so we shook hands on it.

I had already arranged with John Dexter, whose work I had deeply admired from his direction of *Roots* with Joan, that he should direct her *Saint Joan* at Chichester and come on as an associate to the National. Agreeing with the threesome idea, he advised me strongly to engage William Gaskill as the other associate; but I found William to be playing extremely 'hard to get'. I had to get John to help me to persuade him. In one such session I began boasting, '*And* who do you think I've got to open for us?' They were both disappointingly unimpressed; it seemed that John was very much in two minds about the star system, he certainly had no anxiety to direct anyone of that ilk, and William was irrevocably opposed to it. I explained that a National venture such as this would be next to impossible to put across without any stars at all: people would always be asking, 'But who's in it?' When the permanent ensemble could claim to be the biggest star of all, like the Moscow Arts or the Berliner Ensemble, then we could afford to think in such splendid, altogether higher-minded terms; but even with an established group the public would always winkle out its two or three special favourites, and certain of the players would inevitably emerge as leading men and women.

One of my favourite performances is that of Paul Scofield as the 'whisky Priest' in *The Power and the Glory*; the evilly catalystic Peasant, digging into the Priest's inner life, asks him if he has any children, and in his fascinatingly chosen Birmingham accent Paul, in a way I have never been able to forget in twenty-five years, replied, 'Ovva daw-tah.' In 1963, on 10 January, to my incomparable joy, I was able to repeat that line with the utmost rapture; Tamsin Agnes Margaret was christened in St Mary's, East Lavant, during this second Chichester season. This season consisted of *Saint Joan*, which was a particular triumph for Joan (Plowright!) among a variety of other glories; *The Workhouse Donkey* by John Arden, which was not the success that it should have been, admirably directed by Stuart Burge (known and respected since he had given his transvestite Player Queen to my first Hamlet in 1937). It would have been sheer improvidence, after only twenty-odd performances of *Uncle Vanya* in the first season, not to revive it in the second; and the life in it was vibrant enough for it to be revived yet again early in the first National Theatre season, along with *Saint Joan*.

CHAPTER THIRTEEN

The National Theatre Launched

The plays for the first season of the National Theatre Company at the Old Vic Theatre from 22 October were:

Hamlet
Saint Joan
Uncle Vanya
The Recruiting Officer
Hobson's Choice
Andorra
Philoctetes/Play
Othello
The Master Builder

Nine presentations: ten plays, with the double bill. As soon as possible we introduced, although at the extra cost of two change-overs a week, a repertoire such as I had always dreamt of for the National; not only did we have a different play on every night, but we changed over beween matinées and evening, thus:

MATINEE:	*Uncle Vanya*
EVENING:	*Recruiting Officer*
MATINEE:	*Othello*
EVENING:	*Hobson's Choice*
MATINEE:	*Philoctetes/Play*
EVENING:	*Saint Joan*

This could not be achieved when half the company were on tour or at Chichester, apart from exceptional cases; taking our tip from Princess Margaret when she visited Chichester, Her Royal Highness's helicopter perching beside the theatre in Oaklands Park, Maggie Smith did hop bravely up and down one whole Chichester season each day between Oaklands Park and the heliport at Waterloo.

The history of the years from 1963 to 1974 has been amply covered in a book by John Elsom and Nicholas Tomalin, which can be easily obtained from the book-stall in the National Theatre itself. It seems unnecessary for me to write the whole history of those eleven years all over again when they have been so ably recorded elsewhere.

On 1 January 1963 I condemned myself to a year of total abstinence. A year? Well, call it a drinking man's year – from 1 January to 24 December. I thought I must give myself every chance; I was not what could be described as someone bristling with efficiency; it seemed a pity not to do everything possible to improve the situation. It was only for a year, and if I was lucky enough to get such a pearl of a job, the first of its kind in our country's theatre, then some special mark of respect was due, even if I was the only one aware of it. George Devine and I inevitably drew even closer together than we had been before; he and I had something more in common now, which provided a special brotherhood for consultation and advice; and what a comfortable refuge it was. As the leader of the Royal Court Theatre, he regarded his role in an Aristotelian light; he liked to train his disciples' minds and send them out to bring light to the world. This being the case, when I purloined his two bright young directors, John Dexter and William Gaskill, to be my associate directors he was pleased for them and for me. Tony Richardson was by now regarded as second in command to George, and even he was borrowed not infrequently for outside jobs – *The Entertainer, A Taste of Honey*, and other fine productions in London or New York. I was delighted to welcome George himself to direct one production – *Play* by Samuel Beckett.

We started the National with a company of fifty, largely

recruited from the second Chichester season, now strengthened so that twelve were already renowned:

RENOWNED	TO BE RENOWNED
Max Adrian	Frank Finlay
Colin Blakely	Michael Gambon
Tom Courtenay	Derek Jacobi
Cyril Cusack	Robert Lang
Rosemary Harris	Louise Purnell
Peter O'Toole (*Hamlet* only)	Lynn Redgrave
Joan Plowright	Robert Stephens
Michael Redgrave	John Stride
Joyce Redman	
Maggie Smith	
Billie Whitelaw	
Diana Wynyard	
and me	

Administrative director: Stephen Arlen
Literary manager: Kenneth Tynan

The great blemish on 1963 was towards its end – as another President said upon the deplorable occasion of Italy coming into the Second World War against France, 'The hand that held the knife has struck it into the back of his neighbor.' So did it seem to the citizenry of the United States and to all English-speaking peoples and those who feel any love or regard for them. Therefore when the shattering tragedy of 22 November became known to us, we felt that there had been cruelly torn from us a favourite, glamorous young uncle – John F. Kennedy.

After the matinée of *Uncle Vanya* the next day, at which I knew quite a few American visitors to be present, when the curtain rose again at the end I stepped forward raising my hands and said that we would prefer not to receive applause that afternoon as we felt sure that the audience would rather stand with us for two minutes in remembrance and silent grief for the loss of the President. I had arranged that the silence should be broken after exactly two minutes by the strains of the 'Star Spangled Banner'. When this had ended the curtain came gently down and the audience quietly left.

It was during the very first meeting with Ken Tynan on repertoire that he casually slipped in, 'And of course you'll do Othello, you've done all the others. People will wonder why you're ducking this one.'

'Ken, I'm not right for the part.'

'I thought there wasn't any part you couldn't be right for?'

'This is different, Ken. I haven't got the voice. Othello has to have a dark, black, violet, velvet *bass* voice.'

Ken shrugged and turned to some other subject. For the next month or so I was visited by a lot of 'thinks' in variously shaped balloons: 'If I haven't got the damn voice why don't I bloody well go after it and make it happen . . . give myself a month and if there's no sign of any headway I can decide on something else . . .'

I decided to have a bash at that voice. I have always felt nervous about roaring and screaming at home, but would feel no self-consciousness if I could get out into the hills. I remember once screaming King Lear at a group of cows who had formed a ring of curiosity around me. God, I thought, I hope the audience is as patient as they are. I determined to get to the Aquinas Street rehearsal room early and do my yelling before any offices had started work. After three or four weeks it didn't seem to be going too badly and I decided to risk a public try-out – well, not very public; it was one of those more earnest programmes for the BBC which, in unhappy probability, loses them listeners by thousands: a series of Shakespearian speeches by ten or twelve different actors for which I had been given Othello's speech to the senate. I was as bold as I dared be with the two or three lower notes that I had forced into my voice.

When I had finished, the Cassons, who were taking part in the programme, came up to me. Sybil said, 'Darling, what *have* you been up to with your voice, it's quite different'; and Lewis said, 'You've opened up a whole new side to your personality, to your career, if you want it.' It was encouraging. So back I went to my exercises with renewed vigour, calling for some help from Barry Smith, a student from the Central and now voice teacher at RADA. I suspected that just roaring like a bull, trying to roar lower by the semitone as the weeks went by, was probably not all that was required, and that some more classical approach might be helpful.

After many discussions with Johnnie Dexter, I had decided exactly what I wanted to look like. I had rejected the modern trend towards a pale coffee-coloured compromise, a natural aristocrat; this was, I felt, a cop-out, arising out of some feeling that the Moor could not be thought a truly *noble* Moor if he was too black and in too great a contrast to the noble whites: a shocking case of pure snobbery. He is described as 'the thick lips', as having a 'sooty bosom'; he describes himself as 'black':

> Haply for I am black
> And have not those soft parts of conversation
> That chamberers have . . .'

(He can put them on all right when he thinks they're called for: he can positively *pile* them on to the senate.)

I think it would be difficult to disagree with the view of Shakespeare's tragic theme as dealing with rare characters who are brought to their destruction by the existence of one ineradicable fault; indeed, he puts his own definition of this into the mouth of his greatest invention, the most complex and enigmatic of his heroes, Hamlet:

> So, oft it chances in particular men,
> That for some vicious mole of nature in them,
> As, in their birth – wherein they are not guilty,
> Since nature cannot choose his origin –
> By the o'ergrowth of some complexion,
> Oft breaking down the pales and forts of reason,

> Or by some habit that too much o'er-leavens
> The form of plausive manners; that these men,
> Carrying, I say, the stamp of one defect,
> Being nature's livery, or fortune's star,
> Their virtues else, be they as pure as grace,
> As infinite as man may undergo,
> Shall in the general censure take corruption
> From that particular fault.

This passage is followed by two lines of gibberish over which the commentators in the *Variorum* make gluttons of themselves for quite some pages. They should have consulted an actor; why does your researcher always apply to a professor rather than to a practitioner? Here is the explanation of one such: 'From that particular fault' was the cue for the Ghost's entrance, which must have been missed by the Ghost at a certain performance and the wretched Hamlet had to gag, filling in with whatever nonsensical words came into his mouth – all faithfully taken down by the shorthand plagiarist present at this performance. In *Richard III*, when I had played it too long and too often for the memory to be faithfully retentive, I had had to do the same. Possibly my inventions made even less sense than the young Hamlet's, but the audience will stand for quite a few lines of such stuff; provided you keep in rhythm they'll accept that it's an abstruse bit of Shakespeare – within limits of course.

In many Shakespearian heroes there exists a companion fault, that of self-deception. Macbeth does not suffer from this weakness, Othello most certainly does. It is almost impossible to believe seriously that any human being on entirely uncorroborated evidence, as flimsy as a handkerchief embroidered with strawberries, could *that same night* strangle his wife in her bed and afterwards, in all sincerity, describe himself as '. . . one not easily jealous'.

By the way, if I may delve into the field of medical science, I will say that I have reason to feel sure that Othello's fit is not the result of accelerated self-hypnosis, but a plain case of physical dysarthria, which is also brought about by over-heightened emotional stress. Othello's crisis is not the result of a frightening series of kaleidoscopic images, but an interruption of the connection between the brain and the speech mechanism. In the scene that follows, Iago may not just be boasting to Cassio, but from the constancy of his attendance upon Othello he could well have had previous experiences of such a fit and know that the only way of dealing with it was to leave the sufferer to recover in his own time. The best advice to an actor, I think, is to follow as livelily and as literally as possible what is indicated in the text from Act IV, Scene i, from 'he with her' to his fall in a trance.

In comedy, Malvolio is a self-deceiver, Benedick not; the 'Shakespeare man' (our Shakespeare men include the Bastard in *King John*, Hotspur, Benedick, Berowne and Mercutio) is the refreshing character-invention who utterly disdains it.

People ask me, 'What is the most important attribute of a successful actor?' so frequently that I have been obliged to think more deeply than it costs to make the quick reply, 'Talent, of course.' I would now say that there is an equal trinity of contributing qualities:

Talent	*Luck*	*Stamina*
This must develop into skill	Though this must vary, it must be good enough to believe in the truth of it yourself. You must see that it has provided you with the right opportunities at the right times.	A gift seemingly not affected by disease, unless worn down by constant onslaughts.

Here is the best example of luck that I can remember in my own case: until the main dress rehearsal of *Othello* in 1964 I had forgotten to be careful of the way my bare feet were behaving. I had not too happy a memory of Alfred

Lunt's remark to me after *Oedipus*: 'I was fascinated by your feet; the more intense you got, the more rigidly did your big toes stand straight up in the air!' I was horrified as well as disappointed. So on this night, as I started down the passage behind the back wall of the stage at the Old Vic, I tried to keep each foot flat to the ground as it trod the floor; this stiffened up the foot and constricted the leg muscles and, I feared, looked rather comical. I then tried to relax the foot, without placing the heel down first but putting my whole weight on each foot in turn as it touched the ground, thus introducing those swaying hips so generously commented upon, and regarded as the keystone of an elaborate characterisation that even went to the lengths of studying the gait of the barefooted races! I indeed had a feeling that I had stumbled on to a good thing as I rounded the corner at the end of the passage and went through and on to the stage.

That is what I call luck. Alfred can never have guessed the ultimate usefulness of his good-natured mockery.

Perhaps I might insert here a shrewd but partial letter concerning the same part; it is from a professional as well as a wife:

My Dearest Darling, most wonderful Boy,

Just want to send all my love and thoughts and energy to you for your second opening. Don't let any doubts creep in about your Othello; I know this is about the time one begins to bite one's finger-nails and think only of the bits one is still dissatisfied with. No harm in that . . . as long as you remember also that in the greater part of the play you are wildly exciting, beautiful, superb and head and shoulders above anyone living today. Don't know about those who went before, but I'm pretty sure you are way above them too!

Your characterisation is fascinating, original and absolutely valid in human terms . . . the split personality of a man who has had to overcome one powerful part of his nature in order to achieve a certain position in the world.

I know your main problem is that of getting the progress of the character through the play to just flow through your bones without having to think about it. Naturally a great deal of that can only come with playing it but maybe a long quiet mull over what you have already created might help to get the shape and feeling clearer in your mind.

Am going to jot down random thoughts and impressions which might ring a bell somewhere and, if they don't, no harm has been done!

(*'Ha Ha or No . . . No . . . False to me'*)

I think it should be agonized doubt sooner than certainty. He says earlier, 'When I doubt, prove'. So, as yet, it is only doubt . . . and he follows the Farewell content speech with a savage request for proof. All that you do magnificently anyway and there is nothing more to be said about that.

I remember you saying about Brenda de B. that she 'tries to cry' on stage, whereas in real life one tries to stop crying.

I think you are maybe trying to believe Cassio's kisses have been on her lips, instead of trying to stop yourself believing.

I know that Othello's baser, hidden nature probably wants to find her guilty, but the 'noble facade' could still struggle this early in the play to keep up its head a little longer . . . You don't want yet, if it is humanly possible, to reveal yourself as the naked animal you really are . . . but you want proof . . . but if you can get proof and still cling desperately to the last vestiges of the man you once were, it still leaves you plenty of opportunity in the next scenes with her for the final revelation of the mad beast.

This is probably just something *I* feel, but I have felt each time I've seen it that your passion is too great and openly displayed for her to top it and try and pretend it is a game. If the first part is shouted . . . as now . . . and then there is an awful effort to be sane and cunning (which she takes advantage of) and then the rage and pleading break out again . . . you've still got somewhere to go when you finally lose control completely with her.

Also it would make her rather puzzled 'I ne'er saw this before' when you have gone off not quite so much like the understatement of the year.

No other suggestions, my love. And I bet you don't like those! And you are probably quite right! Just one of those ideas of people who come in rather late on a production and don't realise that you discarded all those ideas weeks ago!

Oh . . . I do love you.

JOAN

In preparation for the second season at the National (1964–5) some cast changes had become necessary. Very much to my disappointment Michael Redgrave was not keen to come back. It was early days for anyone, let alone eminences such as he, to remove themselves from the company. Our ideal was to maintain a permanent ensemble, in so far as possible. He had, it goes without saying, done much superb work for us. But he was not happy. He had, I think, a slight sense of disappointment; he should by rights have felt more grieved with me as his manager than with himself. Anyway, I lost him – a proper Koh-i-noor in the crown of any company.

The last part Michael played for us was Solness in Ibsen's *The Master Builder,* extremely well directed by Peter Wood. Maggie Smith did not have in it quite the success I was so hoping for, Hilde being the third of the fine parts by which I hoped to prove that a really good actor need not be type-cast. Watching Maggie's brilliant work in light comedy, I felt compelled to offer her a change of climate. By the end of the season *Master Builder* had only played twenty performances, and it had been by far the most costly small-cast show we had put on. In those days one had a fierce conscience about the spending of public money improvidentially, so I asked Michael if he would mind if we ran the play on into the next season, and if I took over his part. Since Maggie had touring dates for us, Joan took over some performances from her.

During a short holiday in Ibiza, Joan and I learnt and worked on our new parts in the revival of *The Master Builder*, which was to come on early in the season, with only five days of rehearsals on our return. During the first few years of our association and marriage I had sometimes felt anxious lest out of my personal pride in Joan's prowess I might have cast her beyond the powers of any actress, however versatile. She proved me wrong. At our first reading her grasp of Hilde Wangel amazed me.

On the morning of returning to work I went straight into the first reading of *Hay Fever*, for which Noël himself was conducting rehearsals. During the succeeding four weeks there are also references in my diary (which was pretty wretchedly kept as a rule – I can't have dreamt that there might one day be such a thing as an autobiography) to production meetings, rep meetings, even some Chichester meetings. To justify continued use of my name as director of the Chichester Festivals, we made the management of it part of the National's responsibility. It worked very well; by using the seasons there as a try-out ground we were occasionally able to avoid mistakes and thereby save public money.

In early preparation was *Much Ado About Nothing*, which brought Maggie Smith and Robert Stephens together as a stage team. Also in preparation was my own production of *The Crucible*. It may be imagined that regular gym training was asking too much of myself, but no; I have always had the strongest belief in exercise as a builder-up of stamina, and I think that rather than exhausting me it gave me extra strength to resist the expected *faiblesses*.

As the fourth week of this activity came to an end, a shrill note of alarm came from Manchester, where *Hay Fever* was trying out from Monday to Thursday. Up I went, and Noël met me with the words, 'Larry boy, you've got to fire Edith tonight!' I told him I was just not capable of firing Dame Edith Evans on her first night; I would go and see the show, and we would talk afterwards.

I have to say the show was a shock. Dame Edith was vague, without any grip on her part. She was not familiar with her lines and was fluffing about, quite lost and at random. The rest of the cast made me preen with pride and were a credit to themselves and to the National. Maggie, the two Bobs (Lang and Stephens), Anthony Nicholls, Lynn Redgrave, Derek Jacobi and Louise Purnell – they really looked like a company.

With lead in my spirits I went round with Noël to dressing-room No 1 to bluster it out with Edith. The situation was very strange. As I was doling out the bubbling greetings of an old colleague, I caught sight of a pair of unworn eyelashes beside her make-up tray and burst out, 'Edith, dear, why on earth didn't you wear those?' 'Well, dear,' she said, 'I didn't want to think of it as a performance!' Only with difficulty did I hold back the tempting rejoinder. Noël and I stared incredulously at each other. On the way back to the Midland Hotel I told him that nothing more could be gained that night; I would see the show through again on the Thursday three days later and, if I found the results of her efforts to be still damaging, I would bring down the bloody but necessary axe. The axe, in the event, did not fall.

Returning to London, I went to the gym and then the office for the usual discussion of the agenda with Tynan, Gaskill and Arlen, before a run-through of *Builder* at 1.30 on the Old Vic stage. Halfway through it, Joan had that expression on her face I know well enough of anxious, strained, despairing resignation, and said, 'I think I'd better lie down.' I looked searchingly into her face and knew that our third infant was kicking up and said, 'You *lie* down and don't think of getting up. Don't you move – stay on your back and don't think of moving. And I'm sorry, but this is too precious a thing to run any risks or fool around with. Don't think any more about either Hilde or the play – just forget it. Don't move at all. I'll get a nurse and an ambulance, and you get carried up to bed into which you get, my darling, as calmly and unhurriedly as you can.' I knew so well her passion to have babies and I never knew how many more I might be confident of siring at fifty-seven. 'I'll get hold of some universal aunt for the night and a meal brought in from wherever it is. I'm bound to be back a bit late now, I'm afraid, but worry not – all shall be fixed and fine. Bye now. I'd better get on. All my love, my darling.' Her understudy, Jeanne Hepple, a name forever engraved upon this grateful heart, was a splendid, first-class actress who possessed not only talent, but brilliant efficiency as well. She knew every word and every move, so it was mercifully only a question of running it as many times as we could cram into the next two and a half days.

I was late back, of course, and I found Joan wakeful but calm. I felt much cheered and confident that we have staved off the danger for this night anyway. My own state of exhaustion had reached the degree at which one's worst fear is that it may make sleep impossible. I felt so certain that such would be the case on this particular night that, though I very seldom do so, I took two sleeping-pills, for I knew that sleep was vital if I were to get through all that lay ahead. Joan seemed to be drowsing off and, stoked up with pills, I was almost at once in a deep sleep. But I had been too optimistic. Soon after one in the morning, I became gradually aware of a gentle kicking from the beloved one beside me. As if from a great distance I heard her voice, gently but with unmistakable urgency: 'He-i-gh. I'm sorry, my love, but I'm afraid you have to get the doctor . . . I'm so very sorry . . .' I hope without groaning or moaning too much, I phoned her gynaecologist/accoucheur doctor in Brighton. I daresay this may well sound a bit eccentric when there were two or three doctors we knew about in London who could have come along in infinitely less time, but they would have been quite unacquainted with any strangenesses peculiar to Joan when in this particular condition. It turned out to be the right thought. The blessed fellow who had brought our two elder ones into the world eighteen months and two and a half years previously, who was by no means a young man, leapt up instantly, jumped into his car and somehow got to us, just off Victoria Street, from Hove in less than an hour and a half. He examined Joan and told her there was no hope of saving the child; then he advised her what should be done. She did as she was bid and, after not too agonizingly lengthy a time, she came back and gently collapsed breathlessly on to the bed. Then, having told me to fetch blankets, Ken MacKenzie wrapped her up in them and we carried her into the lift and down and into his car. He drove smartly off. It was by now around five. He phoned up two hours or so later to tell me that he had got her on to the operating table in Hove by seven o'clock and that she was now well and not to be worried about further. For me the sleeping-pills had not been prepared to play ball any more and I could only drowse between their leaving and the comforting call from Ken. He was a truly wonderful doctor, always encouraging me to participate with my presence in the births of all of our three. I have always felt that it was the proper thing for a father and husband to do.

Next day we had a *Builder* run-through at 10.30 with a mass of interviews in the afternoon. With the evening free for both Jeanne and me, we managed to get quite a bash at it. Quickly home and to bed, comparatively early that evening (no Noël to inveigle me into staying up). On Thursday, a run-through of *Builder*, one or two appointments and then off to St Pancras for the 2.25 back to Manchester. I did not relish the thought of joining the mêlée again, but after one year of preparation before the National had become a reality and another year of the sort of work that it was created for, trouble was something I was growing immune to. Not personal or family trouble, of course.

Sitting in the Opera House that evening it was clearly not only now possible but reasonably safe to proceed with the announced intention of opening at the Vic on the following Tuesday. Again I had a late supper at the Midland with Noëlie, followed, next morning, by another early start for a lighting run-through and then a full dress rehearsal in the afternoon. During this I had allowed myself to give way to some feelings of misgiving about the performance that evening. I strove to rid myself of any such unwelcome thoughts, assuring myself, probably rightly, that they were obviously the result of natural enough over-fatigue. I have, in earlier parts of this auto-history, described the devious, weevil-like way that my particular guilt complex works, starting as it did with a superstitious or possibly semi-religious fear that some over-blown claim to pride in myself would be bound to find the punishment that it deserved. Such punishment was now served upon me almost immediately in the form of a terror which was, in fact, nothing other than a merciless attack of stage-fright with all its usual shattering symptoms.

Now, of all times, I had allowed two spectres to take firm root in my mind. The two previous occupants of this dressing-room had been Edith and, before her, another eminent actor – about both of whom I was guilty of harbouring despising thoughts. They had neither of them known their parts, or had been indolent or incompetent in the study of them. Now, in the time between the dress rehearsal and our first performance, an appalling thought possessed me: 'I think I'm too tired to remember it.'

My courage sank, and with each succeeding minute it became less possible to resist this horror. My cue came, and I went on to that stage where I knew with grim certainty I would not be capable of remaining more than a few minutes. I began to watch for the instant at which my knowledge of my next line would vanish. Only the next two now, no – one more . . . and then – NOW. I took one pace forward and stopped abruptly. My voice had started to fade, my throat closed up and the audience was beginning to go giddily round (why is it always anti-clockwise?) when with a sickening feeling I realised that Noël was in front, and would inevitably write me off into the wasteland like Edith.

Not only was he in front, but so too were Tynan, Dexter and Gaskill, as well as numberless eminences, not to mention the press who would make a regular banquet out of it; for me, it would mean a mystifying and scandalously sudden retirement. I retraced my step. With unusual inaudibility, owing to my tightly clenched teeth, I somehow got on with the play which I was paying myself to perform in.

That should have been that. But unhappily this malaise

had a most obstinate reluctance to come to a conclusion. It persisted, and continued to torment me, for five whole years. *The Master Builder* remained, for as long as I was in it, a source of much anxiety. What no one could have foreseen was that the disease proved contagious, not to other people, but to other roles and finally to everything that I tackled.

A shy performance as Othello is an absurdity. Early on in the course of it I had to beg my Iago, Frank Finlay, not to leave the stage when I had to be left alone for a soliloquy, but to stay in the wings downstage where I could see him, since I feared I might not be able to stay there in front of the audience by myself. Finally, everyone who had scenes with me had to know what was going on, in order to be able to cope in case of trouble.

The 30th of January 1965 was the day of Churchill's funeral. It was more than a day of national mourning, it was a day of celebration of a nation's overwhelming gratitude for the life of their 'Valiant Man', to whom they owed so incalculably much. The whole day was superbly managed, confidently pervaded by the nation's acknowledged mastery of ceremony. The BBC and ITV each had its separate programme of the day's events; I was fortunate enough to speak the commentary for the second of these networks which, I was proudly informed, gained the greater viewing audience of the two. Our team had fixed itself up with a supreme position for the final shot, their camera placed on top of the tower of the Shell Building on the South Bank, looking down on to the tiny distant train with its plume of white smoke pouring upwards from the funnel of the engine, bearing to its last resting-place the coffin in its single carriage. The camera followed the smoke into the heart of this glorious view of London before swinging smoothly to zoom in on a huge Union Jack flying from the House of Lords tower.

Our Building Committee meetings with Denys Lasdun took place every month. It was to take us five years to find the actor-audience relationship for the larger 'Upper House' as it was referred to then, and one week to find the same for the medium-sized Proscenium House. We still had to find a space within the precincts in which to house our Experimental Theatre. This was to many of us potentially the most important part of the National Theatre.

'An open space' sounds comfortably vague, but that vagueness contained mysteries (I use the word in its old guild sense). The Upper House was to be a purely open-space theatre: 'A room with a stage in the corner of it,' was Lasdun's precription. The Proscenium Theatre, again, was to be uncompromising, a theatre of pure confrontation. The Experimental Theatre was to be entirely adaptable – easily and quickly transformable from being completely in the round, to Elizabethan, to pure confrontation with any compromise imaginable, the audience in the middle and the actors all round them – if you like, an amoral theatre.

Our beloved George Devine died on 20 January 1966. A show was got up to honour him in gratitude for his work at his Royal Court. Were it not for the fact that his first struggle to create an author's theatre had been at the little Kingsway Theatre in Great Queen Street, he might be thought to have inherited his ideas with the building; for long before the Royal Court became, well, just a not very useful theatre only to be taken as a last resort when others were unattainable (it was one of Barry Jackson's London theatres – I was in one season there when I was under contract to him in 1926–9), it had known great *réclame* in the Vedrenne/Granville Barker/Shaw seasons in the early part of this century. But for many years to come, the Royal Court will surely be thought of as George Devine's theatre, newly created by him in 1956.

We took our National to Moscow in September 1965, opening *Othello, Hobson's Choice* and *Love for Love* (its first performance) on three consecutive nights; this engagement put us very much on trial and all of us felt on the tips of our toes. Since the publication of Stanislavsky's *My Life in Art* in the 1920s, Moscow had for my generation and for some years after been the mecca of theatre arts. I think our first performance at the Kremilovsky Theatre had that little extra something, and at the end the applause continued without sign of stopping for thirty-five minutes. The first word of my curtain speech, which I had carefully learnt phonetically, brought a shattering thunderclap of cheering: 'Tovarischi.' The relief was so great – Madame Furtseva, the Minister of Culture, had come backstage to express her pleasure – that I seemed to need the refreshment required by a man lost for a week in the desert. I proceeded to satisfy this need in strict alternation between vodka and champagne until the not-so-early hours of the morning, and Irma la Douce – the name we have given to the forbiddingly large ladies who sat, their thick arms folded upon a desk, at the end of each corridor, eyeing us dangerously – half-rose from her seat as we approached her to turn the corner to our room. I was palpably staggering, though held in a vice by Joanie, from whom with a victorious gesture I freed myself to enter the linen cupboard. Joan somehow got me inside our room and locked the door. She turned to find me on the floor, where she undressed me; she got into bed and coaxed me towards it, whither I obediently crawled on all fours; finally she pulled me up on to the bed.

It was unfortunate that the next day a great luncheon was being given in our honour by a group of the foremost figures in the arts. Magical as had been the power which Joan had been master of at bedtime, she found that more was required than she was able to muster at getting-up time. Periodically she made determined attempts to waken me, but for the brief second-and-a-half that consciousness returned, 'Impossible' was all the murmur that she could distinguish. The excuse she made for me would have scared the crossbar off a scarecrow. 'He has,' she declared, 'been rehearsing *Hobson's Choice* all night and all this morning, and I fear has now collapsed with exhaustion.' I do not know by how craggy a descent this story went down, she told me that it seemed to be accepted with reserved but scrupulous politeness; at any rate nobody looked at her with a deadly level gaze and said, 'You, madam, are a damned liar and your husband is a drunken lazy slob.'

There were two unusually delightful experiences for us; one was an enchanted visit to Leningrad which I found, for sheer beauty, to be a strong rival to Paris. Our hotel was old-fashioned and beautiful with its large lift, open all round, circled about with a grand staircase, and really quite a semblance of service. Leningrad takes justifiable pride in its *pièce de résistance*, Peterhof. Originally built and lived in by Peter the Great, it had to be bombed to smithereens by the Germans. But after the war it was laboriously and devotedly built up again by other Russian hands exactly as it had been before, to the nearest ounce of carved plaster, every carefully secreted treasure, every painting and valuable to the smallest bibelot exactly arranged and placed. One can percieve a two-fold propaganda purpose in this effort: it shows what a superb classical technique they can still demonstrate if they wish to; at the same time they can say, 'Look how these aristocrats threw your money around.' Moscow in contrast seems to take pride in its drabness, which is somewhat put out of countenance by the remains of a romantic past that still lives nostalgically round and about the onion towers of the old Kremlin itself. One of our number asked at the desk of our Ukraine Hotel, 'Do you get many complaints about the service here?' 'Certainly not, there is no service,' came the reply.

Another delight for us both was meeting Moscow's senior critic, whose name is pronounced Aneext. He was extremely agreeable as was his wife and son, all of whom spoke passable English, but his was exceptional and extremely erudite. He held forth long and intellectually on *Othello*; I might have been even more apprehensive about choosing *Othello* to open with had I realised that the play enjoyed such popularity and was more constantly revived than any other, and that any actor of any repute at all had played the part, not only in Moscow but all over Russia. It holds the place in their regard that the rest of the world accords to *Hamlet*. I felt pleased beyond measure that he had so gratifyingly commended me in his criticism. *Love for Love* he was inclined to dismiss as a pitifully bourgeois example of English eighteenth-century would-be witty flippancy, and as for *Hobson's Choice*, he really couldn't understand why we had brought such old-fashioned nonsense to Moscow. I explained that I had hoped that the Russian audiences might be amused by the early hints of social message in a British comedy; he smiled faintly and changed the subject.

Could there be more of a contrast than West Berlin to this dip into Russia? For the sake of Soviet *amour propre* we were requested to travel by an elaborately roundabout route so that we should not appear to be proceeding straight to the suppurating outpost of the world which they held in utter opprobrium – 'First stop Moscow, next stop West Berlin.' So we flew from Moscow to Copenhagen, from there to Hamburg and so to West Berlin, where, let me say, we found an audience of the highest sophistication. We eyed the stage with great envy; the theatre had been designed to house three scissor-sliding stages so that one set could be pushed straight backwards and another slide on from either right or left. We only required two of these for *Othello* and *Love for Love*; I could endure with equability the agonies of *Othello* matinées when I could see off-stage right the *Love for Love* set sitting happily waiting to be shunted on at the end of the show. To our delight the audiences for *Love* were astonishingly quick and clever, both in their comprehension of our language and appreciation of Congreve's wit; the play fetched some laughs in West Berlin that proved to be too subtle even for London.

There is one entry in the 1966 diary, on 24 January, which reads: '*Othello*: Stage fright – painful tautness.' Next day I went, as so often, to the Cassons, now both well into their eighties, and asked what I should do. Sybil promptly answered, 'Take drugs, darling, we do.' A few performances later, traversing that passage behind the stage before my first entrance, in no way influenced by drugs let me say, I found myself lurching so badly that I was ricocheting from one wall to the other. When I was led on to the stage by Frank Finlay, whom I had warned about my condition, I found it impossible to stop myself staggering; all too soon I had to lurch further downstage and, sure enough, the hissing whispering started out front, the content of which I could well imagine: 'You see? Look at him, I wondered how long it would be before he had one too many, didn't you? Oh yesss.' It quietened for a little and then started again: 'But itssn't it marvellouss the way he keepss it out of hiss voice and sspeech? Oh yesss it certainly isss – marvel-loussssss!' I allowed myself to feel a little flattered by that one. After the show the doctor came round and informed me that my condition was called labyrinthitis and sent me some pills to be dissolved under the tongue; they worked; and in a day or two I was myself again.

Our next baby was looming large, and we were a little apprehensive; there were mysterious irregularities. There appeared to be a slight depression down the middle of Joan's normal protuberance, which suggested that there was a possibility of twins: the doctors did not like to take an X-ray and I did not like the idea either. Ken Mac was worried enough to order Joan into White Haven, the familiar home-from-home twice visited before; he told me that he was thinking seriously about a Caesarian section. I was anguished enough to beg him to get on with it as soon as he could, as Joan's pain was continuous and obstinately unproductive; that night was her second in labour, and at 6 a.m. Dr Ken made the necessary incision and pulled forth a tiny female child of only four pounds.

It took the theatre sister and the anaesthetist eight minutes to make the desired cry escape our new daughter's lips. I feel I may take some small credit for this when it came. Husbands are often quite welcome to take part on these occasions, provided they are cool and firmly resistant to hysteria. I, who up to now had been a model member of this brotherhood, who do have their uses as hand-holders, head-strokers and whisperers of encouragement, could contain myself no longer from spluttering, 'For God's sake, why don't you smack its damn bottom?' They did, and the cry came immediately.

In the meantime our Dr Ken was finding out about this other lump. It became apparent that there had been a leak in the placenta; this brilliantly clever membrane is normally pretty flat like a hand-sized loofah, but this one had swollen to the size of a large old-fashioned bath sponge. This was the cause of the baby's minute size; it was reckoned that she had had for the last six weeks an insufficient supply of nutrients, as well as an insufficiency of oxygen; so that cry, when it came, was in fact something of a miracle.

Our paediatrician, Dr Nash, and I took the mite in an incubator to the Brighton General Hospital. As I was leaving they asked if I would like them to baptize her, just in case. After a second to absorb the implication, I said, 'Why yes, of course.' 'What name?' I had thought of Julia, on account of her Caesarian section, and Katherine. 'Julie-Kate,' I said echoing the combination that Joanie and I had hit upon. Next day Dr Nash explained to me that this hospital lacked the comprehensive facilities necessary; he had managed to secure a vacancy at the Children's Hospital in the heart of the town. Here the baby would be given round-the-clock surveillance: the nurse on duty would not take her eyes off her charge for a second.

I was playing again most nights now, returning to Brighton at midnight, and after *Othello* not until one. I'd go straight to the Children's Hospital and peep round the ward entrance; and, sure enough, there would be the splendidly constant nurse, her elbows on the incubator, gazing down, watching the tiny infant's every breath. At first Julie-Kate got everything wrong with her that an infant in such circumstances can be afflicted with: St Vitus-like spasms of the arms and legs (the doctor hated this), then a turn of flu, then nausea, etc., *ad infinitum*, but she responded at once to whatever treatment she was given. Since the earliest days of her doubtful pregnancy she had shown a determination to live that was endearingly impressive.

The actual birth was close to being fatal to both mother and child. Four days after, my diary has written in it: 'J. still very low.' Our surgeon was so worried he was considering a second operation. Mercifully, the anaesthetist begged him not to, as he had reason to believe that Joan might not survive it. Early every morning I would go in to see Joan in her nursing-home to report on how I found things the night before with our new daughter. Julie-Kate was recovering much more quickly than was her mother. It seemed an eternity before this giver of life showed any definite signs of improvement but, thank God, after eight weeks I was able to take her away for a gentle change for a few days in Portugal.

At the beginning of 1967 fortune brought me a kindly and refreshing up-lift. Geraldine McEwan, as everybody knows, is a sublimely funny and delicious comedienne, but I was anxious to enhance her career by finding a dramatic role for her. What should come to light but Strindberg's *The Dance of Death*; she seemed to rise to the challenging prospect of playing Alice and I felt encouraged to play Captain Edgar, her husband. Their relationship was a variation on the common love/hate theme: it was ten per cent love and ninety per cent hate.

There is a great – and may I say welcome? – difference between playing Ibsen and playing Strindberg. Ibsen's dialogue on the surface gives the impression of honesty and candour, but underneath is a subtext of evil sexuality, elaborately wrapped in symbols. Strindberg is different. His people say frankly what they mean, no matter how merciless it may be. Captain Edgar is the way he is because he has been passed over; in his fifties, he is still no more than an army captain. Alice is what she is because Edgar has made her so. The first part of the play could stand on its own; the second half is an exercise of variations which bring in the next generation, and throbs with a bit more danger. You might say that in the first part Edgar is only firing blanks, whereas in the second he's firing real bullets. They are two wonderful parts and we were lucky to have such a masterly director as Glen Byam Shaw.

When troubles come, they come not single spies but in battalions. They also have the cutest way of pushing all other troops aside; troubles have not the faintest conception of what 'being in turn' means.

During the year of 1967, loath as I am, I am bound to report that the relations at the National between its chairman and its director started to deteriorate, and by 1970 had fallen to a depth beyond any hope of recovery. It all started over a play called *The Soldiers*, by Rolf Hochhuth, which I have dealt with in an Appendix to this book.

In March 1968, I unhappily also found myself violently at odds for the first time with Peter Brook, whose work I admired wholeheartedly. He was making for the National a brilliant production of the Seneca *Oedipus*, starring John Gielgud, who unquestionably gave a perfect tragic performance, but I think no performer playing Oedipus in this production could have competed with the dazzling handling of the chorus by Peter. It was a wonderful show, infinitely clever; but to my growing horror it was clear to me that Peter was determined to risk the whole work by being clever-clever. He was convinced, no doubt with historical support, that the Greeks' way with tragedy was to finish their evening on a note of rude and vulgar jollification, as if to mock themselves for the tragic nobility of the main event of the evening. Peter's way of reconstructing this was to set the company, following hard upon Johnnie G's last tragic exit, dancing with pathetically forced gaiety, entirely unchoreographed, up and down the aisles, desperately hoping the audience would be highly amused, to the tune of a hideously jazzed-up version of 'God Save the Queen'. The effect, far from being funny, was just childishly insolent and couldn't have provoked anything other than puzzled boredom in an audience.

I begged Peter to reconsider or at least to modify it so as not to end a production which might prove to be his finest achievement with incomprehensibly infantile larks. Peter listened to me and thought up something that would have a far more savage kick in it, embarrass me to the utmost, and give an even greater shock to the audience. Just before the end, a curious shape was brought on and placed in the centre of the stage; it was about six feet high, and covered with a cloth. It was a monolith of some kind, about eighteen inches in diameter at the suggestively rounded top. There is stood shrouded as our blinded Oedipus was led off by the chorus, the leader of which returned almost immediately and walked in a thoughtful manner round to the other side of the monolith; then with a sharply dramatic gesture he seized hold of the shroud and brutally tore it off. The object now exposed was, of course, a huge phallus. After perhaps twenty seconds the house lights came up.

Thank God there was now no national anthem to accompany that vision. In trying to talk Peter out of his original jazzed-up version of 'God Save the Queen' I had bargained with him that if he would agree to cut that out I would undertake that the anthem should not be played again at any performance at the National, so long as I was its director; to this he gleefully agreed, knowing what was to him, as to quite a few others, the laughable extent of my patriotism. I think the playing of the national anthem has completely disappeared from theatrical fashion now. I recalled Ruby Miller's remark of nearly fifty years before: 'Oh yes, it's a very good thing, you have to stand straight up, even behind the curtain, and be made to feel a good girl again, no matter how naughty you've just been on the stage!'

But I can't really slide out of it so light-heartedly. After a session that went on all night, we had to meet again the next evening as the matter of the phallus had to be settled. Peter was adamant; in my deepest conscience I believed I too had to be adamant. I was alone in my convictions. Ken Tynan and Frank Dunlop clearly did not share them and, obviously dying to bring matters to a close, when Peter left us for a moment, they immediately started to persuade me to give in. Ken produced a cunning little ace: 'You know what will happen if you persist in refusing him? Pete will go straight down to Fleet Street and report that Stratford and the National are at open war.' I felt weak; I was weak; and weakly I gave in. Peter came back in and I told him the decision. Almost with a crow Peter said, 'Well, I'm going for a drink, anyone join me?' The others said goodnight and left, and I was alone, naked in my misery.

Peter had, in fact, dealt a shrewder blow to my *amour*

propre than he could have known, not that any victor broods to excess over the fate of the one defeated; but, like a defeated boxer, I knew I should remember it as the punch that started my undoing; that little inner voice squeaked, 'You're only allowed three like that, you know.' Well, there were two more to come then.

The next job I bagged for myself was the production of that divinest of plays, Chekhov's *The Three Sisters*. The cast got better and better and I grew more and more happy and pleased with their progress, but as winter changed to spring a nagging worry started to obsess me – a pain in my innards which grew ever sharper and less possible to dismiss. I took myself along to two surgeons, who after some disagreement decided that the best thing for me would be hyperbaric oxygen irradiation; for what I had contracted was cancer of the prostate gland, generally conceded to be the least likely to be terminal of the many varieties of this terifyingly deadly disease. I went into St Thomas's and Dr Churchill Davidson, whose invention this treatment was, ploughed in with his hyperbaric magic.

At first one took the extra oxygen through a mask; this increased the oxygen in the blood, which had the effect of setting the cancer into an ultra-active state; while in this state it is also at its most vulnerable, and at that moment it is blasted by two huge artichoke-shaped containers at the heart of which there nestles a radium-soaked morsel of cobalt. After a few of these introductory treatments the technique becomes a bit more scarifying; I was slid into a torpedo-like coffin, with a square of glass over the face to reduce the likelihood of claustrophobia. This coffin is now pumped full of oxygen with much greater effect on the blood's content, and round the inverted artichokes slowly circle, borne by two huge metal arms. I was allowed out for little breaks in between treatments and thus, albeit feeling dreadfully ill, I just saw the final dress rehearsal of my beloved *Three Sisters* through on the Sunday. When I got back they found I had pneumonia; I obviously wasn't to be allowed out again.

Joan at home, sitting beneath a portrait of herself as Masha in *Three Sisters*.

First introduction to Chichester.

My dearest and my closest: Joan and George Devine at the Royal Court, 1964.

Before the National Theatre opened: (*above*) with mighty chairman Lord Chandos (first Viscount), and (*below*) with great architect Lasdun (Sir Denys).

Flanked by Black Rod and the Lords Goodman and Nugent on my introduction to the Lords in 1970.

Dance of Death, 1967.

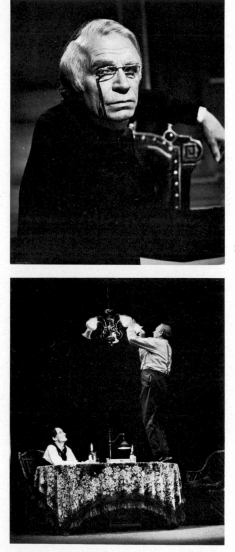

Shylock in *The Merchant [of] Venice*, 1970.

With Ronald Pickup in *[Long] Day's Journey into Night*[.]

With Ken Tynan.

Compagnie Renaud-Barrault.

With Michael Caine in *Sleuth*, 1972. I beat the pants off Michael at snooker. How lucky I happen to be a great player!

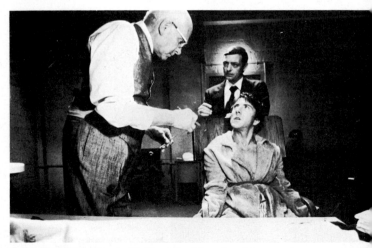

'Is it safe?' With Dustin Hoffman in *Marathon Man*, 1976.

Dearest Larry – I believe every word you say!
Love Trigg

With George Cukor on the set of *Love Among the Ruins*, 1974.

Franco Zeffirelli directing Frank Finlay, Joan, me and Gawn Grainger
in *Saturday, Sunday, Monday*, 1973.

Four of my six 'best' plays for Granada: (*above*) with Alan Bates in *The Collection*, 1976; (*left*) with Joanne Woodward – *Come Back Little Sheba*, 1977; (*opposite above*) with Robert Wagner and Natalie Wood in *Cat on a Hot Tin Roof*, 1976; and (*opposite below*) directing *Hindle Wakes* with Roy Dotrice, Rosemary Leach and Donald Pleasance, 1976.

A Little Romance, 1979.

With Jeremy Irons and Anthony Andrews in *Brideshead Revisited*,

General MacArthur in the as yet unreleased film *Inchon*.

With Elizabeth Sellars in *Voyage Round My Father*, 1982.

After the first night on the Wednesday, three of my beloved troupe came up to see me and tell me everything about the evening; Joanie, of course, such a wonderful Masha, Louise Purnell, ravishing Irina, and Robert Stephens, our splendid first Colonel Vershinin. They brought some champagne and we had a wonderfully wicked little 'feast in the dorm'. The performance had been sensationally successful and was lauded to the skies in every report. The set by Svoboda was acclaimed.

I had made an important discovery with *Uncle Vanya*: Chekhov holds his grip on an audience much more securely if his plays are only allowed one interval in the middle. The plays are much better concerted and the audience much better concentrated; with three intervals, the gentleman who has been dragged not too willingly to the theatre is now on his third double and is grumbling, 'This really is a bit tough to take, I mean are they going to Moscow or aren't they?' And his friend is saying 'With any luck they'll *be* in Moscow by the next act.' Four acts make an evening a bit unendurable.

When Svoboda asked me if I could give him any line on the style I had in mind for *Three Sisters*, I said: 'I'll tell you one thing, Swobbie my dear, I don't go for heavy velvet mantelpiece covers fringed with bobbles and I don't think you do either.' 'It must be grey,' he interrupted. 'Certainly it must be grey,' I said, 'but I must, I'm afraid, give you one great problem; there will be one minute only between acts three and four. From the bedroom to the garden in one minute – it's not easy, I know.' But Swobbie found a way to make it easy. By making the side divisions and background from thick groupings of string stretched tautly from grid to stage, these were transformed from interior to exterior or woodland according to the lighting thrown on them. The much jazzed-up Imperial national anthem had the audience very nicely forward in their seats by the end of the minute, ready to be enraptured by Swobbie's transformation. Moura (Baroness) Budberg made our translation and with Joan, Bob Stephens, Tynan and me helping with the final touches to the dialogue, the play ran off like woven silk.

* * *

Once again, from giddy delight to grievous anguish: Jack Merivale rang me in the hospital at eight in the morning, four days later, to tell me that Vivien had died in the night. Guessing there would be one or two pressmen hovering about in front of the flat in Eaton Square, I went in through a secret side-entrance on the basement floor; Jack was waiting just inside the front door of the flat. Guessing my feelings, he then opened the bedroom door and quietly closed me in to be alone with the one with whom I had shared a life that had resembled nothing so much as an express lift skying you upwards and throwing you downwards in insanely non-stop fashion.

I stood and prayed for forgiveness for all the evils that had sprung up between us.

There is a spirit in us that so to speak drives our engine, puts temperament, energy, alcohol in the nature, that makes those of us who call ourselves artists *tick* in our work, puts verve into the exploitation of our gifts, essential vitality into the illumination that makes our brass to blare and our cymbals crash – all, of course, supported by the practicalities of trained lung-power, throat, heart, guts; and when one's reward for all this hard usage seems to be nothing more than utter exhaustion, one can still find some useful resources in that final state. I would say an all-out performance of a part like Titus Andronicus or Othello will teach you all that there is to be known about this drive; high in importance among its components is, of course, sex.

In the first years of Vivien's theatre-acting there was not the passion, the flare, the flame necessary to set the stage alight. It was therefore hard to make her understand, at those times when she was sadly disappointed in the results of my intimate passionate endeavours, that all *that* had gone into my acting, and that you can't be more than one kind of athlete at a time; a sexual athlete is not likely to find sufficient energy for work of another athletic kind, and the acting of great parts most definitely was and always will be athletic, depending on inner if not on visible energy. Members of other professions that depend on the expenditure of physical energy must, I believe, find similar difficulties when attempting to double up on their energies; one has often heard that the most magnificent specimens of boxers, wrestlers, and champions in almost every branch of athletic sport prove to be disappointing upon the removal of that revered jockstrap.

She found the stuff of which great acting is made eventually on the stage, starting in the comic vein with her Sabina in *The Skin of our Teeth* by Thornton Wilder in the mid-1940s; and in the field of big emotional drama all eyes were opened by her Blanche Dubois in the great tragedy by Tennessee Williams, *A Streetcar Named Desire*, in 1949; this she crowned by her performance in the Warner Brothers film version which gained for her her second Oscar (the first was for her Scarlett in *Gone With the Wind*, after which her gift for cinema acting had been amply confirmed by *Waterloo Bridge* and *Lady Hamilton*). The 1950s saw her emergence in the alternately performed *Cleopatra* plays of Shaw and Shakespeare; these were triumphant and were subsequently taken to New York – and there began the dreadful history of mental illness.

It was in the 1960s, some time after we had parted and each found other partners, that she really came into her own, *on* her own, no longer half-shadowed in a partnership popularly but unwelcomely known as 'the Oliviers'. Though her friends and associates were still put through difficult times, in between these she was able to bring off two Hollywood films and two New York successes, though there was one disastrous musical, the timing of which was not strictly enough 'in between'.

But once more 'to the heart of the ulcer'; it has always been impossible for me not to believe that I was somehow the cause of Vivien's disturbances, that they were due to some fault in me; in spite of assurances to the contrary from every one of the many psychiatrists with which our situation had made it necessary for me to come into contact. Enough to drive a fellow barmy, isn't it? 'I think we may have got to the bottom of something,' the reader may well be murmuring.

Looking for the last time at that beautiful dead face, I

discerned a drawn look in her expression that I knew to be one of faint disgust. When I went to Jack in the sitting-room I asked him if he would mind telling me something about the circumstances of her departure. He told me that when he got back from his theatre he crept along the passage and softly peeped in at her door. All seemed quiet and at peace in the dim light; she seemed to be sleeping normally with her Siamese purring as usual beside her on the pillow. He closed the door gently and went to get himself a can of soup. Soon he himself was ready for bed. When he opened the door he found that she had fallen on the floor, obviously on her way to the bathroom. She was dead. He picked up her body and laid it between the sheets and covered her over, leaving her face and a little of her hands, which he had crossed, showing.

What had perplexed me then became clear. While I was keeping my short vigil in the bedroom, I had noticed that between the bed and the bathroom was a stain, and connecting this with the expression on her face which had caused me to wonder, I now realised what must have happened. What a cruel stroke of fate to deliver that particular little death-blow to one as scrupulously dainty in all such matters as was she. Knowing that I was quite ill and in hospital, Jack had thoughtfully refrained from ringing me till eight. He undertook to see to all the funeral and other arrangements as I obviously wasn't in any condition to do much in that line.

As soon as I could get out from under again, I concentrated on preparations for the Canadian tour; I begged off Othello as I really didn't feel up to the strain of it in those exhaustingly huge theatres. Binkie Beaumont, ever useful in professional matters on the board, suggested that it might be considered a greater compliment to send our latest success, *Dance of Death*; anyway, that was our story and we stuck to it. I had been careful to get myself well played in to *A Flea in her Ear* as well.

I wasn't myself too happy about taking on quite such a load as an overseas tour, and neither were the doctors.

They told Joanie that the treatment that I had been given was apt to have an extremely depressing effect upon a patient, particularly if he were to feel at all lonely; it was arranged that she should join me in Montreal which was likely to be especially festive in their Expo Year. So I had her visit to look forward to right through Vancouver, Edmonton and Winnipeg, which did make a marvellous difference to my moodiness and my continued crippling stage-fright.

Playing in Edinburgh at the end of February 1968, I began to feel not at all myself on the Thursday night during *Dance of Death*. Something made me excuse myself from the usual supper with Geraldine and Bob Lang and get to bed with a bowl of soup. Next day Dear Diary tells me I had 'pains all over abdomen'; a Dr Angus Hepburn examined me and was for operating at once. I pleaded that to spend up to a couple of weeks in Edinburgh would cut me off from all contact with my highly responsible duties, and couldn't I please fly up to St Thomas's in London by the very first plane that morning? He reluctantly agreed; Peggy Gilson, my wonderful secretary, worked her usual miracles at the airport and I was on the operating table and under Ken Shuttleworth's knife at 7.30. 'Just in time,' he said, 'the appendix was just about to explode and make a 'orrible mess.'

A new young actor in the company of obviously exceptional promise named Anthony Hopkins was understudying me, and walked away with the part of Edgar like a cat with a mouse between its teeth.

After the appendectomy, there sailed in the usual friendly dose of pneumonia, and with it the ever-expected dose of gout. I have not mentioned this word before because I would rather spare my reader the dreary details. The cruel fact is that I had since 1948 been a martyr to this venomous thing which provokes only laughter in those from whom you hope for some sympathy. This time the attack was rewarded with a visit from the charming Dr John Anderson, the Professor of Physic at St Thomas's Hospital. He prescribed vast doses of zyloric allopurinal to be started forthwith, and every time another attack threatened it was to receive the same treatment. I followed these instructions exactly and in two years – for the twelve years since, in fact – I have been blissfully untroubled by the painful menace.

CHAPTER FOURTEEN

National But Not Velvet

1969 was not a good year, as one might describe a disappointing wine. But in the month that made Rupert Brooke long for England, an exceptionally welcome invitation came from New York. The Antoinette Perry Award is an annual event honouring all branches of achievement in theatre arts; and would I please come on over and pick up a 'Tony' (the diminutive used for the prize in memory of that most distinguished manageress) on behalf of the National Theatre of Great Britain. It was very pleasant to know that our reputation had made the journey and flown a high enough flag to justify this regard, and off I went dreaming that the Tony might be the first of a glorious display of 'rowing-cups' in the dress-circle foyer.

I got to the Algonquin just in time for a shower, a sandwich, and to throw on my tuxedo before diving into the waiting car which sped to the backstage entrance of the Mark Hellinger; I greeted a few pals among the expectant prize-winners in the wings and we were on. After a charming citation from Alex Cohen I uttered the deeply moving, completely spontaneous lines I had thought up on the plane and, clutching my beautiful Tony, was hustled into another waiting car at the stage door and raced, to the thrilling wail of a police escort, to the airport to climb into the eleven o'clock plane with a few seconds to spare; our kind American cousins, as well as being generosity itself, are masters, as we have seen before, of this sort of organisation.

Hard upon my return I was in the Fitzroy Nuffield in Bryanston Square for a haemorrhoidectomy – too charming.

*   *   *

One of my greatest managerial ambitions for the National was to persuade the famous Ingmar Bergman to give us an English production of *Hedda Gabler*; I heard he was staying at the Savoy on a short visit and so I asked him and the lovely Liv Ullman to lunch with me at their hotel (Liv in Swedish means 'life' – I'll drink to that). It is to be expected that in matters of business a great genius is apt to play hard to get, and so I was not surprised by his skilful evasions. When there were only a few minutes left and I was beginning to give up the ghost, I was rescued by a lightning life-saving job by the lovely Liv. 'How can you be so naughty?' she said to him in her enchanting accent. 'You know perfectly well you are going to do it, why don't you put the poor man out of his misery and tell him so?' And that is how, giddy with incredulity, I realised that I was to be the first manager to persuade the great man to do an English production in London, a place he clearly detested.

I had lined up for him a brilliant cast, headed by Maggie Smith; the company and he got on so well that when, in most unusual custom after one week, he told me he had done all the work that was needed and that now the company could get on perfectly well by themselves, they were undismayed, provided he would come back to see them through the dress rehearsals and on for the first night. They made it quite clear that they didn't want me around trying to pinch-hit for him, and neither did he. A mite hurtful though this may have been, I had just wisdom enough to leave things as they were; back he came as promised, and the show was one of the great prides of my time at the National.

My next bold bid for managerial genius was about as maljudged as anything could be. There was a date in the early spring for the company to go to Los Angeles to open *The Beaux' Stratagem*, which was to play with *Three Sisters*. There was some excitement about this project. A strong section of the company was to go including Joan, Maggie and myself. As the rehearsal period approached, I began to sense a dangerous situation at the National, which gave me cold feet about leaving London. I decided to cut myself adrift from the Hollywood plan, and egotistically assumed that Joan would stay too.

I had developed the habit, common to many over-busy people, particularly those in the acting profession, of rehearsing a conversation in advance. Possibly owing to some little nervousness that this change of plan might not go down at home as smoothly as I had chosen to hope, I rehearsed this imagined conversation with Joan quite often, so often in fact that after a while I believed that it had actually taken place. One evening I airily mentioned some mooted engagement in London that spring. Joan was flabbergasted: surely we would be in Hollywood?

L: But I *told* you, darling, that's all had to be changed.
J: You certainly never told me any such thing.
L: But . . . you surely wouldn't want to leave the children?
J: They would have come with us. I have arranged it all with Nanny. You could have taken a house on the beach for a month, we could all have had a perfectly marvellous time – for a change!

I could see that the cancellation was particularly galling to Joan as I myself had been constantly urging her to get herself into the wider media; I was not going to live for ever, and when I passed out for the last time she might well find it quite a shock facing all her responsibilities alone. My inconsistency must have been hard to understand, let alone bear; here was I apparently now taking this exceptional chance of being seen in the film world away from her.

It is always hard, I suppose, when a busily committed executive, who is expected to be creatively artistic as well, gets caught up in a turmoil that threatens clear-headed thinking – when the triple complexities of business, artistic and domestic life really get going in their clamourings for priority, particularly when Our Subject has never been capable of thinking of more than one thing at a time. Hard, I suppose; but if you take it all on there is no excuse for failure and there was none for me.

I flailed about ineffectually: my stipend and her performance fees at the National hardly amounted to a fortune . . .
beach houses at Malibu weren't exactly cheap . . . the fares
for the whole family including the nanny – God, six
thousand miles *return* . . . I would never have thought it
was a luxury we could possibly afford . . . No good; no
good whatever. I could find no convincing grounds for
excuse. It was all the result of hopelessly muddled thinking.
I was beginning to lose my grip on what I had proudly
considered my good judgement; I had slipped over the edge
in allowing the demands of my job to outweigh the importance of my family. Worst of all, I had hurt Joan; hurt her
deeply. Besides all this, she was a superb Masha and had
made a dazzling success in the part.

The list of my shortcomings pierced me, and my remorse
increased as time went on. This crisis was body-blow No 2,
and it hurt more and more lastingly than either of the
others. (One past and one to come.) It must be twelve years
ago now, but it remains with me as some mortal sin remains
with a practising Christian despite the mercy of absolution.
Like Peppino at the end of Act Two of de Filippo's *Saturday, Sunday, Monday*, one can only repeat 'God damn my
life, God damn my life,' until time shall relieve us all.

This might be a felicitous moment to call to mind a quote
from our seven-year-old son Dickie, relayed to me by a
friend: 'Daddy doesn't know he does these things because
he does have a busy life, you know.'

The 1970s started graciously enough, thus: Miss Joan Plowright, CBE. Bestowed by Her Majesty Queen Elizabeth, the
Queen Mother, on 4 March.

We opened the 1969–70 season with a dazzling performance from Joan in *The Advertisement*. Then, during a
touring week of *Three Sisters* at Brighton, Alan Bates
stayed with us at home and played himself in to the part of
Vershinin for four performances before joining us for the
six-week film of the play, for which Paul Curran generously
yielded his part of Chebutikin to me, so that there could be

two known film actors in this somewhat highbrow-sounding enterprise.

Early in the year Tynan mentioned to Joan that he had discovered an amusing attack by James Agate on *The Merchant of Venice*. This started us on discussions about how one might approach this unpleasant play. Ken suggested that Jonathan Miller should direct and we all thought it was a brilliant idea; his undoubted genius had shone through so brightly in the Cambridge Footlights and in *Beyond the Fringe* that it was completely clear to me that a touch like his would be ideal for this conception.

Cruel and revealing, the relationship between Antonio and Bassanio is not sentimental, as Antonio would have it be, but depends on Bassanio's need to be kept. Gainful advantage is also the motive for his romantic approach to Portia who is entirely aware of this fact but, finding him attractive and suitable enough, with perfect frankness strikes the bargain. Shylock is a respectable old Jewish gentleman, cynically aware of the deadly Venetian prejudice against his race; it is only when, almost for a joke, his daughter is stolen from him and married to a Christian that the fires rage, this being the very most appalling disaster than can happen in an orthodox Jewish family. It has been the same since Christianity started, and I believe will be so for all time to come. As I was informed by Jonathan Miller, the strict Jewish family in such circumstances holds a funeral service for the errant girl, whose name is struck from the family records, and from then on she is dead to them. When it happens to Shylock as a Christian 'joke', he is stirred to the boiling point of fury and proceeds to his vengeance, as is not only natural but in fact his expected duty.

In my time Shylock has been played with varying degrees of highly emotional sentimentality, the actors determined to wring from the trial scene a pulsating sense of nobility. I honestly feel this is pitching it a bit high. I find it impossible to think of Shylock as a really nice chap; he is just better quality stuff than any of the Christians in the play. They are truly vile, heartless, money-grubbing monsters and when

Shylock makes his final exit, destroyed by defeat, one should sense that our Christian brothers are at last thoroughly ashamed of themselves. *The Merchant of Venice* is horrid, cruel and one of the most popular plays in the whole collected volume. What is more, it is thought to be eminently suitable for schoolchildren! I must admit to having been so impressed by the interpretation of Disraeli by Mr George Arliss in an exceptionally good talkie made in 1929 that, to be honest, I lifted it ('pinches' is such a common word) for my playing of Shylock. A few among our critical brethren did, I am afraid, being better endowed with memory and observation than I had given them credit for, see through this little ploy.

For some reason I had never been drawn to the part of Shylock; perhaps because the piece always had such a 'school play' association, perhaps because I had so greatly admired Michael Redgrave's universally acclaimed definitive portrayal and did not think I could successfully follow it. I told Jonathan all the ideas we had so far had about the problems of presentation. Although our approach to the play might be modern, there were always disconcerting incongruities in modern dress; the clothes feel awkward with the words and the words feel uncomfortable in the costumes; and the actors somehow feel uninspired by Elizabethan costumes though they are, of course, to the manner born. I suggested that the year 1880 might perhaps be ideal for our purposes; photographs of this period are probably familiar to most people, and still redolent of successful merchandise. Jonathan excited us beyond measure by the limitless variety, the originality and the fascinating colour in the expression of his ideas. He was the only man; we were thrilled by him and remain so.

For the first dress rehearsal I had made up with great care; he popped in to have a look at me. 'You don't want everybody to talk of nothing but George Arliss and Disraeli, do you?' I obediently scraped the whole lot off. I did cling to the special front row of teeth I had had made, with its companion extra lower gum; these two little friends made my mouth area, from just underneath my nose to the top of my chin, protrude enough (one feature is sufficient) to lend a semitic look to my whole countenance without further sculptural addition.

We opened at the end of April (with a special preview charity performance attended by Princess Marina) in order that a little tradition I was hoping to maintain, namely that there should always be a Shakespeare play at the National on his birthday, should be upheld. Lovely laurel wreaths were generally bestowed on the director, the Portia and the Shylock; and indeed the whole production, which was faultlessly cast, made a glittering impression.

The Merchant of Venice also marked the end of my years of paralysing stage-fright. I had been ridiculously nervous shortly before when I took over the role of A. B. Raham in *Home and Beauty*, in which for policy reasons – unwise, I thought, to risk causing a stir just at this time – I put myself down in the programme as 'Walter Plinge'. (This is a professionally though not generally well-known *nom de théatre* used for various reasons, from uncertainty of final casting to merely wishing to even up the columns on a bill.) I feared what a general turn-out of the critical faculty would do to my performance in my wretched state of mind. This may well be thought a wicked advantage to have taken of my position; but for me it was a necessary exercise. I had Shylock, a Big One, coming up. This presented a formidable danger, but one for which there was no other treatment than the well-worn practice of wearing *it* – the terror – out, and it was in that determined spirit that I got on with the job.

As the much-dreaded performance drew near, I tried to concentrate all I could on Joan, whose Portia made it an occasion even more important for her than it was for me, but the fact that her first-night nerves were not much more than normal, restored, I hate to admit, the selfish balance to myself. Before the curtain went up, I begged Tony Nicholls and others to do something that I knew went against the conscience of all of us who had worked so long for a genuine company spirit: I asked them not to look me in the eyes in any of my scenes. They generously agreed, and managed to look attentively to either side of my face. For some reason this made me feel that there was not quite so much loaded against me.

The show at last over, the reception was warm and vociferous, but I ungratefully gave that less credit for the lift in my spirits than the fact that I had got through at all. This seemed a crack through which I could spy an end to my long, distressful torment. It had started in October 1964, within a day of the first anniversary of the opening of the National at the Old Vic, and the finish hove in sight in April 1970. I had, unbelievably, endured five and a half years of agonising dread. I have sometimes thought that if I had endured more normal stage-fright at seventeen I might have forced myself to expunge it then; for those demi-gods Thespis, Mnester and Genesius to level this particular bolt at my head when I was approaching sixty seemed to me almost too cruel.

The greatest benefit of all from this blessed relief was that now I could feel free to retire from stage-acting, if I wished and if funds allowed, without the personal trauma of knowing for the rest of my life that it was fear and not choice that had driven me from my principal métier. As it was, illness was to settle that for me.

I have always had a natural sense of responsibility towards my fellow actors, and at this particular time of life a strong feeling of protectiveness for those who, like myself, must be aware of old age racing with undignified speed towards them. I felt the need to be sensitively chary of making any move or change of a drastic nature which might cause dismay, depression or even despair in those for whom the consciousness of ever-increasing years was dismal enough.

Once more, then: *it* was over. *It*, I realised with hindsight, had all started with my abortive soprano solo during the evensong of Trinity Sunday in 1921.

It was during that week in Edinburgh in 1968 playing *Dance of Death* that I received an exceedingly kind and giddy-making letter from the Prime Minister, Harold Wilson, inviting me to accept a peerage. My immediate reaction was No, Absolutely Not. The idea of separating myself from my colleagues by the kind of class distinction that this would suggest was abhorrent to me. Knighthoods were altogether different; there had been quite a generous sprinkling of these around the profession since Sir Henry Irving at the turn of the century; besides, there was something glamorous, something chivalrous about a knighthood. But about a 'lawd' there seemed only something a bit stuck-up. I phoned Joan who agreed with me, and I wrote at once to the PM and politely refused, saying that I didn't feel a peerage was suitable for me, nor I for it, and we proceeded to forget about it.

But the PM did not. He wrote again, saying that it was particularly interesting to him that people in the artistic professions should have a forum from which to speak on behalf of their own and other artistic matters. I wrote again giving all the reasons for which I felt bound again to refuse.

At a dinner party to which we were invited a few months later at No 10, Joanie and I were sitting at opposite sides and separated by some length of the table. The gentleman next to her said, counting the table, 'H'm, forty; that means everybody is here for some very definite reason; I wonder if you know the reason why you are here?' Joan replied that she did not. 'Ah,' said her neighbour, 'I expect you'll find out before the evening's over.' Dinner came to an end, the guests were vaguely circulating; Joanie and I had just about met up when the PM took me by the elbow and said, 'Now look, I'm serious about this thing, you know.' Then, turning to Joan, he said, 'You will see he does it, won't you?' Joanie, who hadn't the faintest idea what he was referring to, said, 'Oh yes, of course I will!' When I told her what it was all about, she knew at least what *we* were there for.

Early in 1970 Arnold Goodman, who is a lawyer of exceptional brilliance and acknowledge eminence, Chairman of the Arts Council and a member of the South Bank Theatre Board, sent for me and put the thing to me, once more. I explained that I would rather have almost anything else; Joanie was a 'Ladyship' already – not that she had welcomed that very much; couldn't I have a pretty ribbon or two or three letters after the name – GCMG or something? He explained that any amount of those kickshaws would undoubtedly come my way in time but that they were purely selfish things, giving nobody other than myself anything to preen about; but by accepting a peerage I could stand up in the House of Lords and gain things for other people, support reforms, make claims for my own profession, speak on matters about which I had strong opinions; didn't I have any views on the Common Market? He was very persuasive. Joan said, 'Oh well, dear, they obviously very much want you to have it; I think that perhaps you should take it.' Hence my diary entry for 13 June 1970: 'Baron, B'ess & Hons!' And on that day I was also privileged to dig the 'first sod' for the National Theatre in London.

On 1 August I was taken to the Harley Street Nursing Home with a whopping great thrombosis in my right leg from mid-thigh up to the vena cava. The incredibly young-seeming Professor of Surgery at St Thomas's, into which Ken Shuttleworth had quickly shifted me, pronounced that it was a direct, if delayed, result of my cancer treatment. Poor Shuttle stood staring out of the window, chewing the inside of his cheeks. He needn't have worried on my account, I would never have nursed the slightest feelings of blame for him; besides, I would gladly be a guinea pig for medical science any time. But this was not the end of it; ten years later in 1977 the ureter belonging to my left kidney developed a double loop which was firmly caught up in a small mass of fibrous tissue, innocently floating around still from that old treatment. This necessitated more surgery, and the most serious yet.

My constant indisposition had inevitably created a dangerously unhealthy situation in the National Theatre leadership. The introduction of an undisputedly star performer such as Joan into the administration could only be salutary. Oliver Chandos disagreed strongly with my proposal. Although I have reason to believe that he had actively supported my recent honour, our relations grew more sore and more sour, so that my inclination became ever stronger to go to Arnold Goodman about the National's troubles.

Early in November I asked Arnold for a private meeting, at which I explained as calmly as I could that – God knows how reluctantly – I had come to the conclusion that I was quite unable to go on serving the organisation, since it was impossible for me to continue with the situation as it had now developed between Chandos and myself. When Jennie (Baroness Lee of Asheridge, Minister of the Arts) arrived to join him for dinner he said at once, 'Jennie, Larry says he can't work any more with Oliver Chandos.' She replied, 'Well, no one'll blame him for that.' And that was about it, really; I was stroked and patted and told just to carry on as usual – and what would I think of Sir Max Rayne (now Lord Rayne), the financier, who had lately been elected to the board? I had only comparatively recently met him at a D.Litt. ceremony at London University, but had found him nice, quiet, simple and reasonable and clearly extremely gifted in his own field. I felt composed in the knowledge that all would be well before too long now.

The chairman only chaired one more board meeting. It was an unusually simple agenda and he got through it with dignified despatch; there were no questions asked, no announcements made. As it broke up and members and secetariat were shuffling out, he turned to me and said quietly, 'Well . . . it seems they've decided to get rid of me.' I don't think I said anything, just looked at him questioningly, much as I had done on the rare occasions when he would bring his face, flushed with fury, uncomfortably close to mine – though now it was in half-averted profile: 'Well, I suppose I'm getting on a bit . . . or something.' I felt really sorry for him and said, 'Oh, Oliver, that must seem terribly ungrateful – after all you have done to bring about a National Theatre in our country.' I was as nervously pompous as that. Either out of delicacy or kindliness, he did not ask, 'Did you know anything about this?' He just shrugged and we parted.

On 24 March 1971 I was introduced to the House of

Lords as Baron Olivier of Brighton by Lord Cottesloe, a former chairman of the Arts Council and at this time chairman of the South Bank Board of the National, whom I used to know as John Fremantle in much younger days with Vivien, and Lord (Tim) Nugent, erstwhile Lord Chamberlain and censor, whom I had consequently faced across his desk often enough. Oliver Chandos, whom I would naturally have asked in spite of all, was not eligible as he was a viscount and so a rung above us. Stricter class distinction obtained in the Lords apparently than in Solihull. I gave my one and only splendid lunch in the House of Lords on that day and invited all relations and friends who had had a hand in establishing me or influencing me to this point in my life. I had asked the catering manageress for sausages and mash, but the most homespun thing I was allowed was steak and kidney pie. The big money went on the wine.

On the last day of February 1972 Kenneth Rae called at my office late in the afternoon to say, 'Oliver went into hospital today. I think it's just a little minor surgery; he told me it was "just one of those elderly gentleman's little troubles".' I knew what that meant well enough. Next morning I sent him some flowers with a note of the most warmly encouraging words that I could muster. He died the next day, I expect without ever knowing of my thoughts for him.

Sir Max Rayne had assumed the chair when Oliver retired. I asked for an early appointment as there was something I particularly wanted to say to him. I told him that if he had any inclination towards some other director, or if he felt that I had been there long enough and a change might let in some fresh air, he would find me entirely co-operative, and that I would help all I possibly could in the search for a successor; I had spent a great deal of thought on this question and had indeed yielded many a production I would dearly like to have taken on myself to some other director whom I thought might be a possibility for the future.

In my own heart, of course, I would always go for an actor to lead a company, but the general consensus among my superiors was obviously that they would like a change from this particular animal. I had tried to interest Albert Finney in the idea but his own acting prowess was so marketable that he could naturally see little point in vastly increasing his responsibilities and decimating his income.

In the directorial line, I strongly favoured some youthful talent who coupled imaginative flair with a sense of responsibility and natural authority: a young Tony Guthrie, in fact. I suggested two or three names, but the answer was always, 'Not enough stature.' In vain did I point out that the job would surely create the stature; had they ever heard of Trevor Nunn before he took over from Peter Hall at Stratford? But they were obdurate.

At some unrecorded moment in 1970 Tynan hit me with a dazzlingly brilliant idea – to put on *Guys and Dolls* at the National Theatre. I belong to a section of Anglo-American society that believes this to be the greatest of all American shows, so I set about talking the board round to it. After the first few seconds of uncertain silence, Shaun Sutton said almost defiantly loudly, 'I think it's a marvellous idea.' I was quite prepared for the objection that would assuredly be raised, and not unreasonably – namely the proverbially botched American accents attributed to English actors.

I had laid my plans quite well this time, and before going any distance at all on this project had contacted my friend Garson Kanin, the brilliantly clever dramatist, author, stage director, original film story-writer, film director, script writer, famous for writing and directing both the play and film of *Born Yesterday*, to name only one: could he come over and direct this production, IF, and a very big IF I knew it to be, I could get it passed by my board? Garson, whom I had known in Hollywood since 1938, was Brooklyn-born, as was Danny Kaye, and they would regale me time and again with long colloquies in their native jargon until I could almost do it convincingly myself. Those members of the company that I was choosing to play *Guys and Dolls* (secrecy obligatory, of course) were not only clever but known by me to be expert mimics. I knew enough to start them off on the usage of consonants, individual I believe to New York and essential to the Damon Runyon dialogue. 'Dthon' Tthell *me*' would be the initial exercise. Garson was to bring over an acrobatic dancer to teach us the song-and-dance numbers.

It did not take as long as I feared to persuade the board into sanctioning the production; the company started some exploratory work and I was happier in the job than I had been for ages. All looked promising when bang went my leg to the size of an elephant's with that infuriating thrombosis. A condition of the board's agreement was that I should be part of this company, and it was also conditional with Garson that I should play Nathan Detroit, and here was I in no state to move, let alone dance.

When I had to go into hospital it was thought better to postpone this enterprise indefinitely; alternative plans must be made and the people especially attached to this production, in particular our American visitors, could not be kept hanging around. We would all have to be patient and pray for another opportunity. I did not feel too pessimistic about this, though I knew from long experience how much more difficult it is to get a whole big machine together a second time when it lacks that initial sizzling enthusiasm.

Meanwhile, when I had recovered enough I was allowed a couple of weeks to play de Witte in the *Nicholas and Alexandra* film; I had some records to make of the New English Bible, Joan would be opening in *A Woman Killed with Kindness*, and I had to get *Guys and Dolls* past the board again. They couldn't very well refuse, I supposed; and my future glowed with those roseate dreams of 'the greatest company in the world' again.

Almost since the time when Ken Tynan had started pressing me into Othello, he had been trying hard for *Long Day's Journey into Night* by Eugene O'Neill. My resistance to this marathon piece was on quite different grounds. It was not that I felt inadequate for this role, it was too clearly within my compass; but I had always felt a strong resistance to playing an actor. It is part of the conventional tradition when portraying a member of a profession so automatically mocked that he should be a stereotype: vain, florid, flamboyant, affected and more than a trifle absurd. I remember musing upon this when I was watching the great Freddie March giving his magnificent performance in New York and thinking, 'Not for me, boy, thank you, every single trap is in this part.' For once, when people say, 'You were born to play that part,' it isn't all that cheering.

However, as soon as we started to work on it, enthusiasm began to mount. With Constance Cummings, with Denis Quilley and Ronald Pickup for the boys, with Michael Blakemore directing us, we knew we had what the doctor ordered and that was a money-making hit. We were not in the finest fettle moneywise and when it looked, as it did, that we were going to lose £100,000 by the end of that financial year (may I say we had not lost up till now, 1970, since we had started in 1963) I had said to Ken T: 'All right you've had your wicked way, *Long Day's* it is, not because we want to, Kenny, but because we have to.'

I thought of a good way to learn our long parts. We would meet for an afternoon once a week and just read together for the six weeks before rehearsals were due to start. I am sure that if we had read through six times in one day or once every day for six days we would never have known it in the time; it must have been that lull in between, filled with all the other things that we all had to do, that somehow allowed the words to seep in gently. Anyway, it worked and by the time we came to rehearsal we were all pretty well 'perfect'.

Joanie had taken a box for the first night, which was most unusual, but she was determined the two elder children should be there. She was always funny in her habits on my first nights; she felt she had to be in the theatre but not necessarily to watch, except from time to time. She would sit at the side of the stage or in a dressing-room so that she could turn the tannoy up or down at will. She could slip in and out of the box, and the children too if necessary; it was a very long evening and might be a bit of an endurance test for them. During the long drunk scene with Ronnie Pickup she decided to take leave of absence herself, and sat on a step outside the box.

It felt right for some reason to direct the most difficult part of the scene towards the roof of her box. Sensing that two unusually small people were sitting there I lowered my eyes to find them met by two pairs I knew intimately well: one belonging to a nine-year-old son and the other to an eight-year-old daughter. I dried up as I have seldom done in a long life of speaking other people's dialogue. The scene invited long pauses; even so, a full half-minute made Ronnie aware that all was not well. I was not only helpless but unhelpful, not even having the wit to say, 'Well now, I wonder what it was I was going to say,' or some simpler cypher for 'HE-E-E-ELP'. Ronnie saw my empty gaze fastened upon him, and somehow hoisted me back into the scene. Joan all this time was sitting on the step outside her box acutely aware of what was going on and, though in agony, grateful to be where she was.

In spite of this hiatus the show turned out even better than we had dared to hope and brought our audiences clamouring back again. With more successes to follow we were able to make good the £100,000 loss of the year before, which set the manager side of me all a-purr again; I've never felt quite happy about the idea of billing the government for one's failures. This is not meant to imply that it is possible for such theatres as the National to make out without government subvention, because that would be absurd.

But I am avoiding a sore subject; this is not a success story composed of strongly-maintained up and bravely-outfaced downs. As usual the hurt I do to myself is worse than that intended by the one who delivered the blow; the tap on the jaw can be quite light, it is the heavy weight with which I fall that does me the injury.

This hurt that was done me was not intentional, it was thoughtless, or rather it was caused by wrong thinking. To my sorrow the doer of the deed – let us call him 'my friend' – was one with whom I had been very pleasantly acquainted for some twenty-five years. At the time of this occurrence I was well and truly loaded with work, being in active production directing Gerry McEwan and Chris Plummer in *Amphytrion 38*. As usual this was not the only iron in the fire; *The Merchant* was doing a mini-tour. After Newcastle and Oxford with *Amphytrion*, we faced a production weekend at the Vic.

Over the weekend I heard that my precious *Guys and Dolls* had been cancelled in my absence from all future plans by a board meeting held behind my back (I being on provincial duties) at the instigation of none other than 'my friend'. I talked to him on the phone and, sure enough, he admitted to being responsible and even seemed to be a little boastful about it; he made strong representations on account of the costs, but this was sheer blather. All that had been argued over and over and been passed by the board on two separate occasions, each a year apart due to my interrupted health, and it had been finally agreed that it was a risk worth taking. My friend then said something that really pinned my ears back: 'I wouldn't have objected if the proposed musical had been – *Oklahoma!*' Oh God, the man was now pitching on my preserves: the preserves of the director, who had sole charge in the matter of choice of plays and players, and the final word on every detail in the running of the organisation.

I felt drained of everything except a helpless exhaustion. I had lost my courage. I knew that I should make complaints to the chairman, insist on another board meeting which, with Arts Council backing, I felt pretty sure that I could bring round to a different conclusion. But I felt gutless and hopeless; a board that could be persuaded to go against a twice-made decision in the absence (on duty) of the man most formidably affected by it, and that man their director, was not going to feel inclined, as a favour to that creature, to give him much of a hearing, nor much sympathy. Just as a boxer (yet again! No one was ever less like a boxer than I) who knows he cannot last the round may hesitate to drag himself from his corner, I gave up, I opted out, I allowed myself to be cut adrift from my will. If one finds that one's colleagues and friends are content to take actions that they must know are acts of treachery, then it is more than hard, and in my case impossible, to continue the grotesquely unequal struggle any further. I was tired right out, I was utterly exhausted. I must stop.

My sulks are understandable, I think; since 1963 I had been proving the company's worth, their virtuosity, skill and versatility. 'Let us prove there is nothing this company cannot reach!' would be my constant pep-sentence to them. Complete accuracy of accent is a lifelong passion of mine. In 1965 they achieved perfect Scottish in *Armstrong's Last Goodnight*. In 1966 they achieved Sean O'Casey's Irish for *Juno and the Paycock*, in spite of the more smarty-pants critics who, knowing that Colin Blakely is an Ulsterman, detected as much in his accent; but Harry Hutchinson (whom some may remember as Joxer with the Abbey Players, the first eye-opening time that we saw them in England at the old Royalty Theatre in Dean Street in 1924) had helped me during the direction of *Juno and the Paycock* by keeping a careful watch on the accents; he, with all due respect to the smarty-pants, expressed his entire satisfaction that Colin's Irish was properly Dublinesque. The early Cromwellian English spoken in the period of Arthur Miller's *The Crucible* was, I'm afraid, only a director's guess. And now the rare bird that was due to fall into the company's laps, the opportunity to exploit their prowess at Damon Runyon New Yorkese, was to be taken from them by one for whom the gentle charge of excess zeal is too kind.

For it was against the company that this sin was committed, much more than against me. And here was I, incapable of action, impuissant almost to a state of paralysis, a dull and muddy-mettled rascal, like John-a-dreams unpregnant of my cause, who could say . . . nothing. Were I a woman – which may be wondered about at times owing to a tendency in my writing to emulate Ella Wheeler Wilcox – I might say it was as if my mother's milk was being taken from me and fed to some marauder's brat. Anyway, though there are plenty of things for me to feel guilty about during my incumbence of the driver's seat at the National, faulty accents are not among them.

It was not the wound that this treachery – for that, I'm afraid, we must call it – inflicted, it was my acceptance of it that constituted my body-blow No 3, the one that let me know I was not going to be on my feet much longer. Indeed I expressed this feeling in my diary on 21 June 1971: '*G's & D's* cancelled after twice laid on – decided not stay much longer – 9th year.'

I wondered if anyone else felt the same. The cast had been taken all through the music by Marc Wilkinson, our composer/conductor; Walli Strauss from New York had been working on the dancing and movement, Geraldine McEwan had actually had a course of special singing lessons for which she had paid, one or two others may well have done the same and not told me, the designs had all been completed; it might seem it wouldn't have cost all that much more to put on the show.

Michael Blakemore and John Dexter were now officially associate directors. On 2 February 1972 I went to see Max Rayne, to whom I explained that I was concerned about appointing my successor, feeling as I did now about the job; I plumped strongly for Michael, knowing well that Johnnie wouldn't want to take it on. Once again I got that irritating stuff about 'not being the stature'. I made it as clear as I could that the job was really beginning to get a bit thin on top for me now. He said he would be sure to let me know if he had any suggestions, and I had to be content with that.

Sir Max Rayne sent for me on 24 March 1972 when he spoke of the termination of my directorship of the National Theatre and informed me it had been decided by the board that my place would be taken by Peter Hall. This was a bit of a shock as I had expected to be consulted, and had indeed requested to be; after ten years' hard labour one might feel it was almost an obligatory courtesy, so I had two surprises – the second being that Peter should happily follow me in a job; I had always thought Stratford would be his Ultima Thule as the National was mine. It was a good thing now that our rivalry had claimed so stoutly to be a friendly one.

I phoned Peter to congratulate him and to say that I felt flattered by his decision; he was extremely nice and most apologetic that he had not been frank with me about it, but he had been sworn to secrecy and so in an impossible position. I had no blame whatever in my heart for Peter, but there was a little 'moth' that troubled my mind's eye: why all the secrecy? Why the shoddy treatment? On 3 February 1973 I again went to see Max and complained bitterly about his manners or lack of them. It appeared that he regarded the whole episode as being purely a routine matter; a little back and forth followed, at the end of which he graciously let me 'have the last word' as he put it.

I then turned to the other, hopefully more pleasing aspect of my visit. I was going to find it a little unhappy to continue for the coming months in a hamstrung sort of way; I would always be feeling obliged to refer any important decision to Peter, in case it went against the interests of some policy he might have in mind; so why not be frankly 'co-directors' for this six months? It would clear the situation and ease the public's mind. This went down well all round. So the bills with the usual National heading now boasted: 'Co-directors Peter Hall and Laurence Olivier'; I've always found alphabetical order to be the most practicable and unhurtful way out of a billing problem – except in a mixed partnership, where I have always emulated Gerald du Maurier, who would strictly, like the fine gent he was, cling to the 'ladies first' rule. Anyway, Peter's and my partnership worked out easily and happily, and at the end of the six months I said an affectionate goodbye and good luck, and disappeared.

Determined not to risk being an embarrassment, I did not pay a visit to the National for quite a long time; when finally I did and no one recognised me I was furious, of course, and had to remind myself with a little self-inflicted kick that I *wanted* to be anonymous.

Shortly after being told that Peter Hall was to take over from me I got leave to do the *Sleuth* film. Through the rehearsals I found Michael Caine wonderfully good company, ceaselessly funny and a brilliant actor. Two days or so before shooting, Joe Mankiewicz directing us said privately he was a bit worried about me; I seemed to lack the essential authority for Andrew Wyke's stature in the relationship. It did not take me very long to work out why. I had developed a habit of being an audience to Michael, a foil for him. This was disastrous to the enterprise; if the character of Wyke does not completely dominate the younger man there is no dramatic peak when the positions are reversed. Moral: be religiously firm on a character even at possible risk to personal relationships. Joe also asked me, a little wistfully, whether I couldn't possibly do something to make myself look a little more attractive. 'Nothing easier,' I said. Since I was twenty-four in Hollywood I have had recourse to one panacea to which I always fly should a little beautifying be required. I stick on, if there is not time to grow it, a Ronald Colman moustache; I appeared with this adornment on my upper lip next day and the shock of the transformation ran through the studio. Everyone thought that now they had a certain success on their hands, as indeed they had. It seems almost too simple.

Well, it is.

Joan was for Chichester, under John Clements now, to play Mrs Dubedat in *The Doctor's Dilemma* and Katharina in *The Shrew*, richly gentle in one, deliciously dangerous in the other, wondrous witty in both. I am reminded that when Joan took over Beatrice in *Much Ado* from Maggie Smith a little before this, Tynan found a delectable comparison: 'Maggie,' he said, 'is the Lemon and Joan is the Orange.'

I will never know whether I should be ashamed of the little confession that follows or not; with a life-style that would seem to be expected of people in our sort of position, the modest stipend from my permanent appointment of the previous ten years was not enough for us and it had to be augmented somehow. Which accounts for the occasional two- or three-day film appearances being welcomed by me from time to time. Government education requires that the choice of school be limited to the locality in which you live. I'm afraid we wanted something different. Like most people who pay the stratospheric income tax charged for the undoubted privilege of belonging to our country, we found it next to impossible to save enough to pay school fees. The authorities are not touched by this plight, they have no sympathy for our educational ambitions for our children, they want every man-jack of us to love the state school. They refuse to recognise in what shallow waters they flounder, against the flood of intelligent opinion and inclination.

People who like to think of themselves as artists are inclined to regard their profession more in the light of a vocation and seem to cheapen themselves by advertising some commodity, at least I fancy that is so in our lovely old country; and so when I fell for this means of gaining an extra bob or two – or even three – I felt compelled to exclude Great Britain from view or sound of the advertisement I made for the remarkably clever camera created by the brilliant engineer, Dr Land, for Polaroid. I felt sure enough that the European countries with the US would not disapprove, but only sympathise with any guy who needed a buck.

Noël, at last Sir Noël, had been living in Jamaica for a few years now, coming home every eighteen months or so for a visit. Towards the end of one of these in 1972, a magnificent party was given for him and some three hundred of his most intimate friends – oh yes, very funny, but he could certainly boast that many. Our host was Swifty Lazar, an exceptionally gifted Hollywood writer's agent, and this was a mighty gesture to do honour to a matchless talent, outstanding and glistering at the peak of our profession for the past fifty years, on both sides of the Atlantic. It was a wonderful occasion but there was a hint of the ominous about it.

After the delicious Claridges dinner was finished, the company started to clamour for Noël to go to the piano and do something for us all. I think most of us who counted ourselves among his true intimates worried a little about this; he had suffered more than his fair share of illnesses over the past ten years and didn't seem at all his old unassailable self. His hands were markedly shaky, he was walking very lamely and referring to his 'leg trouble'. However, he politely rose from his seat and limped to the piano, sat down and played the intro to 'If Love Were All'. Tears sprang to most eyes at the clumsiness of those formerly agile fingers slipping off the black notes, and 'The most I've ever had is just a talent to amuse' became a really tragic message. Some of us, I'm afraid, took a little heavily to the bottle; poor Binkie Beaumont was over-wrought enough to have to traverse the pavement to his car on all fours, and indeed most of us were well on the way to the same condition. Some of our hands helped Noël into his car; as it drove off he looked through the back window straight at me, waving gently and grinning; I was doing the same back to him as he receded from me, and I knew that we both knew that we would not see each other again.

When one reaches the sixties it is difficult at first not to feel a grievous sense of shock at the disintegration of the Clan, the ever-increasing frequency of the departure of one's friends, hopefully to Paradise. The first three years of the decade seemed particularly rich in their crop.

1971   *31 July: Michel St Denis*, an eye-opening director and *homme de théâtre*, very much a part of an almost closed circuit of friends of which I was proud to be one.

1972   *19 January: Stephen Arlen*, a wonderful partner and warm friend of enormous value at the beginnings of the National, when he shared the administration between Sadler's Wells and ourselves, having to relinquish his responsibilities to us when he became director of the Wells.

21 January: Lord Chandos, eminent statesman, Minister of Supply and Secretary of State for the Colonies under Churchill; interested in all the arts, the theatre in particular, most especially in the National which could not have been built without his powerful backing.

1973 *19 January: Max Adrian*, invaluable actor and resourceful *diseur*. He and Laurier Lister, who directed such brilliant revues, were close friends of ours and his sudden death was a sharp shock.

26 March: Noël Coward, not unexpected, but his death was difficult to take in. Ginette Spanier and I agree, still, that we don't really believe he is dead. We remember his talents, the masterliness and the variety of them, his originality, brilliant wit and understanding, his generosity, his inventiveness, the protean range of his gifts: his musicality, gift of melody, as a lyricist, playwright, actor, singer, tap-dancer. With his dazzling prowess as a light comedian, he was the most complete master of the stage in this century, and adored by his friends, and many millions of others.

22 May: Binkie (Hugh) Beaumont, a close friend and a rival manager of unique supremacy and as such an unusually helpful adviser.

Six in three years; quite a little holocaust.

Nineteen seventy-three was the year, if not of grace, at least of the EEC. The festivities celebrating this great event began with a finely constructed set of ritzy music-hall turns compèred by the scrumptious Judi Dench, Max Adrian and myself at the Royal Opera House, Covent Garden, attended by HM the Queen and other members of the Royal Family. On 2 May took place the topping out ceremony of the National.

On 24 June our dining-room was broken into. It was a neat job. Our man was not over-ambitious and knew when enough was enough; he simply placed all the silver candlesticks, ornaments and cutlery into the centre of the table-cloth, which happened to be a handsome lace one, picked up the four corners to make a sack, which he presumably knotted at the top, and went out through the window, which he left open.

Three months later there was another intrusion, not so light-hearted, in fact very heavy-handed indeed. This man had obviously been watching our habits. We had been staying in our country cottage for our three-week summer holiday; on my return I had pulled up in the Mews, and while I was unloading the car Joan went up to the library with Tamsin – aged ten now – to get herself a drink, and then down to the kitchen. I stopped for a drink at the bar on my way in with the luggage, and carried the glass upstairs in my right hand, with a large heavy suitcase in my left hand. I pushed the library door inwards with the hand with the glass in it, and bent to put the case down before getting myself a refill from the library. As I rose, a cosh from behind came straight across my right eye, the heavy bit landing on my nose. Knocked almost senseless for a second, the thought flashed, 'That was a bit much, Dickie really must learn to pull his punches.' I straightened up to see a young man in jeans, with bobbed hair, disappearing upstairs round the first half-landing, keeping his face well averted. I seized a British Oscar from the library but, finding it too weighty for me, set it down again. Never a brave man, I wasn't for chasing a youth with a dangerous weapon in his hands. Also my nose was pouring blood, and I started screaming for help from the family.

It turned out that Joan asked the kids if that wasn't me shouting? To which one of them replied, 'Oh no, Mummy – *Hamlet*'s on the telly tonight and you know how he roars and screams in that.' But when after a while it became apparent that the vociferous distress was mine, not Hamlet's, up they came. Tamsin was first round the staircase corner to see the front of my new pale fawn Glenurquhart jacket apparently covered in a crimson cloth, my nose having done a thoroughly good drenching job.

When we summoned up the courage to go upstairs we found the top back bathroom window open – he must have jumped through this, landing on a projecting piece of building, from which he hurled himself across to the drain-pipes on the back wall of the house to the right of us, and shinned down these into the outside basement. The lady next door, who was taking a bath, saw him flash past her window.

In phoning the police I was guilty of some over-dramatics. *'He,'* I said, 'took to his heels and *ran*, whereas *I* . . . *held my ground*!' The police brought fistfuls of photographs for me to identify. I had to keep telling them I had only seen the back of his head, which might well have been a wig. They obviously didn't think much of me for not giving chase and collecting a brand new criminal for them. Our friend Dr Binning came over and took me to the Eye Hospital, where they couldn't find anything obviously wrong. This turned out to be a mistake. I accepted for some years that one lens of my glasses would have to be different from the other; but recently I was recommended to an eye surgeon, Mr Bedford, who told me that the blow from our young escapee had, in fact, resulted in the formation of quite a bit of scar tissue in my right eye; this had caused considerable pressure in the eye-ball and consequently on the optic nerve, causing loss of sight. I made a second visit to Mr Bedford for a progress report; he saw some improvement, but said that I must continue with his drops or the sight would go again. So that is the charming little visiting card our uninvited young guest of eight years ago left with me. All will be well, provided I don't get stranded on a desert island with no eyedrops.

At the end of October 1973, Tynan had come upon a very exceptional Italian playwright, Eduardo de Filippo. It was high time Franco Zeffirelli directed for us again, as it seemed a long time since his *Much Ado*, and we asked him which of de Filippo's plays he would choose. 'If you want his Chekhovian style, then *Saturday, Sunday, Monday,*' he replied. 'But if a domestic comedy-drama would be better for your programme, then *Filumena*.' We chose the first because it had many more parts in its cast – ever a prime consideration with a large company.

It was a lovely success, and before leaving I persuaded

Peter Hall that if he was making changes in the company we could at least give this section of the old one a little extra innings by setting *Sat., Sun., Mon.* up in the West End. We did, and it was a huge success. It was financially rewarding to the company, to the National and to Zeff and Eduardo.

There was time for one more part for me under our combined auspices. I asked Joan what she thought I should do. She replied with that typical candour that I have always appreciated and found so endearing, 'If you do anything as predictable as King Lear, I really don't think I shall speak to you again; do something modern, for heaven's sake, give one of your younger contemporaries a showing.' I did not have to look for long. Johnnie Dexter had a play he wanted to do and brought it for me to approve. I read it and was thrilled. It was by a left-wing author, Trevor Griffiths, and called *The Party*, and that was just what it was about. What excited me was that the author was too good a playwright to let his play be overwhelmed by political bias, too good an artist to be a pamphleteer. Like many of his inclination he is wretchedly dissatisfied with the state of the Communist Party in England, and so in his mind his play is a tragedy.

I told Johnnie that we would certainly put it on; of course he should direct it; and I offered myself for the character of Tagg, one of three remarkably fine parts in the play. Tagg is based on a well-known representative of the Party, but the character is prevented from being too vulgarly recognisable by being made a Glaswegian. For this accent I was mercilessly schooled by Paul Curran, a Glaswegian in the company.

I have grown to appreciate frank direction, it is what we elderly actors need. So many directors are too impressed by the celebrated to risk giving offence, whereas the older we get the more we need the support of others' experiences and skills; particularly do we need the reactions of the younger generation, who represent our future audiences. I'll never forget Jonathan Miller saying to me, when directing the film of *The Merchant of Venice*, 'I wonder if you realise how many times you have said that sort of line in just that sort of way and that tune of inflection, please avoid it for ever more!' Well, I'm sorry but we oldies need it.

Two other outstanding roles in *The Party* were played by Frank Finlay – the leading part really – and Ronnie Pickup. I have always accounted this product of John Dexter's skill his finest to date. The terror in my part was a speech twenty minutes long, and I was never able to confront it without fear of making mistakes and ultimately being forced to dry up. I had taken four months through the summer to learn it, legs stretched out on a garden seat from six to eight every morning, adding another twelve or fifteen lines a day.

It's no use hiding it for the protection of my contemporaries: the sixties do bring problems to the faculty of memorising. It's better for us to face the difficulty and make allowances and provision for it. When the brain is at its clearest, probably in the early morning, is the best time for learning; when you're young, late at night is all right – well, any time's all right for anything when golden youth is yours. The last entry in my 1973 diary is a quote from Gough Whitlam, the Australian statesman, in 1969: 'When you're faced with an *impasse* you have to crash through or you've got to crash. I crashed through.' I don't think it's particularly applicable but it's striking.

Peter Hall gave us a lovely farewell present at the National, though I was past the co-director stage now. He was very anxious that both Joan and I should be seen to be overlapping our time with his; we were happy to co-operate in the avoidance of a severance. He asked Joan to play and me to direct *Eden End*, to my mind J. B. Priestley's most lovely theatre work. The piece is set in 1912, and his title has a double meaning; apart from being the imaginary name of a village in Yorkshire, it is a reference to the final phase of that wealthy, happy, easy, unworrisome time when everything in the civilised world seemed settled, secure and absolutely all right, before the Great War bust everything asunder. It is almost seventy years ago now, and still every nerve is a-jangle, and scare abounds in this world of universal insecurity. To some of us only to be associated with the National's first phase, the title also applied a wry unguent to any scars that might be smarting a little.

It was a lovely experience. Jack Priestley was delighted with the show; it is a most gratifying experience to please an author. He said that Joan's first entrance had an uncanny magic about it. The door opened and a woman came on to the stage, smiling a little wistfully, a little apprehensively; it was not Joan at all; it was his Stella.

I had a lucky snip just after this; two months later, in May, Katharine Hepburn, George Cukor and I were shooting *Love Among the Ruins* for television. I had known Katie since 1934 when we were in two different plays in New York, she in *The Lake*, I in *The Green Bay Tree*. I had known George even longer, but had never worked with either before. George had directed Kate, of course, many times; we had all talked about working together over the years, as one does, but it was happening now for the first time, and it was an unforgettable six weeks; it passed like a lovely pink shooting-star, so memorable but quickly gone.

CHAPTER FIFTEEN

L'Envoi

In August 1974 all the family went to stay with our dear friend Franco Zeffirelli among his cascade of small villas near Positano; he is a wonderful host and we were blissfully happy. There is not much of a beach there, it is rock bathing with I personally enjoy even better; all the children could swim by now so there was no need for alarm. One rock in particular was a nice easy height to dive off, about ten or twelve feet. One day as I was taking off, just too late I saw one of the kids swimming across underneath; I made an absurd attempt for a split second to arrest my flight through the air; I plunged, of course, perfectly safely beyond the child, but I jarred my back a little. I would have thought no more about it if a dull pain in my back had not persisted. As time went on pains seemed to spread from my neck to my shoulder, down my upper arms to my forearms, eventually to my hips and quadruceps. When I got home I made an early visit to my osteopath who thought that it all stemmed from ricking my back halfway through the dive.

In a little while there were stranger symptoms: funny things seemed to be happening to my skin, an acute sort of dryness, and before I knew it my face was swelling up all over. There was an inch-deep triangle of dead white under each eye; both eyes had almost disappeared into the swelling, through which they could be seen to peer like boot-buttons. Next, the outside corners of my fingernails began to feel very sore. On a day up in London I went to see a doctor who told me it must be my teeth; my dentist said there was nothing wrong with my teeth, it might be my eyes. My oculist said there was nothing unusually wrong with my eyes.

Finally I went to my Brighton skin specialist, Dr Pat Hall-Smith, who was quite a friend of mine. He looked very interestedly at me, touched my face once and asked if I had noticed anything else unusual; I told him about the sore corners to the fingernails. He asked if I had mentioned these to anyone before. I said, 'Certainly not, I don't want just to be told to trim my fingernails more carefully.' He told me to sit down and relax while he made a telephone call. When he came back he said there was a doctor, a lady, thought by him and his brethren to be the best consultant physician in East Sussex and maybe beyond; she would come and see me at six o'clock that evening.

Dr Joanna Sheldon turned out to be a very handsome woman with whom one felt an immediate rapport. She gave me a complete examination, during which I told her about the accident to my back and its strange sequels. When she had finished she sat in thought, and then said very carefully, 'You have a disease called dermato-poly-myocitis' – explaining that 'dermato' stood for skin, 'poly' for much or general, 'myo' for muscle, and 'citis' for inflammation, and that it could be a lot worse than it sounded; I must prepare myself to be in hospital for six or even nine months. I reacted to this as heroes do in melodrama when faced with some excruciating death, cool and unmoved. She told me a little later that I was as brave a chap as could be; well, there you are, that's yer actor's training for you. Joan, I may tell you, showed every bit as sound a grounding in actor's training as I. So, a few duds in a suitcase and in I went to the Royal Sussex County Hospital.

The disease, as it took hold, turned out to be rather scary. People seem to know so little about it, very few doctors have ever seen a case, one of my doctors had heard of it but was without any experience of it, another had never heard of it. Pat Hall-Smith had just happened to have had a case through his hands and had passed that on to Dr Sheldon. She had had a few cases – I think I was her fifth. All that anyone knew, apparently, was to feed it with steroids in large doses, 80 mls a day – I still take 15; but such very large doses can have an alarming effect. I actually went out of my mind; poor darling Joan believed that I was to be like it for life. It was an appalling feeling, as if there was something right through my face and head turning at a steady pace round and round, about on a level with my right eye from front to back, churning like a wheel; I kept complaining to Joan that the thing was going round and round 'like this', facing my right hand to my face and turning it wheel-wise.

I was obviously in great distress; Joan, distraught, called a nurse and told her to get hold of Dr Sheldon as quickly as she could. She arrived quickly and reassured me calmly; perhaps, she said, she had overdone the doses of Prednisone, but they were all so encouraged by the way I had been reacting to the medicine that they thought I was going to escape this condition which was a pretty usual side-effect. She would reduce the Prednisone significantly and make it up with Immuran. I only half understood what she was saying, but at least Joan was relieved when the doctor told us that the condition should improve quite quickly – which it did, but it left me feeling and seeming, I'm afraid, a little strange and odd. Friends such as the Millses would come to visit; everyone stared a bit but managed not to look perturbed. Ralph R. contrived to treat me with such ultra-calm, as if there was nothing in the least out of the ordinary, that, knowing him as I did, I was confirmed in my suspicion that my condition was critical in the extreme. Joan came to see me daily and as always was a benison with her own special kind of comfort. She didn't encourage the children to come very often because for quite a lot of the time my swallow was inoperative and there was a tube up my nose for liquid feeding, and the look of that upset the poor pets a bit.

After eight weeks Dr Joanna examined me with extra care; when she had finished, she said in a way that gave me a good feeling of confidence, 'Right, physiotherapy now.' Mrs Cook, an expert at her job, came daily and put me through my paces. At first, as I had no strength at all, unable to lift either arm or leg, she would lift and bend these for me, gradually increasing the exercise until they began to lift and move themselves. After a time I was able to stand and attempt knee-bends and balancing on one leg. On Christmas Day I was picked up in a car and taken home for tea; I stayed for supper, though it had been forbidden, but I got back and in bed about nine and was forgiven. I had to convalesce in bed for another eight weeks, and was finally allowed to go home at the end of February 1975.

Then, as I suspect always happens, I found myself the target for every breath that blew, including some that blew in through the window. Colds, flu, a wicked wisdom tooth that had to come out, followed by a quinsy on the back of my tongue which swelled up against my soft palate so that again I thought I was in for the definitely not-to-be-chosen death by asphyxiation – but again, as it never ceased to amuse Tony Guthrie to describe it, 'I was spared.'

About this time two letters were sent to me in the space of eighteen months, both of which in their vastly different ways thrilled me beyond words. First:

Dear Lord Olivier,

During the past two years we have re-introduced the old railway practice of naming locomotives and this month the Rt Hon. Harold Macmillan will name a locomotive 'Harold Macmillan' in an official naming ceremony at London, Euston.

We would now like to extend this by inviting you to honour us by using your name on one of our electric locomotives at a naming ceremony at Euston next year.

To give you just a little background, we have found that locomotives given names provide an individual character to each one previously known by numbers only . . . . Others carry such historical names as Sir Francis Drake, Sir Winston Churchill, William Shakespeare and Robert Burns.

The locomotive to be named 'Laurence Olivier' will haul the 12.40 Inter-city service to Wolverhampton . . . .

GENERAL MANAGER, *British Railways,*
London Midland Region

And the second letter:

> Dear Lord Olivier,
>   The Queen has commanded me to say that it would give her much pleasure to confer the Order of Merit on you. Her Majesty hopes that you will find this proposal agreeable . . . .
> (Sir) PHILIP MOORE

As a result of the second and most overwhelming of these celestial twins came this, from Lord (Bernard) Miles:

> My dear Larry,
>   . . . . Quite honestly, and to be brutally frank, I don't mind if they make you a Duke – and bloody well deserved too – SO LONG AS I CAN HAVE AN ENGINE NAMED AFTER ME, *even a little shunter would do*. That's where the honours lie – in the goods yard.

In the meantime a little action started; after getting home, when I had left my bed and begun going out and taking the air, some encouraging hints of professional activity appeared. By the end of May, John Schlesinger was telephoning me to talk about *Marathon Man*. To a mere man and a career man at that, there is nothing so revivifying as the bewitching appearance of opportunity, and I have always regarded John as my restorer of life; through him I felt that life, real life was starting again and I seemed to breathe nothing but oxygen. This new breath carried me forward through some twenty films from 1975 to 1981. In 1975 I did *The Seven Per Cent Solution* and *Marathon Man*; in 1976, *A Bridge Too Far*.

From June 1976 to July 1977 I was busy with my *Best Play of 19*– series for Granada Television. While I was still in the Royal Sussex County Hospital Joan's brother David Plowright, Controller of Programmes for Granada, had started to interest me in the idea. I had a wonderful time producing six plays in thirteen months, each chosen as the 'best play'

from any year in the last seventy-five years. All except one
of them I reluctantly played in; *Hindle Wakes* was the only
one that I directed myself. The other five were *The Collection*, *Cat on a Hot Tin Roof*, *Saturday, Sunday, Monday*,
Come Back Little Sheba and *Daphne Laureola*.

Between 1977 and 1980 there was more film work – *The
Betsy, The Boys from Brazil, A Little Romance, Dracula,
Clash of the Titans, Inchon, The Jazz Singer* – and the
television serial *Brideshead Revisited*. From March 1980
this book, referred to by all the gang as 'that book', has
taken precedence over almost everything else, only interrupted in the summer of 1981 by the television production
of John Mortimer's *A Voyage Round My Father*.

The wide media of films and television do not usually tax
one's energies beyond their normal capabilities. But the
playing of a great stage role does exactly this, demanding
abundant reserves of vitality and verve – in fact an auxiliary engine, and to drive it a firmer and more versatile
technique of control, discretion and shrewdness. I can no
longer be sure I am master of these strengths. Although I
have not yet dared to take the risk, I cannot entirely stifle
the hope that one day I may defeat these scruples.

Before I start getting too pleased with myself let me, in
the name of Love, remember my rapturous family and,
more particularly, the extraordinary forbearance of their
mother. I Have Suffered, as the very young read the three
letters at the top of the Cross, most certainly, and I
wouldn't have it otherwise; everyone on earth does, or has,
or must. 'Man is born to suffer as the sparks fly upwards,'
Solomon sings. But we do not realise enough how that
inescapable suffering spreads itself to our fellows. Sickness
is not always borne with patience except by superior characters, or ones who achieve superiority. Of course it is
harder for the naturally active, who incline to an extra
testiness, which continues through months of recurring
convalescences. What my beloved, my Joan had to stand
from me, and to some degree our children too, has since
caused me much wonderment, as well as deep, loving,

inexpressible gratitude, forever.

For these and for all my other sins, which I cannot now remember, I firmly purpose amendment of life and humbly ask pardon of God and of you, Reader, counsel, penance and absolution.

APPENDIX A

L'Histoire de Hochhuth

I intended to tell this story through documents alone, in order to give a safer conveyance to the facts, perhaps less guided by prejudice than the author's telling of it. Unfortunately this has not proved possible for reasons of copyright; permission to print has not always been obtainable. I therefore summarise where necessary.

I think this would be a proper moment to declare that in the history of partnership there can hardly have been two men with less in common than Lord Chandos and myself – save for one very big exception, the intensity of enthusiasm which we shared for the erection of a National Theatre of Great Britain, in London.

The recorded history of this moral conflagration begins with a note from Ken Tynan concerning *The Soldiers* by Rolf Hochhuth, which dealt with Winston Churchill's actions during World War II and with the death of the Polish leader Sikorski:

3 January 1966

Dear Larry,

What follows is probably an attack of stage fright in anticipation of the Board meeting on Monday. Anyway, here goes.

I'm worried. Nothing really specific: just a general feeling that we're losing our lead, that we are no longer making the running, that what the NT does has become a matter of public acceptance rather than public excitement. At a time when – as I Cassandra-like keep saying –

audiences even for *good* theatre are dwindling all over Europe, we are doing nothing to remind them that the theatre is an independent force at the heart of a country's life – a sleeping tiger that can and should be roused whenever the national (or international) conscience needs nudging.

We have had no *Marat-Sade*; we have no *US*. Meanwhile, Barrault has gained the respect of Gaullist France by staging *Les Paravents*, in which the French army is reviled for its Algerian atrocities; the Royal Dramatic Theatre in Stockholm is playing to full houses with *O What a Lovely Peace!*, a show that bitterly arraigns its country's politicians for their cowardly neutrality in World War II; and a millennium or so ago a Greek playwright derided his own country's heroes for their *wanton* devastation of Troy.

Hochhuth may not be Euripides and *Soldiers* may not be *The Trojan Women*, but it is in the same tradition and in this country that tradition is in our hands. Subsidy gives us the chance – denied to movies and TV – of taking a line of our own, with no commercial pressures and without the neutralising necessity of being 'impartial'. In a way, I think Hochhuth is the test of our maturity – the test of our willingness to take a central position in the limelight of public affairs. If the play goes on under our banner, we shall be a genuinely national theatre, and, even as the stink-bombs fly, I shall be very proud of us.
Love,
K.T.

On 23 December Ken sent me a memo concerning changes Hochhuth was willing to make and with the postscript: 'I don't know whether this is a great *play*; but I think it's one of the most extraordinary things that has happened to the British theatre in my lifetime. For once, the theatre will occupy its true place – at the very heart of public life.'

In early January Ken sent a list of the opinions of ten distinguished historians and journalists, whom he later described as recording 'an open verdict'. This was to be disputed. He also mentioned that Hochhuth had copies of statements given to him in confidence deposited in West European banks which could be examined in fifty years' time.

Anthony Quayle had been serving on Gibraltar at the time of the death of Sikorski and raised several points when consulted. Ken fielded these as best he could on 24 January.

A press hand-out stated that Ken and I hoped to present the play in the West End, and I noted on it, 'I was never partner to this hope.' It also says more accurately: 'L.O. does not want to talk any more about it. These are the facts and he humbly suggests that there might have been quite enough quotes on the subject as things are.'

On 24 April 1967 came the Board Meeting, of which these recollections are as close as I can get to the original conversation without breaching etiquette:

CHANDOS We have got to make up our minds about this play, and this is the way I propose to deal with it. The Board have now had a full script, followed by a certain amount of errata (which are not significant) and I propose to deal with it without anybody present except the Director. Before that happens, before we simply have a closed meeting, I would like to ask if anybody has anything to add, particularly the Director and Kenneth Tynan, so that we can consider that before we make our decision, and have a full opportunity to hear their views.

OLIVIER I am afraid that what I have to say is bound to be a bit stumbling, because it is to do with over-exercised feelings and conflicts within my soul on this matter. I have not been idle in the pursuit of the delicate and brutal difficulties surrounding this play for us. I have in your service gone to a lot of trouble over the matter in trying to determine a decisive attitude in myself. I have been torn between my prejudices as an Englishman and my wishes for the National Theatre as its Director. And some time along the line in my search for some precept that might help me and might also help the Board, being much foxed by all sorts of suggestions that theatre plays have little or nothing to do with history, etc, and what the business of the dramatist was; trying to find some comfort and some sense in order to guide me more clearly than I had found myself able to guide myself; in going through the play very much and being very much conscious of all the obvious objections to it on political grounds, grounds of wisdom, fears of legal action, etc, I traced through all the objections that I could find for myself and for the Chairman and the Board or anybody who would have anything to do with the play, I found that these were so preoccupying in me that even if the relevant questions were disposed of – like Bomber Harris and that is easily cured. There are ways round a good many of the objections; I don't know if ways can be found round the main central objection concerning Churchill and Sikorski. It then struck me that, having resolved all these questions, they had been obliterating my true judgement of the play as a play. And in my searches I decided that I would see so that I didn't find myself with every objection erased that I wasn't able to make much sense out of the play itself. So I devoted my attention to the play as a play. In doing so, I found a bit of Aristotle, who says in *On Poetics*:

'From what we have said it will be seen that the poet's function is to describe, not the thing that has happened, but a kind of thing that might happen, i.e. what is possible as being probable or necessary.

'The distinction between historian and poet is not in the one writing prose and the other verse – you might put the work of Herodotus into verse, and it would still be a species of history; it consists really in this, that the one describes the thing that has been, and the other a kind of thing that might be. Hence poetry is something more philosophic and of graver import than history, since its statements are of the nature rather of universals, whereas those of history are singulars.

'By a universal statement I mean one as to what such or such a kind of man will probably or necessarily say or do – which is the aim of poetry, though it affixes proper names to the characters.

'The poet must be more the poet of his stories or plots than of his verses, inasmuch as he is a poet by virtue of the imitative element in his work, and it is actions that he imitates. And if he should come to take a subject from actual history, he is none the less a poet for that; since some historic occurrences may very well be in the probable and possible order of things; and it is in that aspect of them that he is their poet.

'The poet being an imitator just like the painter or other maker of likenesses, he must necessarily in all instances represent things in one or other of three aspects, (a) as they were or are, (b) as they are said or thought to have been, (c) as they ought to be.

'It is to be remembered, too, that there is not the same kind of correctness in poetry as in politics, or indeed any other art.

'As for the question whether something said or done in a poem is morally right or not, in dealing with that one should consider not only the intrinsic quality of the actual word or deed, but also the person who says or does it, the time, the means, and the motive of the agent – whether he does it to attain a greater good, or to avoid a greater evil.'

I think one of the first things that supported me in my search for unbias came with a letter from our lawyers who, quite gratuitously I imagine, after going through various difficulties and dangers concerning libel, summarised the situation: 'We think that there are inevitably some small risks involved, as to both civil and criminal libel and most of them it would be impossible to obviate without drastic revision of the play. Nevertheless it appears to us that the play as a whole is a serious contribution to historical record and we are of the opinion that from the legal point of view there is not much to fear.'

I was struck by that at the time. I thought that, having given the play quite a weight of study on its own merits divorced entirely from prejudices, that I might find myself in trouble with the author, if it were accepted; that he might be an intractable author who refused to have anything altered. I got in touch with the author and he came to see me, and I spent last weekend with him. He was anything but intractable. He agreed with everything I suggested, including a complete reconstruction of the play, and he is pleased with the ideas I gave him. He wants to re-write the play on my suggestion. I had to be sure that even if we got to the bottom of the objections that we might have an evening's entertainment. My major concern attached to this, but indeed attaching to every minute of my working life, is the image of the National Theatre. And I must compare it to the image of the Royal Shakespeare Company. The list of plays we will have in the repertoire between now and this time next year is: *Othello, The Royal Hunt of the Sun, Much Ado About Nothing, Love for Love, A Flea in her Ear, The Dance of Death, Three Sisters, As You Like It, Tartuffe, Volpone, The Pretenders* by Ibsen, Seneca's *Oedipus* and *Rosencrantz and Guildenstern Are Dead. Rosencrantz and Guildenstern* is the only fresh little piece we have at all. It doesn't look dazzling in its audacity as a programme. I do not want the repertoire to look like Lord Goodman's showcase filled with antiques only. We are at a disadvantage in the National Theatre as against the Royal Shakespeare Company, as against the Royal Court Theatre and as against almost any other theatre. The RSC has the advantage and privilege that is extended to it by subvention from the Government, which if you include the twenty weeks of the year they play to £15,000 a week (which amounts to £200,000 more than we can play to in the like period), you can then claim that altogether Stratford probably receives more than we do, but at the same time they can do what they like. I know their Board is not appointed by the Treasury, but I feel this is an unfair disadvantage on anybody who directs the National Theatre. I do not think we can avoid looking a bit dead in comparison. If we turn down this play, which I am fairly sure we are going to, this play is still going to be done. The censor may not pass it for the National Theatre. At the time of *Spring Awakening,* the censor actually said to me, 'I don't have any objection to it anywhere else, but I don't like it being done at the

National Theatre.' I think that is a most unfortunate attitude for us. The rest of the world is certainly going to do this play. New York, with its thousands of Irish, is going to do this play, shooting down Churchill as hard as they can. I don't know about the rest of the countries. Jean-Louis Barrault has presented a play, controversial in the extreme, and has been allowed to present it. He had some prejudices against it, as I have against this play, but he put it on because of his love of his artistic integrity. His theatre is a fully supported state theatre.

There are not very good illustrations in Shakespeare, because most of his plays were entirely responsive to popular opinion or fear of the throne. But we don't mind an idiotic characterisation of Saint Joan in *Henry VI.* We didn't object to Christ being criticised in a play put on here by John Osborne. It is understandable, but not reasonable, that we object to a play about Churchill. Hochhuth's previous play, *The Representative*, which was about the Pope, raised no objections at all, and it was every bit as critical about the Pope as this play is about Churchill. This play is not really critical of Churchill. The play says that if Churchill did take part in the Sikorski episode, he was doing the right thing. I understand our attitude – I mean the attitude of people of my age – but the attitude of people under forty is quite different. People under forty think he was a splendid chap, and have said they think it is a marvellous thing to have done. They don't have the particular God-like worship of Churchill that my generation has. We must attend to the people under forty in the National Theatre, or our audience will all be over forty. We have our image to look after, and I want us to look after it sensibly and wisely, considering the younger members of the audience. My wife, who is thirty-six and is a very sensible girl, cannot understand the objections. The play does not diminish Churchill to her; it rather increases her admiration for him.

Are we going to offer a stage with some freedom for men of ideas or not? This is a very vital question. I maintain that this play is a far finer piece of work than *Andorra, The Royal Hunt of the Sun* or *The Crucible*. It is a far more important piece of work. I am going to ask the Board, if I am allowed to do so, to consider giving me back this play. The conduct of its process in arriving at the Board went against the precepts the Chairman laid down. After the Wedekind episode, he laid down that if the Drama Committee did not approve of a play, then it was to be decided between the Chairman and the Director, and only by a document counter-signed by both of us would it be sent to the Board. I would like to have that chance. I would like to be given back the play. I don't want you to vote against this play. I want you to give me a vote of confidence. In my time I think I have earned a certain amount of confidence from you. If it wouldn't make you feel weak-kneed or easily swayed, I would be very willing to give a reading of this play to an extremely select audience (a few well-known writers and critics or anyone else you would like to be present) to find out their opinion. I am perfectly willing to do this. It is difficult to follow the terms of my contract exactly, but my understanding is we have all signed that: 'Sir Laurence shall (a) determine in consultation with the Board the plays and other productions to be presented by the Board; (b) be generally responsible for carrying out the broad artistic policy of the National Theatre both in London and on tour as laid down by the Board in consultation with him.'

CHANDOS I don't know if you wish me to answer that now. We will leave this till later. Would Mr Tynan like to add anything?

TYNAN I have very little to add, except that I speak not as a member of the Board but as someone who gave up a career as a critic in order to serve the National Theatre, and I am very proud of what we have done. And one of the things that I promised myself that we might see at this theatre was that drama should be re-established to the same level of eminence that it attained with the Greeks; that the theatre should be a place where great matters of public concern were presented, and it did seem to me that this play was an opportunity for that sort of confrontation. In these days, when the churches are empty, there is nowhere except the theatre where such matters can be properly debated as the Greeks debated them: matters of supreme conscience, of the highest level of importance, moral concern with great events and the motives behind them. That is what theatre is for. That was my principal reason for supporting this play. I met the author briefly over the weekend. I was afraid that perhaps he was a crank, a man obsessed. I was astonished to find a very quiet, gentle, deeply rational man, whose honesty I could not but trust completely. He understood all the objections, was quite agreeable to make the point of the play even more precisely clear. He cannot prove in court that there was complicity by Churchill in the Sikorski affair. He doesn't know whether this is proved. He says that if it is true, Churchill is a greater man than even he thought him: it is a crime against the one man to save all men. That is what he wants to say in some of the many modifications he agreed with Sir Laurence. I am glad that we are talking about this play and shall continue to do so, because it is going to be done all over the world. This play came to us and I think it is a test of our maturity and of our audiences' maturity as well as a vote of confidence in Sir Laurence's ability as a person to select plays which will be justified – for example, the recent great success of the Tom Stoppard play. It is not the time for any of us to say that Sir Laurence's judgement is at fault. The Lord Chamberlain question is another matter. We do not know what the result of that will be. My own feeling is that if this theatre does it, he will have respect for this Board and its Artistic Director. If another company were to attempt to do it, he would perhaps look at it in another way. If Sir Laurence decides to do this play, it may be its first and last chance in this country.

CHANDOS We will consider these matters. I must answer one point. In your memorandum you said you had consulted contemporary historians who had given you an 'open verdict'. You said you had consulted Hugh Trevor-Roper. Trevor-Roper wrote to me, and I think you ought to hear the second paragraph in his letter. He says: 'It would be interesting to know who the contemporary historians are whom Tynan says he has consulted and to whom he ascribes "a very open verdict". If he explicitly named me among them, I can only say that he has ascribed to me, at least by implication, an opinion diametrically opposite to that which I very clearly gave him. I cannot think that any reputable historian would have given him an answer different from mine.' That should have been stated to the Board at the time.

TYNAN   I was asked in detail what the historians said. I said I preferred to postpone detailed discussion until the subject was raised again. I have my notes here. Hugh Trevor-Roper's comment was that the theory was 'bizarre'.

CHANDOS   You reported to the Board that contemporary historians said it was an 'open verdict'. You misled the Board. You never mentioned this diametrically opposed view.

TYNAN   I was asked would you please tell us what they said. I said that since discussion was to be postponed to a subsequent meeting, I was not going into it then. I said Hugh Trevor-Roper was one of the historians consulted, but the consensus of all of them was that it was an 'open verdict'.

CHANDOS   I can't accept that. It is usual when you consult people to say that they hold opposite views. This play is based upon a lie. It is simply untrue. You are entitled to put on a documentary play about atrocities in Algeria which are facts. No theatre is entitled to invent facts and then erect a theory upon them. You can't do that. I think you made a very eloquent plea, and so did the Director, and we must now decide what we must do.

TYNAN   If the Director wishes I would go into the historical evidence which we have. I don't know if he wishes to go into it now or in the course of your deliberations. I have all the research here, and it is available to the Board if the Board wishes to consider it.

CHANDOS   Your allegation is that this is true?

TYNAN   I think it is a possibility.

CHANDOS   You set aside the findings of the Court of Enquiry?

TYNAN   I could spend about two hours giving you evidence to the contrary, including evidence from eye-witnesses.

CHANDOS   I have other evidence, which I don't propose to produce here, in a completely contrary sense. Never mind. As you made this point about the 'open verdict' I thought the Board should know that you failed to mention that the most eminent historian said the opposite. Whatever the consensus of opinion may have been, that fact should have been brought out quite clearly. Nor is it right to describe Saundby as acting for Harris. This is not true.

TYNAN   I said Sir Robert had vetted the text on points of technical accuracy. As to the historians, there are others who agree with Trevor-Roper. Alan Bullock thinks it was an accident, but we do have the journals and day book of MacFarlane, the Governor of Gibraltar, over the period in question.

CHANDOS   Most of this is a pure myth.

TYNAN   We have his diary and private journals.

CHANDOS   I have a document which shows how the accident actually happened. It shows how the accident happened to the first plane and to a second plane and how it nearly happened to a third plane. The point is that Trevor-Roper's opinion would never have come out if he hadn't written to me.

TYNAN   If a jury is divided, wouldn't you say it was an open verdict?

CHANDOS   This is not a jury, but if a jury is not agreed then the prisoner is not guilty.

TYNAN   I did not say *this* was a jury, I was alluding to the body of historians as being a jury.

This sentence was only half heard, being over-ridden by the chairman's following order. Anyway what else was the NT

Board being at this moment? An in-camera meeting of the Board and the Director then followed.

The possibility of my resignation from the National Theatre appeared in the press and some welcome letters of support rolled in. On 7 May 1967 I left the following telephone message at the National Theatre:

The last time I spoke to Lord Chandos I begged him to let the matter rest and for my part write my letter to *The Times* which I hoped would have the desired effect. I completely appreciate the Board's wish to have a written guarantee but know equally well that the proposed letter will not bring this about nor shut the fellow up. If Lord Chandos will leave it to me to come to a personal understanding with T. – I can guarantee truce for 6 months.

I have a quite appalling programme between now and coming back from Canada and honestly cannot cope with having to replace the Literary Manager which would be the result of the proposed letter. I am working quite terribly hard and getting more and more tired with work on *Three Sisters* all day and acting in *Dance of Death* all night.

K.R. [Kenneth Rae] to implore Lord Chandos 'please leave it to me'. If the Board ask Lord C. why he has gone back on the letter, could he not say 'I decided to leave it to the Director.' I can pretty well, I am sure, and with the help of my wife, guarantee a truce for 6 months. Please, please try to let me have one more chance. We really must have a truce now – between now and nearly Christmas. If Lord C. will leave it to me, I will appreciate it as much as anything he has ever done for me. Please give my kindest regards and devotion to Lord Chandos.

My dear Oliver,

Thank you for our talk yesterday. There was one aspect of it which took a little bit of sleep away from me last night and that was the thing about Tynan.

Your conviction that he is dishonest goes back a long way to circumstances which, to put it mildly, were not in my opinion ones out of which any of us emerged with any very great credit. I remember thinking at the time (wishing of course that you had never warned me of your intention because although my relationship with Tynan has never been one of extreme closeness, such as it is it would, I think, come well within the precincts of the title of friendship) it did not seem to me that he was given more than a very meagre opportunity to explain himself, and my own reading of this incident was that he was guilty more of over-stating his case than bare dishonesty – you can of course call this dishonesty – but again I must say that I do not regard the conduct of any of us as being immaculate and I can never do so.

I think anyone in any such job as his, or indeed as mine, is entitled to slight ups and downs in the matter of bulls-eye-hitting.

A great many things which have given us the aura of success have come from him which people, Board members for instance, may not be conscious of, and quite a few of our failures are things for which he has not been entirely, if at all, to blame.

Our record stands, as was described in the last copy of the *Sunday Times*, as 22 hits out of 38, in comparison to 1 in 12 in the West End.

1963/64

I don't think there was anything criticiseable about the first ten plays for 1963/64. The most successful in this season, and possibly for some time to come, was *Othello*. This was in the first place due to his insistence on my undertaking this rôle which, as has been said many times, I was extremely unwilling to do.

The Master Builder did flop initially because it was a bad choice, and anyhow this was remedied later.

Though a lot of people may have questioned the style and adaptation of *Much Ado*, it delighted many audiences for a long time. (The adaptation only, of course, was Ken's department.)

1964/65

I know a lot of people don't like Brecht but even those very people would consider it wrong of a state theatre to ignore him entirely, and this production of *Mother Courage* was as much the result of my Associate Directors' enthusiasm as it was Tynan's.

1965/66

The package deal over *Flea in her Ear*, to be adapted by John Mortimer and directed by Jacques Charon of the Comédie Française, was entirely initiated by him.

Nobody liked the Osborne *Bond Honoured* very much but before it came on I know a lot who would have grabbed at it.

1966/67

The Storm – The choice of this play needs no apology though one could feel differently about its presentation. Surely we should resurrect rare birds occasionally.

Rosencrantz was acquired for us as a result of deft and expeditious nabbing by Tynan and could be our greatest money-spinner remembering its New York run and movie deals.

1967/68

Tartuffe was a second choice since we were nipped in the bud for *Misanthrope* by Peter Hall (for which John Gielgud had been engaged) who afterwards and too late went back on it.

Volpone had been announced a good six months before its West End presentation and we had gone too far in promises to director, designer and cast to go back on it.

Seneca's *Oedipus* cannot surely be a surprising choice, and to choose the acknowledgedly most dazzling director of our time can hardly be regarded as a howler.

Edward II, more my choice than anybody's. I personally think it is infinitely preferable to the Marlowe which can only boast one 'mighty line' and even that not a very mighty one – the one about 'the antic hay' (can't quite remember it, I am afraid). Incidentally, my choice was fortified by the fact that it does happen to be the only Brecht play that I like at all.

The *Triple Bill* is something which, as I told you, came in by result of a last-minute disappointment, and it had to be got together and designed within a few days. We had, again through Ken's initiative, secured the rights of the Lennon and it was a question of showing a couple of other things with it and very quickly too.

1968/69

The Advertisement. Neither Ken Tynan nor I can help it if the critics occasionally turn out to be cretinous clots; if they cannot see the difference between tragedy and melodrama, and see nothing but banality in a lovely piece of work. Almost any human situation can be regarded as banal if you choose to think of it like that: then nobody can be to blame except the critics. Incidentally, I think the records now show that well over half of these gentlemen were in favour of the play.

Home and Beauty was done against the strongest resistance from Ken Tynan.

I do not in any way wish to make anything that might be construed as being an ultimatum out of this letter, because I do not believe people in my sort of position should talk in that sort of fashion, but it would not be right to do other than to tell you that were Ken Tynan to be got rid of I should be not only extremely unhappy but most unlikely to find a replacement who could in any way compare to him in the way of theatrical brains, or provide the National Theatre with half his value. I would be quite stricken if a partnership such as this were to be dissolved.

Altogether let anyone say what anyone will, the fact is we would have been a hell of a lot duller if it had not been for Ken.

Laurence Olivier

Monday 28 October 1968

My dear Larry,
I ask you to withdraw *in toto* your letter of the 24th which has angered me beyond measure.

The suggestion hidden by the ambiguous word 'us' in the second paragraph that my conduct and truthfulness are to be rated no higher than his has overstepped the limits of my forebearance.

If you still wish to send the letter I must reply in full, and that would really cost you some sleep and perhaps damage our relationship irreparably.

I don't want to see Tynan go immediately, but I do not want his appointment to be regarded as permanent or for that matter sustained beyond its usefulness to the National Theatre by threats however discreetly veiled.

Yours ever,
Oliver [Chandos]

To Lord Chandos   *Sunday 3 November 1968*

Dear Oliver,
To me it appears certain that the time has come to be mindful, and I ask you to scorn easy or ready replies to anything unintended to provoke – such as, 'about time' or 'a bit late' to this opening remark to this letter. And mindful *now* of the nobly generous services and patronage which you have voluntarily given to my profession and metier, and aware *now* of the precipitate dangers of the slightest irritant fuel to the flames which have sprung up between us, so quickly and so alarmingly, and the

utterly disastrous end that this situation could quite well bring to our dreams and labours, I am agreeing herewith that my letter to you of 24th October 1968, marked Private and Confidential, be withdrawn.

I hope you will appreciate that it is these same motives that stop me now from making any answer to yours to me on Monday last, beyond acknowledging it.

Let it be recognised that while it may be that my services have been more arduous these last 5 years or so, yours have been of far longer duration and acknowledgedly of far greater influence and usefulness (benefit?), moreover, with no reward to you.

Larry

It seemed apparent that, since my letters to Lord Chandos must inevitably inflame him, no matter how strenuously I tried to keep them on a conciliatory note, I would be wise to have them vetted by my lawyer, whose suggested simplification of mine of Sunday 3 November 1968 follows herewith. I probably sent this on his advice:

My dear Oliver,
I understand you persist in asking me to withdraw my letter of 24 October. If for the good of the National Theatre I do so it is not to be construed as altering my belief in the facts I stated. It was intended only as a factual statement. I still think it reads so. It contained no threat, ultimatum or attack. If it be withdrawn I want it on record that I strongly consider that Tynan has considerable future value for the National Theatre and should be retained.

A complicated correspondence in *The Times* included contributions from Winston Churchill MP, Professor Trevor-Roper (now Lord Dacre) and Kenneth Tynan. I planned this lengthy letter:

16 January 1969

Dear Sir,

I have been asked to say that at no time during my connection with the Hochhuth play was my interest in it brought about by any historical evidence; this I do herewith and at the same time beg the opportunity to explain a little my silence in face of the recent conflagration, in which the more sweeping the statement the more authoritative its ring; when a deadly truth lurks beneath every suspicion, no matter how far-fetched, when truth in fact becomes the servant of fancy. 'I take a fancy to a theory and so I choose to believe it and because I believe it I know it to be true and I will therefore swear it to be an established fact' has been rehearsed before our astonished eyes.

Someone has said ('I believe') that he knows 'for a fact' that Hochhuth showed me the evidence supposedly locked in a Swiss bank. This is not so, and if I did not ask Hochhuth for it, it was out of respect for what I accepted to be his avowed intention, namely not to show it to anybody.

This does not mean that I accepted this evidence *in truth*. Nor does it mean that when I pointed out to him that his informant might well have been a malcontent, a drunk, a mischief-maker or an enemy agent that I repudiated the possibility that there could be truth in it.

I must think that everything is possible and that nothing short of the implausible is impossible in history; but this tolerance begets a permissiveness and therein starts the rot, and if your readers have been following this case the ambience of this three-letter word may well, for them, have reached alarming proportions.

It is perhaps a pity that a man of such pure emotional integrity as Rolf Hochhuth should seek to reinforce his moral fervour by historical evidence when as an idea it might have worked without all this fuss. Had he presented it as an abstract idea, the gargantuan figure who endangers his immortal soul to save the lives of all our children, it might have been acceptable to those who find it unacceptable now; but then it likely would not have made the same impact; and so the idea would have passed by, the Churchill family have been unhurt, and his memory unmolested. A play would have been performed which made respectable representations concerning area bombing, and about as much notice would have been taken of it as usually is of such subject-matter. (This question does not in principle disturb me, to be truthful, as I believe area bombing started the first time a burning arrow sailed over the wall of a small town and that if there is to be a war then the civilians are every bit as much responsible for it as the soldiers they hire to shoot it out), but believe in it personally or not, any director of a National Theatre must believe that such a purely humanitarian message has a right to be heard.

History changes shape as various lights are thrown across it; even if, for interest's sake, certain exaggerations become obvious, the case is not entirely lost by over-statement. If in *The Daughter of Time* Miss Josephine Tey must stand accused of partiality by neglecting to mention King Richard's last letter the night before Bosworth this does not demolish entirely the idea that Richard was not the villain painted by Cardinal Bouchier and Shakespeare. Perhaps purists would say that it should but in fact it does not; the face of history assumes a slightly different expression just the same.

I have no way of knowing with certainty how Churchill would have reacted if he had been asked to allow the play's performance in his lifetime. He would have recognised that there would be no way of stopping its production after his death, and I cannot imagine just how he could have permanently discredited the vexed question before this event (somewhere or other in the world).

I am not quite persuaded that it is entirely right to sweep aside the opinion that his assuming this burden on his conscience for humanity's sake enhances his reputation lest its acceptance should give the idea credit. I have found the notion that it would take a lot worse than this to blemish Churchill's memory to be a fairly common one.

I am persuaded that this sentiment is not unacceptable to the generation who was not alive when he was. This generation is not indelibly dyed with the same grateful idolatry that colours the feelings of his own. We hear every day that their alienation from previous generations is more clearly marked than has ever been known before.

At the time when it was concerning the National Theatre, I was deeply disturbed and torn about, and by this play as well as by the various effects it had upon other people and their conduct. Whatever reactions the play produced in people of my acquaintance, these were by no means generally typical and I do not believe that even Churchill's own condemnation of it would have seen the end of it or laid a permanent dust upon it.

If I am guilty of hindsight in this letter may I refer to my letter to *The Times* of 8 May 1967, in which I declared that my chief complaint to my Board was my not being allowed time for unhurried deliberation, and 3/4 months is *not* long to consider a play of the immense size it was as first presented, with the myriad arguable facets it turned up all in concert with the many other concerns attendant on the day's work.

In view of all recent clamour this attitude may now be seen to be justified. No one need wonder that a little later in 1967, in response to my painfully trained senses, I decided that this was too awkward a child for me to bring into the world in consideration of the vibrant family in the Waterloo Road to whom all my cares were, and still are, primarily due.

Before it was sent, I received this:

Friday 17 January 1969

My dear Larry,

The Soldiers

Don't worry. As I raised this hair-split *I* shall have to reply since my veracity will be called into question.

The point is of no substance, the dialogue went like this:

Tynan said that he had consulted a number of contemporary historians who felt obliged (I haven't the exact words in front of me) to return an open verdict.

I – 'Did you consult Jack Wheeler Bennett?' Tynan, 'No.' Did you consult Hugh Trevor-Roper? Tynan, 'Yes'. Trevor-Roper was therefore *by name* included or not excluded from amongst those who had returned an open verdict.

Yours ever

Oliver

  P.S. Your speech at the Arts Council yesterday was a masterpiece and I am more than ever confident that we shall get what we want. I wish, with Arnold, that we had it on the tape – it would be Top of the Pops!

  P.P.S. Tynan should *not* be given either the minutes or the verbatim report which are confidential to the Board without my consent, which I probably would not refuse.

ı the event I was persuaded only to send this to *The Times*:

CHURCHILL AND SIKORSKI   *[20 January 1969]*

Sir, I wish to bring two points to your attention.

One has been requested of me from a member of the Churchill family and that is to say that I was at no time convinced by any historical evidence supporting Hochhuth's theory regarding the death of Sikorski. This I willingly do.

The other is that I feel I must take up Professor Trevor-Roper in one statement in his letter on 17 January. In a memorandum that Mr Tynan wrote for the consideration of the Drama Committee and the Board of the National Theatre he wrote: 'I have consulted a large number of historians and military experts and the result is very much an open verdict.' In saying this he mentioned no names. He did at no time in my hearing (and I was present on all relevant occasions) say that this was the expressed opinion of Professor Trevor-Roper.

Mr Tynan admitted on another occasion that Professor Trevor-Roper had been one of those asked but he did not inform the Board specifically of the Professor's attitude at the time of the memorandum referred to.

I am bound to say that I think there may be some general misunderstanding of precisely what comprises an open verdict.

22 January 1969

My dear Larry,

I have tried my best, as your devoted friend, to keep you out of the Sikorski turmoil, and I am very sad that you entered the fray on Monday. I have been obliged to write a letter to *The Times,* but I have dealt as lightly as I can with your letter.

I do not want you to 'move about in worlds unrealised'. If you look up the verbatim report (which is no more than notes to help Kenneth Rae write the Minutes), you will see that Tynan said 'If the Director wishes I would go into the historical evidence which we have . . . I have all the research here, and it is available to the Board if the Board wishes to consider it.' He said it would take two hours to explain the evidence which he had with him.

What has happened to this evidence? Why does Tynan not produce it now? Does he allege that somebody's life would be endangered if he did so? (This is the Hochhuth excuse.) Has Tynan got a Swiss bank of his own, etc?

Moreover, the statement about the evidence is not in harmony with what he said on the Frost programme: e.g., talking of Hochhuth's documents, he said, 'I certainly believe there is evidence. Whether it's good or bad I have no means of knowing.' Yet at the time of the Board Meeting he had evidence, according to his own statement, which would have taken him two hours to explain.

There are now a number of libel actions about, and I

beg you to be careful, because Tynan as a controversialist is a piece of cake to his enemies, and a disaster to his friends. He is both dishonest and untruthful, and if you recognise this fact it will save you a lot of tears in the future.

Blessings,

Yours ever,
Oliver

I also have this second letter I intended for *The Times*:

DRAFT   *24 January 1969*

Dear Sir,
I wish to say that at no time during my connection with the Hochhuth play was my interest in it brought about by any historical evidence; and at the same time explain a little my silence in face of the recent conflagration.

When Mr David Frost reported on my telephone conversation with him last Saturday I realised that there was an untidy ending to it. God knows there are a thousand such to this case and one day I may find the time and the ink to put down all that has exercised me on this subject during the two years since I first read *Soldiers*.

In the meantime, let me recap my conversation with Mr Frost. 'I never saw the evidence claimed by Hochhuth,' said I. 'Did you ask him for it?' asked Mr Frost. 'I believe I did not, in fact.' (You would do better to accept Mr Frost's words than mine since I am sure he has a tape of them – who, apart from me, has not these days?)

If there is one thing of value that has been elicited from the Hochhuth case it is an enforced reassessment of the nature of Truth, catapulted into prominence by the recent wild graspings or claims for this quality based only upon conviction. This has offered again for scrutiny such terms as truth, honour, honesty, honourableness, behaviour, conduct, code, ethics, standards. There is really nothing surprising or out of order about this. Each generation must concoct its own definitions of these things and must stand or fall in moral judgement by the findings of future hunks of humanity concerned with 'Our Island History' etc, or, more broadly, in more broad philosophical areas. Please don't talk of things like 'Eternal Truths' because they come not within the realms of *pragma*, no matter howsoe'er much they may tickle my fancy. It is such fancies that are largely responsible for the present maelstrom. E.g. 'I take a fancy to a theory and so I choose to believe it and because I believe it I know it to be true and I will therefore swear it to be an established fact' seems to be about representative of present standards.

Someone has said (I believe) that he knows 'for a fact' that Hochhuth showed me the evidence locked in a Swiss bank. This is not so and if I did not ask him for it, it was out of respect for what I accepted to be his avowed intention, namely not to show it to anybody.

This does not mean that I accepted it *in truth*. Nor does it mean that when I pointed out to him that his informant might well have been a malcontent, a drunk, a mischief-maker or an enemy agent that I repudiated the possibility that there *could* be truth *in it*.

I must think that everything is possible and that nothing short of the implausible is impossible in history; but this tolerance begets a permissiveness and therein starts the *rot*, and if your readers have been following this case the ambience of this word may well, for them, have reached alarming proportions.

It is perhaps a pity that a man of such pure emotional integrity as Rolf Hochhuth should seek to reinforce his moral fervour by historical evidence when as an *idea* the Sikorski incident might have worked without all this fuss. Had he presented a purely abstract idea, a gargantuan figure who endangers his immortal soul to save the lives of all our children it might have been acceptable to those who find it unacceptable now; but then it likely would not have made the same impact; and so the idea would have passed by, the Churchill family have been unhurt, and his memory unmolested. A play would have been performed which made respectable representations concerning area bombing, and about as much notice would have been taken of it as usually is of such subject matter. (This question does not in principle disturb me, to be truthful, as I believe area bombardment started the first time a burning arrow sailed over the wall of a small town and that if there is to be a war the civilians are every bit as much responsible for it as the soldiers they hire to shoot it out), but personal reactions aside, any director of a National Theatre must believe that such a purely humanitarian message has a right to be heard.

If I am guilty of hindsight in this letter may I refer to my letter to *The Times* of 8 May 1967, in which I declared that my chief complaint to my Board was my not being allowed time for unhurried deliberation, and, believe me, four to five months is *not* long to consider a play of the immense size it was as first presented with the myriad arguable facets it turned up; all in concert with the many other concerns attendant on the day's work.

In view of all recent hullabaloo, fandango and tittifalla the wish for more time to consider may now be seen to be justified; but on the other side those who may have espied a breach of faith with Hochhuth in my conduct may now no longer wonder that a little later in 1967, in response to my painfully trained senses, I decided that this was too awkward a child for me to bring into the world in consideration of the already large and vigorous family in the Waterloo Road to whom all my cares were, and still are, primarily due.

And that is the sum of the records that I can find in my possession which concern this turmoil; between times were smothered with moody preoccupations, heart-searchings, deep thinking, talks, arguments fierce and arguments reasonable, so that it might well be thought there was no time for any other considerations; but no, during the three years that cloaked this issue from January 1966 to February 1969, the Rep continued with various selections of eighteen presentations, among which I undertook the direction of

Juno and the Paycock, Three Sisters, The Advertisement and *Love's Labours Lost*, adding performances of *Dance of Death*, with take-overs in *Three Sisters, Home and Beauty* and *Flea in her Ear*; the company played twenty-five provincial dates, made a visit to Stockholm, did a three-week season in Stratford, a seven-week season at the Queen's Theatre in the West End, a six-week tour of Canada and a special experimental season at the Jeanetta Cochrane. I was twice hospitalised, and I do hope it's not sticking out my lower lip too far or letting it tremble too violently if I mention that for quite a few months the front of our Brighton house had to be torn down and built up again; the large sum that this cost was money thrown away; when a town council orders something of this nature, one can't exactly stick it on to the sale price: so *L'Histoire de Hochhuth* was hardly the *leitmotif* that would have been so welcome.

If I don't know, it is not for want of telling, that the vastest areas of charred devastation are caused by the smallest cigarette-end. Was it an overheated baker's oven that caused the fire of London? What minute spark was it that caused the combustion through which both reader and writer have been laboriously wading?

Two and a half weeks before that 'heavy emergency' Board meeting of Monday 24 April 1967, the chairman, Lord Chandos, came for a snack with me in my office at lunchtime to have a quiet, grave talk about the proposed venture that was beset by such polarised differences of opinion. I was desperate to play for time to see whether I could not perhaps find some prescription that might just exercise some healing magic and even things up. Supposing I could work out with Hochhuth some more theoretical attitude about his devotion to the Sikorski aspect, removing its emphasis, and build up some other facet upon which to hang the play? Chandos replied that even without Sikorski he couldn't countenance the play's production at the National; when I pressed further, he explained that he was a member of the war cabinet that had sanctioned area bombing with Dresden in particular as a target. I could see that made things awkward for him but felt we could not be expected to feel bound by that, we were infringing no official secrets act, it was a subject of extreme and lively interest to the public and that placed it naturally within the orbit of theatrical debate.

The National Theatre surely could not be expected to allow itself to be kept in subservience outside the circle in which every other theatrical interest was free to jump in and play all it wanted to. He said it wasn't for himself so much as for his friends and partners in those times of such special responsibility; I went further and asked if the National was really to ignore a matter that could be explored by every other theatre merely to spare the feelings and save the faces of his old cronies from more than twenty years ago? He shrugged apologetically. I said, 'I'm sorry, Oliver, you've lost me now. I must be against you on this: I have to fight a decision which puts the National in quite such a wretchedly feeble position.' At last I knew that I must abandon my grimly determined fulcrum position, intent on the tricky problem of pleasing all. I just knew which side I was on and it was not on the side of authority. I had chosen golden youth. Oliver and I, by allowing the comparatively minor matter of what might quite possibly turn out to be an inconsiderable play's merits to develop into a matter of high principle, had started a small but painful little war that was to last for three years.

Appendix B

On 20 July 1971 I gave my maiden speech in the House of Lords:

> My Lords, I have the honour to crave the indulgence of your Lordships' House. During the maiden speech that follows I fear your Lordships may find grim cause to reflect upon the prescient genius of the introducer of this tenderest of courtesies, and if I fail to achieve it then I must beg to suggest to your Lordships that it would be most contrary to the chivalry for which your Lordships' House is so famous to withhold your gallantry and refuse to indulge a maiden of sixty-four.
>
> I stand before your Lordships the second Baron of my name. The first, incomparably much more deserving, virtuous, illustrious, and in service to his country richer than I can ever hope to be, was my uncle, twice Governor of Jamaica, KCMG, friend to Bernard Shaw, the Webbs, and all the eminent Socialists of the day with whom he created the Fabian Society. He entered your Lordships' House the first Labour peer – he seems to have started quite a thing. He served the Government in 1925 as Secretary for India, a title once representing one of the richest jewels in the Imperial Crown and which now sounds perhaps almost quaint to the retrenched ears whose lobes can only boast the holes to show where once such lush gems hung.
>
> But it is not on account of being my uncle's nephew that I am here, no matter what storybook feudal nostalgia might tempt me to allow you to think so. The fact of

my presence can only find reason in what his enemies would describe as his greatest eccentricity, his friends as the only eccentricity of which our recent Prime Minister was ever culpable. For a time I resisted this honour, as I thought was proper and to be expected, I think, in a person of my calling; the breaking of ice in any sense being apt to cause hesitation in most of us. But it does not take all that multi-repeated persuasion, that seethingly passionate ardour to make even the coyest maiden of sixty-four to wonder what on earth she thinks it is she has got to lose. He, Mr Wilson, said he wanted people like me to have a forum.

I believe I can detect among your Lordships a growing sense of uneasiness that your most kindly indulgence is about to become strained. I hope you will find any such apprehension to be unfounded. I should like to say how deeply grateful my fellow Equity members feel for the extraordinary generosity of your Lordships' attitude, the concern, trouble-taken thought and serious consideration with which your Lordships have deliberated upon our problems. Many days and many a late night's work of the business of your Lordships' House have been devoted to certain difficulties of our minority profession.

May I say on behalf of that profession that your tender care will be appreciated from time without end. In particular, will your Lordships allow me to mention in gratitude the right reverend prelate, the Bishop of Durham; the noble Lord, Lord Drumalbyn; the noble and learned Lord, Lord Stow Hill; the noble Baroness, Lady Lee of Asheridge, whose loving and constant guardianship over the interests of our work has always been such an inspiration and such a comfort to us; the noble Lord, Lord Bernstein; the noble Earl, Lord Balfour; the noble Baroness, Lady White; the noble and learned Lord the Lord Chancellor, for his kindly patience for our affairs; the noble Lord, Lord Beaumont of Whitley; the noble Lord, Lord Archibald; the noble Earl, Lord Mansfield, to whom our profession would like to extend their warmest wishes that his recovery to health may be both speedy and lasting; the noble Lord, Lord Henley; the noble Lord, Lord Delacourt-Smith; the noble Lord, Lord Donaldson of Kingsbridge, and the noble Lord, Lord Davies of Leek. If I have made any glaring omissions I ask one more sip of indulgence.

The great problem which has been recognised is the essential necessity of the closed shop for the acting profession. I can personally vouch for this necessity. We quite appreciate that in order to make its maintenance possible, the Government have made what is to them a major concession in the terms of Clause 17 and Schedule 1. Inevitably this concession is in somewhat of a restricted form, so much so that those who attempt to work under it may with justice reckon that it may not achieve its object.

With regard to the so often referred to 'ephemeral manager', once more we ask that some way may be found to make a closed shop unerodable in a part of an industry in relation to which the Commission on Industrial Relations has certified that a 'closed shop is necessary' – Schedule I, part V. Assuming that we may get an approved closed shop, there is no way of bringing this ephemeral manager inside it. If the several methods that have been suggested and discussed have been found unacceptable, then is there not perhaps an onus on the Government themselves to find a way or to outline a procedure which, as the noble Baroness, Lady White, has said, might work? What a pity if, having gone to such exhaustive lengths, as has been done in this closed shop Amendment, there should be found in the end no means to put them into practicable form or, as has been better put, 'We would have a situation in practice where the Government would have willed the end but would have failed to provide the means.'

I appreciate that I am asking for more than is expressed in the noble Baroness, Lady White's, Amendment, and if I am not misinterpreting – and if I am I humbly ask her pardon – I believe the noble Baroness herself would agree that its position in the landscape finds itself uncomfortably and all too familiarly in a last ditch. It may be that this position is preferable to none at all but, by providing for easy entry for the willing while not arranging compulsory entry for the unwilling, the Government are only being asked to preach to the converted without strengthening or enriching the parish.

My Lords, I believe in Great Britain and in keeping her great under the Sovereign. My 'great' is not rhetorical, it refers directly to the continuance of the family of England and Scotland, Wales and Northern Ireland, together with what relationships we can still muster among those peoples with whom, if we lose a relation, we gain a friend. I am proud to belong to this family. The trend of nationalistic feelings has now spread, we are given to understand, to Cornwall. Sometimes it seems to me that we shall be lucky if, when that superb building at present half erected at the foot of Waterloo Bridge on the South Bank finally achieves its sky-line, we shall dare to inscribe a legend more boastful than 'The National Theatre of Surrey'. Here my profession must own a debt of incalculable magnitude to the noble and chivalrous Viscount, Lord Chandos, and the noble Lord, Lord Cottesloe, together with most grateful acknowledgements to the GLC for their tireless efforts in creating this new 'London Pride'.

I believe in the theatre; I believe in it as the first glamouriser of thought. It restores dramatic dynamics and their relationships to life size. I believe that in a great city, or even in a small city or a village, a great theatre is the outward and visible sign of an inward and probable culture. I believe in the Common Market, in the Concorde, in Foulness and the Brighton Belle. I believe in anything that will keep our domains, not wider still and wider, but higher still and higher in the expectancy and hope of quality and probity.

I humbly thank your Lordships for your kind attention.

It may be observed that I only exceeded the statutory ten minutes by two.

Select Chronology

1907	Born on 22 May
1916	All Saints School, London
1917	Brutus in *Julius Caesar*, All Saints School
	Maria in *Twelfth Night*, All Saints School
1920	Katharina in *The Taming of the Shrew*, All Saints School and
1922	Stratford-upon-Avon
1923	Puck in *A Midsummer Night's Dream*, St Edward's, Oxford
1924	Lennox in *Macbeth*, Letchworth
	Suliot Officer in *Byron*, London
1925	Thomas of Clarence and Snare in *Henry IV, Part II*, London
	The Ghost Train, Brighton
	Member of Lena Ashwell Players
	Henry VIII, London
	The Cenci, London
1926	Minstrel in *The Marvellous History of Saint Bernard*, London
	The Barber and the Cow, UK tour
	Richard Croaker in *The Farmer's Wife*, UK tour
1927	With Birmingham Repertory Company
1928	Young Man in *The Adding Machine*, London
	Malcolm in *Macbeth*, London
	Martellus in *Back to Methuselah*, London
	Title role in *Harold*, London
	Lord in *The Taming of the Shrew*, London
	Gerald Arnwood in *Bird in Hand*, London
	Captain Stanhope in *Journey's End*, London

1929   Title role in *Beau Geste*, London
          Prince Po in *The Circle of Chalk*, London
          Richard Parish in *Paris Bound*, London
          John Hardy in *The Stranger Within*, London
          Hugh Bromilow in *Murder on the Second Floor*, New York
          Jerry Warrender in *The Last Enemy*, London
          The Temporary Widow (film)

1930   Married Jill Esmond
          Ralph in *After All*, London
          Victor Prynne in *Private Lives*, London
          Too Many Crooks (film)
          Potiphar's Wife (film)

1931   Victor Prynne in *Private Lives*, New York
          Friends and Lovers (film), Hollywood
          The Yellow Passport (film), Hollywood

1932   *Westward Passage* (film), Hollywood
          Perfect Understanding (film)
          No Funny Business (film)

1933   Steven Beringer in *The Rats of Norway*, London
          Julian Dulcimer in *The Green Bay Tree*, New York
          Screen test for *Queen Christina* with Garbo

1934   Richard Kurt in *Biography*, London
          Bothwell in *Queen of Scots*, London
          Anthony Cavendish in *Theatre Royal*, London

1935   Peter Hammond in *Ringmaster*, London
          Richard Harben in *Golden Arrow*, London
          Romeo, then Mercutio in *Romeo and Juliet*, London
          Conquest of the Air (film)
          Moscow Nights (film)

1936   Robert Patch in *Bees on the Boat Deck*, London
          As You Like It (film)
          Fire Over England (film)

1937   Title role in *Hamlet*, London
          Sir Toby Belch in *Twelfth Night*, London
          Title role in *Henry V*, London
          Title role in *Macbeth*, London
          Title role in *Hamlet*, Elsinore, Denmark

1938	Iago in *Othello*, London
	Vivaldi in *The King of Nowhere*, London
	Caius Marcius in *Coriolanus*, London
	Twenty One Days (film)
	The Divorce of Lady X (film)
1939	Gaylord Easterbrook in *No Time For Comedy*, New York
	Q Planes (film)
	Wuthering Heights (film), Hollywood
	Rebecca (film), Hollywood
1940	Marriage to Jill Esmond dissolved
	Married Vivien Leigh
	Romeo in *Romeo and Juliet*, New York
	Pride and Prejudice (film), Hollywood
1941	*Lady Hamilton* (film), Hollywood
	Lieutenant (A) in the Royal Naval Volunteer Reserve
	49th Parallel (film)
1943	*The Demi-Paradise* (film)
1943–4	Title role and director *Henry V* (film)
1944–5	Button Moulder in *Peer Gynt*, London, Paris and New York
	Sergius Saranoff in *Arms and the Man*, London, Paris and New York
	Title role in *Richard III*, London Paris and New York
	Astrov in *Uncle Vanya*, London
1945–6	Hotspur in *Henry IV, Part I*, London
	Justice Shallow in *Henry IV, Part II*, London
	Title role in *Oedipus Rex*, London
	Mr Puff in *The Critic*, London
1946	Title role in *King Lear*, London
1947	Received knighthood
	Title role and director *Hamlet* (film)
1948	Sir Peter Teazle in *The School for Scandal*, New Zealand and Australian tour
	Title role in *Richard III*, New Zealand and Australian tour

Mr Antrobus in *The Skin of Our Teeth*, New Zealand and Australian tour

1949   Title role in *Richard III*, London
Sir Peter Teazle in *The School for Scandal*, London
Chorus in *Antigone*, London

1950   Duke of Altair in *Venus Observed*, London
Carrie (film), Hollywood

1951   Caesar in *Caesar and Cleopatra*, London and New York
Antony in *Antony and Cleopatra*, London and New York
The Magic Box (film)

1952   *The Beggar's Opera* (film)

1953   Grand Duke of Carpathia in *The Sleeping Prince*, London

1954   Title role and director *Richard III* (film)

1954–5 Title role in *Macbeth*, Stratford-upon-Avon
Malvolio in *Twelfth Night*, Stratford-upon-Avon
Title role in *Titus Andronicus*, Stratford-upon-Avon

1956   Title role and director *The Prince and the Showgirl* (film)

1957   Archie Rice in *The Entertainer*, London
Title role in *Titus Andronicus*, European tour and London

1958   Archie Rice in *The Entertainer*, New York
The Devil's Disciple (film)
John Gabriel Borkman (British television)
The Moon and Sixpence (US television)

1959   Title role in *Coriolanus*, Stratford-upon-Avon
Spartacus (film), Hollywood
The Entertainer (film)

1960   Marriage to Vivien Leigh dissolved
Berenger in *Rhinoceros*, London
Becket, then Henry II in *Becket*, London

1961   Married Joan Plowright
The Power and the Glory (US television)

1962   Prologue and Bassanes in *The Broken Heart*, Chichester
           Astrov in *Uncle Vanya*, Chichester
           Appointed Director of National Theatre
           Term of Trial (film)
           Fred Midway in *Semi-Detached*, London
1963   Astrov in *Uncle Vanya*, London
           Uncle Vanya (film)
           Captain Brazen in *The Recruting Officer*, National Theatre Company, London
1964   Title role in *Othello*, Chichester and National Theatre Company London
           Halvard Solness in *The Master Builder*, National Theatre Company, London
1965   Title role in *Othello*, Moscow and Berlin
           Tattle in *Love for Love*, Moscow and Berlin
           Othello (film)
           Bunny Lake is Missing (film)
1966   *Khartoum* (film)
1967   Edgar in *The Dance of Death*, National Theatre Company, London, and Canada
           Plucheux in *A Flea in Her Ear*, Canada
1968   *The Shoes of the Fisherman* (film)
           Oh, What a Lovely War! (film)
           The Dance of Death (film)
1969   A. B. Raham in *Home and Beauty*, London
           The Battle of Britain (film)
           David Copperfield (film)
           Actor and director *Three Sisters* (film)
1970   Created a Life Peer: Baron Olivier of Brighton
           Shylock in *The Merchant of Venice*, London
1971   James Tyrone in *Long Day's Journey into Night*, London
           Nicholas and Alexandra (film)
           Lady Caroline Lamb (film)
1972   *Sleuth* (film)
           Long Day's Journey into Night (film)
1973   Resigned as Director of the National Theatre

Antonio in *Saturday, Sunday, Monday*, London
The Merchant of Venice (film)
John Tagg in *The Party*, London
1974 *Love Among the Ruins* (US television)
1976 *The Seven Per Cent Solution* (film)
Cat on a Hot Tin Roof (British television)
Marathon Man (film)
The Collection (British television)
A Bridge Too Far (film)
Jesus of Nazareth (television)
1977 *Come Back Little Sheba* (British television)
1978 *The Betsy* (film)
The Boys from Brazil (film)
1979 *A Little Romance* (film)
Dracula (film)
1980 *Inchon* (film unreleased as at July 1982)
The Jazz Singer (film)
1981 *Brideshead Revisited* (British television)
Clash of the Titans (film)
1982 *A Voyage Round My Father* (British television)

INDEX